A History of the Jews of Arabia

Studies in Comparative Religion
Frederick M. Denny, Editor

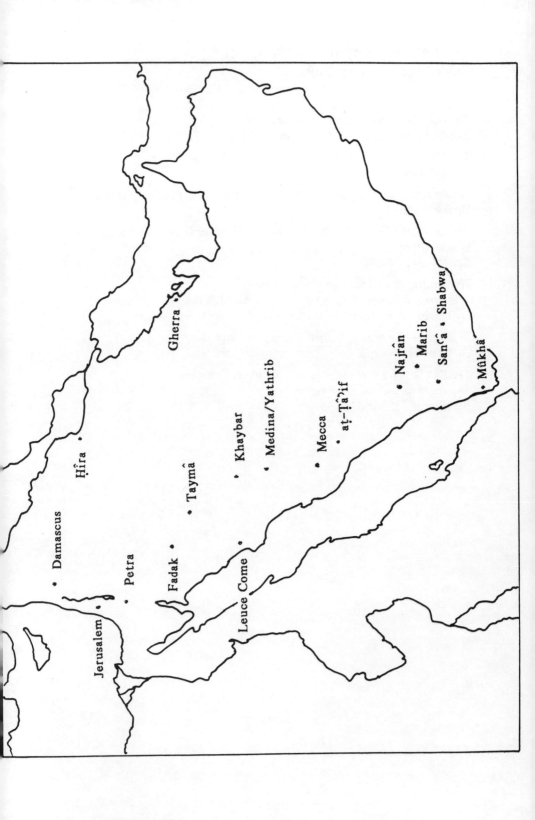

A History of
The Jews of Arabia

*From Ancient Times
to Their Eclipse Under Islam*

GORDON DARNELL NEWBY

UNIVERSITY OF
SOUTH CAROLINA PRESS

Copyright © UNIVERSITY OF SOUTH CAROLINA 1988

Published in Columbia, South Carolina, by the
University of South Carolina Press

First Edition

Manufactured in the United States of America

LIBRARY OF CONGRESS
Library of Congress Cataloging-in-Publication Data

Newby, Gordon D., 1939–
  A history of the Jews of Arabia / Gordon D. Newby.
    p.   cm. — (Studies in comparative reliigon)
  Bibliography: p.
  Includes index.
  ISBN 0-87249-558-2
  1. Jews—Arabian Peninsula—History. 2. Judaism—Relations-
Islam. 3. Islam—Relations—Judaism. 4. Arabian Peninsula—Ethnic
relations. I. Title. II. Series: Studies in comparative religion
(Columbia, S.C.)
DS135.A7N48   1988
953'.004924--dc19   88-11766
                                                                    CIP

CONTENTS

EDITOR'S PREFACE

Comparative religion means different things to different minds, but from the perspective of this series it always means, among other things, serious scrutiny of sources and open-minded evaluation of previous wisdom, theories and interpretations. Gordon Newby's venture of writing a history of the Jews of Arabia will strike some seasoned sifters of the sources as quixotic if not impossible. The absence of such a work in the history of distinguished scholarship on Jews and Judaism should be sufficient proof of the difficulty of the task. No one knows this better than the author of this synthesis cast in the form of an extended historiographical essay. Far from claiming to have produced the definitive history of Arabian Jewry, Newby has instead provided an assessment of the field that should reopen many questions for further study.

This book presents both a narrative history and abundant interpretative reflection for the wide range of readers this series hopes to reach, in this case Jewish studies specialists, Islamologists, historians of the ancient and medieval Near East, Semitists, and historians of religion. At one level, *A History of the Jews of Arabia* can be read as a summary of what is known about the subject; that in itself is sufficient reason to have published the project. But at another level, Newby engages his colleagues in an absorbing and challenging discourse on the nature of historical investigation, the status of earlier claims and theories about Jews in Arabia, and how one's perspective—Jewish, Muslim, Christian, secularist, ancient, modern—definitively influences what one sees. The author himself sees very much due to his creative use of anthropological, literary-critical, linguistic, phenomenological, sociological and historical theories and methods.

The Jewish experience in Arabia has never commanded the scholarly attention that the great Mesopotamian, Palestinian, Egyptian, North African, and Iberian Jewish legacies have enjoyed, whether before or after the rise of Islam. But we have long known that Arabian Judaism played a major role in Muhammad's developing vision of his

x

mission as prophet and leader. And the heavy debt of early Muslim religious scholars to the corpus of Jewish learning in the interpretation of the Qurʾân is well documented. This is not to suggest that Islam is some kind of by-product of Arabian Judaism; that kind of thinking is no longer relevant or sound. But the long history of Jews in the Arabian Peninsula and their substantial contributions to the region's cultures, values and institutions deserve to be widely known, understood and appreciated, both for their intrinsic worth and for their often fateful consequences in the history of Jewish-Muslim relations and beyond.

Frederick M. Denny
General Editor
Studies in Comparative Religion

PREFACE

When Professor Fred Denny first asked me to think about writing a history of the Jewish communities of Arabia, I was of two minds about the project. I was eager to try to put together in one volume the pieces of the Arabian Jewish historical puzzle I had been working on for some time; but I was apprehensive about how comprehensive a picture could be developed. Fred's encouragement, however, gave me the necessary inspiration to persevere, and I ended up even somewhat surprised that we can know as much as we do. Still, we do not know enough. We do not have the personal records, autobiographies, and letters that would really let us glimpse the lives of individual Arabian Jews. For the most part, we can only look at these long-dead Jews at a communal level. Even with that limitation, we can learn much about Jewish courage and survival in a harsh environment after the destruction of the Temple. In the foreword to his book *The Exiled and the Redeemed*, Itzhak Ben-Zvi holds that each "tribe" of Israel may be said to have contributed its share to the common heritage of the nation. The Jews of Arabia lived a rich life in Exile; but they can be "redeemed" only in our memories. In part, this work is a beginning of an ingathering of the memories and heritage of the Jews of Arabia.

I want to thank two colleagues in particular for their long-standing help, criticism, and ideas. David Halperin, with whom I sometimes teach and write papers, has been a special friend and colleague. He continually teaches me much that aids and furthers my work. Steven Wasserstrom also has been a source of ideas, bibliography, and perspectives without which this project would have been impossible. In addition, I have been sustained by the encouragement of Marilyn Waldman, Bruce Lawrence, and my colleagues in the Department of History at North Carolina State. I would also like to thank M.J. Kister, S. Shaked, and the other organizers of the colloquium "From Jâhilayya to Islam," held in Jerusalem in July 1982. The intense collegial atmosphere and the caliber of the participants did much to advance my education. My special gratitude also goes to the Interlibrary Loan xii

staff at North Carolina State University, Allison Greene and the staff
at the Divinity School Library at Duke University, and the staff of the
Middle East Library at the University of Utah whose expertise and
cooperation made my task of research both easy and pleasant.

The bulk of the writing of this volume was made possible by a grant
from the National Endowment for the Humanities and a grant from
North Carolina State University, which made it possible for me to
devote all of 1986 to writing, free from teaching and administrative
responsibilities.

Finally, I would like to thank all my friends who have had to listen
to me perorate on this subject. I am just sorry that I cannot now promise to keep silent.

G.D.N.

A HISTORY OF THE JEWS OF ARABIA

INTRODUCTION

The Jewish communities of Arabia had great influence on the attitudes that Muslims hold toward Jews, and yet relatively little has been written about the history of the Jews of Arabia. This has been due in part to the nature of the sources and in part to the interests of Western writers and scholars.

There are very few sources for the history of the Jewish communities in Arabia, and most of these are Muslim sources, often hostile to Jews and the Jewish communities, which resisted Muḥammad and Islam. And Western scholarship has had its own perspectives on the Arabian Jews. From the time of Abraham Geiger's 1833 thesis *Was hat Mohammed aus dem Judenthume aufgenommen*, the Western scholarly world has shown interest in the history and nature of the Arabian Jewish community. However, Geiger's perspective to show what Muḥammad had taken from Judaism, remained paramount. Some scholars were most interested in proving that Islam was a derivative form of Judaism in the same manner that other scholars were interested in proving that Islam was a derivative form of Christianity. As the academic world grew weary of the inherent polemic in this approach, scholars abandoned interest in the subject altogether. Recently interest has revived in the early period of Islam, and great debates have arisen about the nature of this early material, some of which I discuss in the chapters below. Because of this, I have felt that it is time to write a history of Judaism in Arabia, if only to spell out

3

what it is we know about those long-neglected communities and add to the debate about the nature of early Islam's nurturant environment.

Arabic sources from the early period of Islam remain the greatest source of our understanding of Arabian Judaism. The Qurʾân, the Sîrah, the Ḥadîth, and other early Islamic materials have much to say about the Jews. But the Jews of Arabia are not always objectively represented. Nor, at first glance, does there appear to be any distinction made among the several communities of Jews. Jews are made to fit the stereotypes developed from the particular theological perspectives of Islam. Yet Islamic literature is rich in traditions and stories that can be used to reconstruct the history of the Arabian Jewish communities. As an example, by examining a tradition about a minor military expedition, we laarn that the Jews of the Ḥijâz spoke a particular dialect of Arabic—al-yahûdiyyah, or Judeo-Arabic—during the lifetime of Muhammad and practiced a slightly variant form of the Passover rituals. Through techniques borrowed from anthropology, literary criticism, sociology, and comparative religion, it is possible to reconstruct some understanding of Jewish life in Arabia before and during the time of Muhammad. When the literary and religious material is supplemented by the recent archaeological finds from within Arabia and from surrounding areas, we begin to see the rich textures of Arabian Jewish life.

The first chapters of this volume address the problems of geography and perspective. If we look for Jews in Arabia, which Arabia do we mean, for there were many definitions of that ancient geographic term, only some of which fit with our modern notions. Chapter 2 scrutinizes the legends of the beginnings of the Arabian Jewish communities, particularly from the perspectives of the methodology made explicit in the final chapter.

Chapter 3 reexamines the rich period of Roman interests in the eastern Mediterranean. Jews both as individuals and as members of Jewish states competed with others for the wealth of Arabia. The Romans built defenses against the Arabs and sent troops to try to capture Arabia Felix, and at all times Jews were involved.

Toward the end of the Roman period, a Jewish ruler in the Yemen established a kingdom of Arabian Jews, was accused of persecuting Christians and, according to some theories, tried to establish a trading empire that would have extended into Palestine. The theme of chapter

4 is the fascinating and controversial ruler Dhû Nuwâs, his policies, and his relations with countries outside Arabia.

Chapters 5 and 6 are the main sections of the volume, with their focus on the Jews we know most about, the Jews of the Hijâz shortly before and during the time of Muḥammad and the rise of Islam. These were the Jews whom Muḥammad knew, learned from, and with whom he negotiated treaties. These are the Jews who resisted the spread of Islam, and these are the Jews whose descendants provided information for our knowledge of the period. Chapter 7 contains a short history of the communities after their eclipse by Islam.

As the reader will soon discover, this volume is an extended essay about reconstructing the Arabian Jewish past. I have meant for it to be a synthesis of what we now know about Arabian Jewry, but I have not tried to close the discussion about either the methodology or the content. Chapter 8 contains a discussion of the current historiographic debate into which this work fits. In addition, I have tried to address an audience broader than the few who regularly work in the field of early Islam or early Judeo-Arabic history. I expect that students of comparative religion, persons interested in Jewish history and Islamic history, and historians interested in the techniques of reconstructing pre-modern cultures will find this volume useful.

1

LOOKING AT THE PAST

HAL GHÂDARA SH-SHUʿARÂʾU MIN MUTARADDAMI ʾAM HAL
ʿARAFTA D-DÂRA BAʿDA TAWAHHUMI

[HAVE THE POETS LEFT A PLACE IN NEED OF MENDING
OR DID YOU RECOGNIZE THE PLACE ONLY THROUGH
IMAGINATION?]

ʿANTARA

This book is about the history of the Jews of Arabia, a subject that has interested Western scholars for over a century, and scholars of the Middle East since the time of the rise of Islam. Much has been written that is fantasy, much that is polemic, and some that I shall call history. What I have set about in this study is to recover what we can from a community now long past. Also, and maybe more to the point, I look at some of the ways that we and others have regarded the history of the Jews of Arabia to elucidate our own understanding of ourselves, our past, and Jewish history in general.

Arabia is not usually thought of as a land of Jews. Most histories of Judaism pass lightly over Arabia except for two periods, the time around the rise of Islam and the modern period of the Yemenite Jewish communities, now transplanted in the state of Israel. But Arabia has been a country for Jews and a presence in Jewish history from the earliest legends and continues to be a home for Jews until this century. Who are these Jews? What can we know about them? What impact have they had on the course of events? What can we learn from examining their story? These are the questions that begin this book; we shall finish with others.

For our ancestors, Arabia was not a precisely defined place. It was the land where one found Arabs, of course. But since many Arabs were nomads and, for the most part, were the chief representatives of Arabia to the outside world, Arabia was wherever one found

7

these Arabs. Even the name "Arab" is vague. It usually meant a
speaker of Arabic, by which we now mean the classical North Arabic
exemplified in literary form by the Qurʾân, by some pre-Islamic
poetry and a wealth of poetry and prose from the time after the rise
of Islam, and by its numerous vernacular dialects; but ancient Arabs,
like modern ones, were often bilingual, speaking Aramaic, Syriac,
Greek, Latin, Persian, the languages of South Arabia, or combina-
tions of these in addition to a dialect of Arabic. Often, too, the name
"Arab" was applied to any nomadic pastoralist or bedouin in the
Near East, regardless of the native language. Arabs wandered as far
north as the northern parts of Mesopotamia, and were found in the
Syrian desert, Transjordan, the Negev, and in all of the peninsula
we now call Arabia.

When Rome ruled the eastern Mediterranean, the province of Ara-
bia included all of Jordan, southern Syria, the Negev, and northwest
Saudi Arabia.[1] Between 244 and 249 C.E., the Roman empire in the
East was ruled by Philip, who was an Arab from the area of the Jabal
Druze in the southern Lebanon.[2] During this period, the civilized
world knew at least two Arabias, the Roman Provincia Arabia, a land
touching modern Arabia only at the northwest corner, and Arabia
Felix, the southern Arabian kingdom of Saba and the land of spices.
They also knew of Arabs over a wide expanse of the lands of the east-
ern Mediterranean.[3]

In this study, the term "Arabia" will usually refer to the great peninsula bounded by the Red Sea and the Persian Gulf.[4] But because Arabs
in ancient times regularly came in contact with Jews of lands tradition-
ally associated with Judaic culture, the boundaries of this study's definition of Arabia will be extended to include what even the ancients
themselves regarded as the land of the Arabs.

When we think of Arabia, we imagine *natura maligna* at its worst.
Even the ancient geographers who called the southern cultivable portion of the peninsula Arabia Felix (Fortunate Arabia) did so with
knowledge of the considerable irony of the name. Arabia is a land of
extremes. It is a quadrilateral plateau with a spine of mountains on its
western side. These mountains are 5,000 feet in average height, with
the highest peak, at 12,336 feet, in Yemen. The center of the peninsula
is hard desert with numerous oases, but no extant permanent water-
courses. Around this is a soft, sandy desert that has acted as an effec-

tive barrier for the interior. The most famous of the sandy deserts are the Nafûd in the north and the Rubʿ al-Khâlî in the south. These areas have no oases, and travelers must carry water for themselves and their animals in order to cross. Around the perimeter of the peninsula are areas of rocky steppe, lava waste, and mountains. These are the areas with the greatest population, but even here there are no rivers, only oases tapping ancient groundwater.

Arabia is surrounded by water—the Red Sea, the Persian Gulf, the Gulf of Aden, the Gulf of Oman, the Arabian Sea, and the Indian Ocean—but there are no really good ports except in Aden. The Red Sea is filled with coral reefs, and the Persian Gulf is subject to severe shoaling. There are few offshore islands that have served as transitional lands between Arabia and the sea. Little rain falls on Arabia, the greatest amount being in the highlands of Yemen. The average rainfall is less than three inches a year, which falls in just four or five days. Temperatures have been recorded over 120 degrees Fahrenheit and below zero and can range from freezing to over 100 in a single day.

Malignant Nature has also been a protection. For much of its history, Arabia was never successfully occupied by foreign troops. The desert, the climate, and the sea defended it. And so Arabia became a land of refuge, of retreat, and of mystery. But the desert barrier was permeable by tiny bands, and the interior of Arabia was never cut off from contact with the Mediterranean world or with the Far East. Caravan traffic passed through Arabia to all parts of the world. Missionaries from the Mediterranean came to Arabia singly and in small groups. Refugees passed through the desert barriers to settle in the oases and fertile valleys and were always drawn into the culture of the peninsula, becoming like the Arabs among whom they lived.

Despite the harsh climate and forbidding terrain, Arabia was a land of opportunity and attraction. For Christians, particularly after the Council of Chalcedon in 451 C.E., Arabia was the last great area for missionizing in the eastern Mediterranean. It lay in the center of the struggling groups of Egyptian and Ethiopic Monophysites, Syrian Jacobites, Persian Nestorians, and Greek Orthodox, each wanting to carve out bishoprics for its individual confession.[5] Christian penetration into Arabia and competition for its land and souls were destined to play a great part in the story of the Jews of Arabia.

A HISTORY OF THE JEWS OF ARABIA

The real attraction of Arabia was its wealth. Arabia then, as today, was the major source of a scarce commodity, and all the world powers wanted control of the trade. The commodity then was incense, particularly the two types we know as frankincense and myrrh. These are derived from the gums and resins of certain shrubs or trees found chiefly in southern Arabia and its colonies of Soqotra (the island of Socotra or ancient Dioscorida) and Somalia in Africa.[6] The incense was gathered from the regions of present-day Oman, the People's Democratic Republic of Yemen, Yemen, the island of Soqotra, and Somalia and carried by merchants to the great consuming powers of the Mediterranean. Egyptians used frankincense and myrrh for embalming, and the Romans used it to burn at funerals. According to Pliny, more than a year's output from Arabia was burned by the emperor Nero at the death of Poppaea.[7] Jews used it in ceremonies in the Temple, and Christians used it in the Mass, despite the critics who claimed that this was merely a pagan practice.

Jewish use of frankincense (Heb. *libônah*) is well attested from early times. Its use is enjoined in Leviticus 2:14–16 as an essential part of the first-fruit offering; and in Leviticus 24:7, frankincense is commanded as part of the weekly memorial bread offering. In this last verse, a "pure" frankincense is mentioned, which is usually assumed to be that from Arabia.[8] Imported from southern Arabia (cf. Isaiah 60:6 and Jeremiah 6:20), it was needed for sacrifices, so a supply of it was kept in the Temple (cf. 1 Chronicles 9:29). In the Talmud frankincense is mentioned as one of the components of incense[9] and, because of the Temple association, it was not to be sold to one who worshiped idols.[10] It appears to have been used along with myrrh, which also came from southern Arabia, in the preparation of a drink that was supposed to stupefy someone who was about to undergo capital punishment.[11] As we shall see later, however, there are some problems using the biblical accounts for reconstructing a history of Jewish associations with Arabia, and not all the stories can be taken at face value.

The Via Odorifera (the Fragrant Highway) brought not only the Arabian aromatics; it was the conduit for trade goods from Asia and Africa.[12] At times, as during the period of Hellenistic ascendancy, for example, these goods were borne on ships up the Red Sea, but that waterway is treacherous, as the numerous shipwrecks, both ancient and modern, will testify. The domestication of the camel (*Camelus dromedarius*) and the development of the "North Arabian camel saddle" meant that goods could be transported by "ships of the desert."[13] The trade routes for the aromatics and eastern goods generally went around the perimeter of Arabia, skirting the empty desert areas, starting in the eastern part of the peninsula in modern Oman and proceeding along the southern edge to modern Yemen, picking up goods on the way, and then north along the western edge to end up in Syria or Egypt. The main highway ran from ancient Moscha at the easternmost part of the peninsula in Oman westward along the edge of the great Empty Quarter through Shabwa over to San'â and Mârib in Yemen, then northward to Najrân and Tathlith where one branch crossed back over the peninsula to Gherra on the Gulf. The main route continued north through the northwestern area of Arabia known as the Hijâz, passing by Mecca, through Yathrib (al-Medina), Dedan (al-'Ulâ), Hijrâ (Madâ' in Sâlih), west of the ancient city Taymâ, and up through modern Jordan to Tabûk, Ma'ân, Petra, and on to either Gaza and north or west through Rhinocolura (al-'Arîsh) on the coast and into Egypt. Still in Arabia at Dedan, a branch of the route went to Leuce Come (al-Wajh) on the coast of the Red Sea and then over to Egypt.

The domestication of the camel also brought about a profound change in Arabian society. The camel became not only the pack animal of choice; it was also the main means of military transportation. There were few roads in the Arabian desert, and these would often become covered with sand. For the camels, this was ideal; it covered the stones that could hurt their tender feet. For wheeled vehicles, chariots and the like, it meant that the land was impassable. Camel cavalry was mobile and well adapted to the environment.[14]

Increased dependence on the camel meant that a portion of the population of Arabia had to follow the herds of camels from one pasturage to another depending on the time of year and the amount of rainfall. Even in the best of times, it would not have been possible to keep camels and remain sedentary. Carl Becker has proposed that the increased dependence on the camel produced a process of "bedouinization" in which sedentary and semisedentary Arabians became pastoral nomads in order to follow the camels.[15] Some Western writers, positing a natural progression from the more primitive nomadic pastoralist to the more sophisticated urban dweller, have rejected the possibility that such a transformation could have taken place. But, at any rate, by the time of the fifth and sixth centuries, camels had become such a fixture of Arabian society that great tribes of pastoralists moved about the Arabian peninsula, intimately participated in the political and economic life of the region, and were destined to play a crucial role in the development and spread of Islam. We shall see that Arabian Jews were also bedouin, and had been, apparently, for some time before the birth of Muḥammad.

Some scholars have assumed, primarily on linguistic evidence, that Arabia was the original home of the Semites. By a process of dessication, whereby Arabia's fertility gave way to increasing desertification, these Semites were forced from Arabia into the lands we associate with Semitic cultures.[16] In recent times, most scholars have rejected that theory on grounds of insufficient evidence or have abandoned the quest for a Semitic "homeland" altogether. This has meant that the dessication theory has also been abandoned. But new evidence and a reevaluation of old findings may be cause to revive the dessication theory, not to find a home for the Semites, but to account for social changes in Arabia in historic times. In a private communication, Nicholas Clapp of Jet Propulsion Laboratories informs me that he has seen photo-reconnaissance evidence of a trans-Arabian river known to the ancient geographers under a variety of names, which ran across the Rubʿ al-Khâlî. This river is now dry and silted in with the sands of the area. Nigel Groom cites evidence in the last chapter of his book *Frankincense and Myrrh* that Arabia has undergone cyclical periods of aridity, and that Arabia in ancient times must have had more available water. He points to the existence of numerous large settlements in places where little or no water is available now.[17] While this topic is more germane to the later discussion of the bedouinization of certain of the Jews, it seems clear that Arabia supported more settlements and vegetation in the past than it does at the present, and the wealth associated with an increased yield of frankincense and myrrh would be a powerful attraction to would-be Jewish settlers looking for homes and opportunities after the destruction of the Temple by the Romans.

The result of the process of bedouinization does not mean that there were no urban centers in Arabia. Quite to the contrary, towns and cities were located wherever there was a large enough source of water and livelihood. The settlements that will concern us most are in the southwestern portion of Arabia and north along the western edge, particularly the area known as the Ḥijâz. The best known of the cities of the Ḥijâz, to the Western reader, are Mecca and Medina. Mecca is known to the ancient geographers as Macoraba, a name possibly related to the Hebrew and Arabic word *qurbân* because of the ancient temple there known in Arabic as the Ka'bah.[18] Mecca was not the only place in Arabia to have a ka'bah, or cubical stone temple. We know of such temples at aṭ-Ṭâ' if and Ṣan'â.

In Islamic times, Mecca became the cultic center of the religion of Islam, and the Ka'bah was incorporated into the worship, although in a somewhat modified form from its function in pagan times. Under Islam, it took on much of the aura and many of the legends usually associated with Jerusalem. As we shall see, it is not always easy to differentiate between originally Jewish legends taken from their venue of Jerusalem and applied to Mecca and those legends that developed around Mecca because of Jewish influence and presence.

Legends, along with poetry, inscriptions, histories, biographies, religious texts, the Bible, the Talmud, the Qur'ân, commentaries, and travelers' stories, all contribute to our recovery of knowledge about the Jews of the Arabian peninsula. The majority of the sources available to us were not written or created by these Jews, but are writings or tales from other people who were often hostile to the Jews or indifferent to their activities. Arabs, Greeks, Ethiopians, Muslims, Christians, and even Jews from outside Arabia mentioned Arabian Jews in passing or fulminated against them in religious invective. One of the tasks of the historian of Arabia's Jews is to ferret out these bits of information, evaluate them, and fit them into their places in the puzzle of historical reconstruction. The methods for this type of historical reconstruction are complex and often hotly debated, involving opposing theories and philosophies of history. In what follows, the methods and assumptions are for the most part implicit. In the final chapter, however, the reader can view some of the underlying approaches more explicitly drawn out. But it is said that legends are the precursors of history, and so it is that we shall begin with the legends of Arabian Jews.

2

LEGENDS AND ANCIENT ORIGINS

According to Muslim traditions, the present-day Arabs were not the first inhabitants of the Arabian peninsula. They were preceded by "true" Arabs whom the current speakers replaced. Some traditions link the "true" Arabs to the "original" inhabitants of the peninsula. These were, according to Arab legend, the Amalekites, who occupied the Ḥijâz and were almost totally annihilated by Jews sent by Moses:

>ʾAus b. Danî al-Yahûdî was a man of the tribe of Qurayza. The B. Qurayza and the B. an-Nadîr were called al-Kâhinân [the Two Priestly Tribes] because they were descended from al-Kâhin, the son of Aaron, the son of ʿAmrân, the brother of Moses b. ʿAmrân, may the prayers of God be upon Muhammad, his family, and the two of them. They settled in the vicinity of Yathrib after the death of Moses, upon him be peace. It is said that alʾ-Azd scattered at the time of the flood of alʿ-Aram and the settlement of the [tribes of] alʾ-Aus and the al-Khazraj in Yathrib.
>
> I was told about that by ʿAlî b. Sulaymân al-ʾAkhfash, who got it from Jaʿfar b. Muhammad al-ʿÂsî, from Abû al-Minhâl ʿUyayna b. al-Minhâl al-Muhalabî from Abû Sulaymân Jaʿfar b. Saʿd from al-ʿAmârî, who said: The first people to settle Medina before the Children of Israel were an ancient people called the Amalekites. They terrorized the countryside because they were a strong and unjust people. The tribes of Haff, Saʿd, al-Azraq, and Matrûq were those of them that settled Medina. The king of the Ḥijâz was

from them, a man called al-ʾArqam, who lived in the area
between Taymâ and Fadak. The Amalekites had filled the city
and had many date-palms and fields there.

Moses b. ʿAmrân, upon him be peace, had sent soldiers against
the tyrants of the towns to conquer them, so Moses, upon him be
peace, sent an army of the Children of Israel against the
Amalekites and ordered them to kill all of them when they
appeared before them and not to leave one of them. So the army
went to the Ḥijâz and God, the Great and Powerful, caused the
Amalekites to appear before them, and they killed all of them
except the son of al-ʾArqam, who was a beautiful innocent, so
they refrained from killing him, but said, We shall take him to
Moses to get his opinion. So they returned to Syria, but they
found that Moses, upon him be peace, had died, and the Children of Israel said to them, What have you done? They said, God
caused us to appear before them, so we killed them, and none
remains except a youth who is a beautiful boy, so we were reluc-
tant to kill him and we said, We will take him to Moses, upon him
be peace, and get his opinion. They said to them, This is disobedi-
ence, for you were ordered not to leave one of them alive, so, by
God, never enter Syria. At that they said, How nice were the
dwellings of those we killed in the Ḥijâz; let us return to them and
dwell in them. So they went back until they came to Medina and
settled it, and that army was the first of the Jews to settle Medina.
They spread out in all the regions of Medina up to al-ʿAlîyah, and
they took the fortresses and wealth and crops, and remained in
Medina a long time.[1]

This portion of the story from the *Kitâb al-Aghânî* appears to have little
historical content, although some Western scholars have regarded it and
other similar accounts as reliable sources of Arabia's earliest past. Rather,
this appears to be one in a series of "foundation legends" that purport to
show the antiquity and noble heritage of the community.[2] The *locus clas-
sicus* is the Bible, and the story is a recasting of the story of the Amalekites
as found in the Bible and in rabbinic literature.

The Amalekites are regarded as the first inhabitants of Arabia,
based on the notion of Amalekite priority found in Numbers 24:20
where they are described as "the first of the nations." From 1 Samuel
15, we find that God ordered Saul to destroy all the Amalekites. But
Saul and the Israelites, succumbing to the temptations of wealth and

power, spared Agag, the Amalekite king. By sparing Agag and keeping the best of the spoils, contrary to God's instructions, Saul lost his kingship, and Samuel the prophet becomes the destroyer of the king of Israel's enemies.

The narrative in the Bible is a gloss on the ambivalence of Israel toward its kings and the very notion of royal power. For the rabbis, the story takes on a different emphasis, and the attractions to the spoils are cited as among the reasons that Saul failed to execute God's commands.[3] For the rabbis, the Amalekites were the archenemies of Israel, and the name "Amalekite" became almost a generic term for any hater or persecutor of Jews. Amalik was the progenitor of Haman, and Amalekites became identified with Christians. When the Islamic sources have Amalekites ruling over Egypt, this is merely a reflection of the conflation of the Amalekites and the Egyptians as Israel's enemies. From rabbinic sources also comes the notion that it was Moses who ordered the destruction of the Amalekites.[4] In some rabbinic sources, Rome was identified with the Amalekites, which makes this legend an appropriate introduction to the second of the foundation legends in which Rome's destruction of the Temple is offered as a major cause for Jewish settlement in Arabia.

The second of the two foundations legends from the *Kitâb al-ʾAghânî* concerns the Diaspora after the destruction of the Second Temple.

> Then Rome rose up over all the Children of Israel in Syria, trampled them under foot, killed them, and married their women. So when Rome conquered them in Syria, the B. an-Nadîr, the B. Qurayza and the B. Bahdal fled to the Children of Israel in the Hijâz. When they departed from their houses, the king of Rome sent after them to bring them back, but it was impossible for him because of the desert between Syria and the Hijâz. When the pursuing Romans reached at-Tamr,[5] they died of thirst, so the place was named Tamr ar-Rûm,[6] which is its name to this day.

We shall return later to the historicity of the migration to Arabia after the destruction of the Second Temple, but the story in this form is clearly part of the foundation-legend cycle. It is at once an etiological account of how a place name came about and also a reference to the paradigm of Jewish migrations, the exodus. The detail of the pursuit of the fleeing Jews by the king of Rome is clearly reminiscent of Pharaoh pursuing Moses and the Israelites. This is further confirmed by the linkage between this passage and the previous narrative, which equates Rome with the Amalekites.

These two passages, coupled by their oblique references to the exodus, are paralleled by numerous other Arabic sources, many of which are dependent on one another. Appearing as they do in the context of Arab histories and Arab genealogies, these passages function, in part, to bestow nobility and antiquity to the Jewish tribes of the Ḥijâz. It would appear that the Jews of the Ḥijâz regarded themselves as superior to their Arab neighbors, in part because of their connection with the Bible and in part because of their agricultural successes. Nuʿaym b. Masʿûd, Muhammad's agent against the Meccan confederation and the Jews, reports that "The B. Qurayzah are a people of honor and wealth, while we are an Arab people without date-palms or vineyards; we were only a people of sheep and small cattle.'"[7] In contrast with the values of pre-Islamic bedouin poetry, the wealth and comforts of the settled life are here regarded as bestowing a kind of nobility.[8] When the Arabs proffer their most noble genealogies, as in the case of Muhammad, the references are to local heroes and to the distant ancestors of biblical origin.[9]

Within the communities, groups of Jews themselves used genealogical claims of nobility: "It is said about the B. Qurayza and the B. an-Nadîr that they were the upper class of the Jews [and were] called the Two Priestly [Tribes], so named because an uncle of theirs was called al-Kâhin.'"[10] This is, of course, the personification of the title of priest in its Arabicized form. These two tribes, the B. Qurayza and the B. an-Nadîr, were supposed to have derived from a migration of priests to Arabia some time after the destruction of the Second Temple.[11]

The remaining portion of the story of the advent of the Jews into the Ḥijâz as given in the Kitâb al-ʾAghâni concerns the details of the etiology of their settlement in particular places, around the city of Medina especially. The passage is replete with historical detail, which probably reflects the settlement configuration at the time of the advent of Islam rather than at the beginning of the city's settlement, although preservation of specific details about the acquisition of property would have been carefully preserved in family traditions in a time without fixed deeds:

> When the B. an-Nadîr, the B Qurayza, and the B. Bahdal came to Medina, they settled the low ground and found it plague-infested and hated it. So they sent out someone to find them another place. He went until he came to al-ʿAlîyah, which is in Tihân and Mahzûr, two wâdîs in the lava waste in the hills, a sweet land with potable water, which caused the lava waste to grow trees. So he returned to them and said, I have found a land for you that is better watered than the lava waste with two wâdîs in the hills with good earth and flowing water. So the people changed their abode. The B. an-Nadîr and those with them settled in Tihân, and they had fine camels, which they used as wealth. The B. Qurayza and the B. Bahdal and those with them settled in Mahzûr, and they had the hills and what was watered by springs and rain. And of those who dwelt in Medina of the tribes of the Children of Israel until the Aus and the Khazraj came were the B. ʿIkrimah, the B. Thaʿlabah, the B. Muhammar, the B. Zaghûr, the B. Qaynuqâ, the B. Zayd, the B. an-Nadîr, the B. Qurayza, the B. Bahdal, the B. ʿAwf, the B. al-Fasîs. The ones of the tribes of the Jews who inhabited Yathrib were more noble and rich and power-ful than the rest of the Jews. They had a fortress called al-Khâl, and with them of those who were not of the Children of Israel were the small tribes of the Arabs, among whom were the B. Harmân, a tribe from the Yemen, and the B. Marthad, a tribe from Baliy, and the B. Nayf, who were from Baliy also, and the B. Muʿâwiyyah, a tribe of the B. Salîm, and the B. al-hârith b. Bahthah, and the B. Shayzah, a tribe of the Ghassân.

This section closes with a reference to the Qurʾânic event of the flood of al-ʿIram, the migration of the tribes of the Aus and the Khazraj to Medina, and the intercommunal strife that followed, which resulted in the slaughter of many Jews.

The Jewish communities of south Arabia had foundation legends associated with the destruction of the Temple, this time with the First Temple. According to Yemenite legend, the original Jewish settlers had left Jerusalem forty-two years before the destruction of the Tem-ple. When Ezra called on them to return from exile to help in the rebuilding of the Temple, they refused because they foresaw the second destruction of the Temple. This brought Ezra's curse on them, condemning them to a life of poverty and intellectual privation. They, in turn, cursed Ezra so that he would not be interred in the Holy Land.[12] H. Schwarzbaum has observed that this story has its roots in the Midrash Tanhûma, which employs the words from Haggai 1:6 in which the prophet urges the return and the rebuilding of the Temple. They refuse, claiming that the time is not right. In anger, Haggai asks if it is right that Israel dwells in houses with roofs and God is denied his house, and then delivers the message: "Now therefore thus saith the Lord of hosts: Consider your ways. You have sown much, and brought in little, ye eat, but ye have not enough, ye drink, but ye are not filled with drink, ye clothe you, but there is none warm; and he that earneth wages earneth wages for a bag with holes."[13] The curse presupposes that the edict of forfeiture of property for failure to return to Jerusalem would be enforced on all the remaining Diaspora as God's will and that it was not merely a temporal judgment at the discretion of the counsel of the princes and the elders.[14]

It is difficult to ascertain the antiquity of this legend, although its grounding in Haggai would argue that the tension between the exiles and the forces of return was widespread and early. The folklorist Schwarzbaum assumes that the story is late, but other scholars, like B. Heller, argue for its antiquity.[15] By the time that this story gets its latest and most elaborate exposition, it is only one of many "exile" legends associated with Ezra's pleas for the ingathering.[16]

The Yemenite Jewish communities also derive their origins from the biblical legends surrounding Solomon and the Queen of Sheba. Solomon, according to Islamic legend, was supposed to have converted Bilqîs,[17] the Queen of Sheba, to Judaism along with all her nobles and their subjects. Most all of the elements of the legends can be seen to be paralleled by antecedent rabbinic literature, so it is likely to assume that the ultimate source of these stories is to be found among Jews of Arabia, but there is insufficient evidence to date the origin of these legends, even to the extent of placing them before or after the advent of Islam. If they come before, we may assume that their purposes would differ from the purposes of legends derived from the inter-confessional polemics that grew up between Muslims and Jews (and Christians, for that matter) over the shared stories of the Qurʾân and the Bible.

Western scholars have not been free from the influences of these legends, particularly when the stories can be made to exhibit some relationship to the Bible. It is, of course, beyond the scope of this study to comment on the development of Oriental studies as it was derived from the theological context of European biblical studies, but when one reads the works of R. Dozy[18] or D. S. Margoliouth,[19] the presuppositions of Arabia as a Semitic homeland and the genetic interrelations of Hebrews and Arabs become clear. For Dozy, Jews came to Arabia during the period of the Babylonian exile and brought with them a cultic practice that was established in Mecca. For Margoliouth, both Arabs and Hebrews had started out in Arabia, presumably at a time when, Edenlike, Arabia was able to sustain more life. He entertained the hope that we would be able to discover scientifically the genetic links that would show the evolution of Hebrew from its older Arabic kin.[20] While neither theory gets us closer to actually seeing the beginnings of Judaism in Arabia, we do see that close scrutiny of the texts and legends has perpetuated the belief that Arabs and Hebrews are related.[21]

On the basis of the inscriptional evidence from both Babylon and Arabia, some scholars have assumed that during the reign of Nabonidus (556–39 B.C.E.), the last king of Babylon, a significant event for both Arabia and Judaism took place. After reigning for more than three years, during which time he carried out an extensive religious and diplomatic policy, Nabonidus invaded the northern Ḥijâz, defeated the local inhabitants and established his residence in the city of Tamyâ: "(but) I hied myself afar (usherîqanni) from my city of Babylon (on) the road to Tema', Dadanu, Padakku, Khibrâ, Iadikhu, and as far as Iatribu; ten years I went about amongst them (and) to my city Babylon I went not in."[22]

All of the northern Ḥijâz came under Nabonidus' sway as far south as the city of Yathrib, modern Medina. Most of the cities mentioned in his inscription are both famous Arabian cities and known Jewish settlements in later times: Yathrib (Iatribu), of course, but also Khaybar (Khibrâ), Fadak (Padakku), Dedan-al-'Ulâ (Dadanu), and Taymâ (Tema').[23] Scholars are still puzzled about his motives for the move. Apparently they were to avoid a priest-supported revolution at home, and the choice of the Ḥijâz may have been economic. The same cities are the caravan cities of that section of Arabia.

Nabonidus' armies of conquest, according to Gadd, were drawn from peoples of the western areas of Babylonian influence, and he infers "that Jews, whether from among the captives of Babylonia or from those remaining in their homeland, were strongly represented among these soldiers and settlers in Arabia."[24] For ten years he made war on and peace with the people of Qeder and the land of "Aribi,"[25] evidently amassing wealth for himself and his subjects, for he contends: "In plenty and wealth and abundance my people in the distant tracts I spread abroad, and in prosperity I took the road to my own land."[26] All was not happy for Nabonidus, however, for he seems to have suffered some sort of skin disorder, usually interpreted in the ancient world as a sign of divine disfavor. An Aramaic fragment, usually known as "Nabonidus' Prayer," was found among the Qumran texts, and indicates that he was advised by a Jewish seer to pray to God for a cure.[27] Some scholars have assumed, on the strength of the text, that Nabonidus was advised by Jews taken with him during his sojourn in Arabia. Recent scholarship has questioned those conclusions. Some, like Israel Eph'al, while not doubting Nabonidus' sojourn in Arabia, question what we can glean from the inscriptions, while others, like Ronald Sack, choose to cast the whole story into a Jewish midrashic context.[28]

Even if this event could be shown to be the beginning of the settlement of the Jews in Arabia, we have to wait until after the destruction of the Second Temple for further word on the fate and structure of these settlements. By that time, as we shall see, Jews were well integrated into the land of the Arabs. In particular, linguistic assimilation seems to have taken place, and the Jews by Muhammad's time are represented as speaking Arabic, having Arabic names, and speaking a special dialect of Arabic in addition to reading Hebrew and Aramaic.

Evidence for the existence of a specialized Judeo-Arabic in Arabia in pre-Islamic times is both direct and indirect.[29] Indirectly we have the presence in the Qur'ân of a wide number of words, terms, and phrases derived from Jewish Hebrew and Aramaic.[30] In the Qur'ânic context, they are regarded as Arabic, clear and understandable to all Arabs.[31] This includes common words like *salât*, *sadaqah*, *zakât*, and *nabî* as well as many uncommon words. The simplest explanation for their presence in Arabic and their being regarded in the Qur'ân as "clear" Arabic is that they were assimilated into the vocabulary of the

Hijâz, at least, through the intermediary of the Jews who, both for themselves and for their Arab neighbors, used to read the Scriptures in Hebrew and translate them into Arabic. In other words, in the bilingual environment of Arabian Judaism, the Jews were probably acting as other Jews did in the Diaspora and preparing "Targums" in Arabic.[32]

The direct evidence also comes from Islamic times, but has to be regarded as having developed sometime before the advent of Muhammad. If we assume that Judeo-Arabic was part of the linguistic milieu, we would expect to find statements about such a commonplace cultural-linguistic situation only in those traditions in which it was vital for the point of the narrative to mention them. We find just such a mention in al-Wâqidî's version of the raid against Abû Râfiʿ, the prominent Jewish leader in the heavily fortified city of Khaybar.[33] The leader of this expedition is listed as ʿAbdullâh b. ʿAtîk, although ʿAbdullâh b. ʾUnays was along, did the actual killing, and was the more experienced leader. The reason for placing an unknown in charge of the raid was that Ibn ʿAtîk's mother was a Khaybar Jewess, providing them with an inside contact, but, more important, Ibn ʿAtîk could speak al-yahûdiyyah, a dialect of Arabic. The success of the raid depended on the group's ability to infiltrate the most securely guarded fortress in Arabia, and Ibn ʿAtîk proved equal to the task.[34] Muhammad's amanuensis, Zayd b. Thâbit, is said to have learned al-yahûdiyyah in seventeen days in order to be able to understand what the Jews were writing, an indication that the differences between Arabic and al-yahûdiyyah were matters of vocabulary and script; they were not different languages.[35]

As indicated above, it is difficult to ascertain the beginnings of the development of this phenomenon. If we use the model of other Jews in the Diaspora, the hints we get about the linguistic assimilation of the Jews of Arabia to Arabic do not seem strange, but it must have taken some number of generations for the vocabulary of the Jewish communities to penetrate the regular speech of the Arabs of the Hijâz. It is unlikely, however, that the linguistic conditions prevailing in the centuries immediately before Muhammad have their direct origins in the Jews who came with Nabonidus. It is more likely that the period after the destruction of the Second Temple is the time for the formation of the communities as we come to see them later, and until more archaeological evidence allows us to see the time before the Roman occupation of the eastern Mediterranean, we shall have to direct our greatest attention to events in this millennium. With the beginning of Rome's domination of the eastern Mediterranean, we have slightly more and surer evidence of Jewish events in Arabia.

3

JEWS, ARABS, AND ROMANS

By the time Rome became a Mediterranean power, the territory that the Romans would call Arabia was already ruled by an enterprising, skillful, and peaceful Arab people, the Nabataeans. As early as 312 B.C.E., when a Greek heir to Alexander attempted to conquer them at Petra, the heart of their national homeland, the Nabataean Arabs were controlling a region that extended from the Ḥijâz to Damascus.[1] They were resourceful and wealthy, and their sources of wealth are a good indication of why they were courted and eventually invaded by the world's powers.

One source of Nabataean income was the trade in aromatics from the south. There is no indication that the Nabataeans controlled the trade routes beyond the northern reaches of the Ḥijâz, but they did control the major trade routes into the settled areas of the eastern Mediterranean and the Red Sea. Diodorus states that they procured frankincense and myrrh, as well as other spices, and brought them down to the sea.[2] Their overland route must have gone through the area of Transjordan, across the Wâdi 'Arabah to Gaza and al-'Arîsh (Rhinocolura).[3] Nabataean territory also included the Negev and the Sinai. At the point that they came under the gaze of historians, they appear to have been in the process of becoming sedentary, at least in some of the areas under their control. But their origins were as pastoral nomads, and they retained enough of the bedouin skills to exploit the desert and, for a long time, use it as a defense against invasion.[4]

Until Arabia Nabataea became a Roman province in 106 C.E., the Nabataeans were generally successful in keeping Roman military presence out of the area. The attempted Roman invasion of Arabia around 26 B.C.E. is probably the most famous Roman military incursion into the Arabian peninsula and shows the ambivalence that the Nabataeans had in aiding their new Roman allies, on the one hand, and protecting their territory and trade routes, on the other. When Caesar Augustus cast his eye toward the East, he naturally was attracted to the wealth and position of the Sabaean Arabs who lived in Arabia Felix, the southern tip of Arabia. So he ordered his Egyptian prefect, Aelius Gallus, to undertake an expedition to make the Sabaeans either allies or subjects.[5] Fortunately for us, we have a fairly complete account of this unfortunate expedition by the pen of Aelius Gallus' friend, the geographer Strabo.

Strabo reports that Augustus had heard a report that the inhabitants of Arabia Felix "were very wealthy, and that they sold aromatics and the most valuable stones for gold and silver, but never expended with outsiders any part of what they received in exchange."[6] So he sent Aelius Gallus, "for he expected either to deal with wealthy friends or to master wealthy enemies. He was encouraged also by the expectation of assistance from the Nabataeans since they were friendly and promised to co-operate with him in every way."[7] The expedition's failure was blamed on the Nabataean envoy, Syllaeus, who is reported to have led the force through a difficult route into the Arabian interior. They left from Egypt by boat and landed at Leuce Come in the Hijâz. From there, they went inland and then south to the Sabaean city of Mârib, near which they established a garrison.[8] Lack of water and exhaustion of the troops compelled Aelius Gallus to abandon the siege before his objectives were met and to retreat back to the Hijâz in defeat.[9] Of particular interest to us is Strabo's report that the Roman troops were augmented by "Roman allies, among whom were five hundred Jews and one thousand Nabataeans under Syllaeus."[10] According to Josephus, these troops were sent by Herod, who probably wished to ingratiate himself with the Romans and get a piece of the lucrative aromatics trade.[11] They would have been welcome, for

Jews had a reputation as excellent fighters and were much in demand as soldiers.[12]

For later history, the name "Nabataean" became synonymous with irrigation and agriculture, for it appears that they brought hydraulic technology in full force to Arabia. Archaeological discoveries in the Negev have revealed that the Nabataeans employed a series of terraces, catch basins, and dams to turn otherwise barren land into gardens of abundant dates and grapes.[13] While they applied their agricultural techniques wherever they were, the principal areas of agricultural settlement were in the region of the Hawrân, far to the north of the Negev, where there was extensive settlement.[14] A third source of income was from bitumen obtained from the Dead Sea.[15]

Nabataean settlements are situated along all the major trading routes from Arabia Felix north to Syria and west to the sea. It would appear that the Nabataeans, like others who have followed them in the Jordan and the Negev, recognized that agricultural settlements could provide centers of control in otherwise open land, so they were able to derive strategic reward as well as material wealth. This Nabataean wealth was enticing to those who knew of it, but even without the agriculture, the land they controlled was vital to any power that wished to control the eastern Mediterranean. For Rome, Nabataean lands could be a barrier against the Parthians, their dreaded rivals for control of the East, as well as a conduit for trade.

The Nabataeans are regarded by most modern historians as Arabs, a term that requires some explanation at this point, because understanding this term will help us understand the complex and fluid relationships between Jews and Arabs around Roman times. The Nabataeans were philhellenes and employed Greek art and culture; and after 82 B.C.E. Aretas III began issuing coins with Greek legends.[16] But they were not completely Hellenized either in language or in religion.[17] They used Aramaic for international correspondence with the settled cultures of the Near East and for their inscriptions, but Arabic was their mother tongue. Arabic was also the language they must have had to use for commerce with the Arabian peninsula, and, as Shahîd has observed, this "vast ethnic and cultural reservoir of Arab presence" contributed significantly to keeping the ethnic awareness of the Nabataeans alive.[18] In other words, depending on what situation obtained or who was doing the reporting, the Nabataeans could present a different face to different peoples, Greek, Aramaic, or Arabic. This is, of course, characteristic of the Near East. Even when the same people vigorously defend their ethnic and cultural heritage, they can be international and cosmopolitan, but the Nabataeans appear to have been a cultural bridge between the Hellenistic Mediterranean and the culture of the interior of Arabia. For someone wishing to penetrate into Arabia Deserta, Nabataean culture pointed the way, and the Nabataeans themselves guarded the roads.

Relations between the Nabataeans and the Jewish inhabitants of Judea vacillated between friendly cooperation and mutual aggression. During the period of the Maccabees, Nabataeans received the fugitive high priest Jason and later advised Judas Maccabee and his brother Jonathan.[19] Some seventy years later, around 93 B.C.E., the Hasmonaean Alexander Jannaeus lost a battle to the Nabataean king Obodas, nearly lost his life, and was forced to surrender territory to the expansionist Arab kingdom.[20] The involvement of Rome and Roman interests complicate the relations between Judea and Arabia Nabataea, but the issues ran deeper than politics and economics, at least for the Jews if not also for the fiercely independent Nabataeans. The Jews, whether in Judea or dispersed in the rest of the Greco-Roman world, were often in conflict with the fundamental approach of Hellenism to the world.

Hellenism, while often tolerant of private idiosyncrasies, regulated public conduct through citizenship in the city-state, the *polis*. Through the *polis* one exercised the privileges of tax exemption, the ability to litigate, and the ability to act freely—free, that is, as long as one did not stray from the norms of public life. Mosaic law also regulated public conduct and stipulated certain behaviors that the Hellene found abhorrent. For the Greek, the body was a temple, a measure of all things, and mutilation of the body was barbaric and evil. Thus circumcision, central not only to Jews but to others in the Near East, was regarded as an evil atavism. Further, the pagan Hellene regarded the human body as an object of beauty, to be admired and displayed, particularly in the games. For the traditional Jew, both the nakedness of the athletes and their participation in the pagan religious ceremonies of the games was anathema. Jewish religious observances and customs tended to separate Jews from Greeks, and the Greeks responded with suspicion, prejudice, and hatred.[21]

Not all Jews, of course, despised the Hellenic culture, and the history of Judaism in the period from the Seleucids through the destruction of the Second Temple shows a marked increase in accommodation to the Greek world even among the staunchly traditional Pharisees.[22] Indeed, anti-Hellenic feelings were most pronounced in Jerusalem and Judea. In the Diaspora, particularly in Egypt, Jews coexisted with their Greek neighbors, desirous of and sometimes achieving full participation in the *polis*. One remarkable product of the Greco-Judaic symbiosis was the Septuagint, Scripture in Greek for Jews who had lost much, if not all, of their Hebrew and Aramaic. The Septuagint also facilitated the linguistic Hellenization of the Jews of the Diaspora, and was an Egyptian substitute for the oral law being developed as the Talmuds in Palestine and Babylon.[23]

The destruction of the Temple in 70 C.E. sent shock waves through the Jewish world, killed or enslaved thousands of Jews, but did not extinguish the flame of Judaism even in Judea. Pharisaic rabbis took the lead in transforming and saving Judaism, and the most important figure for the future of Pharisaic Judaism was Johanan b. Zakkai, the student of Hillel and Shammai, and the founder and first president of the rabbinical academy at Jabneh. While his exploits are enshrouded in myth, particularly those associated with the destruction of Jerusalem, it is clear that Johanan b. Zakkai was the moving force in transferring Jewish religious activity from the Temple to the rabbinic academies.[24] He transferred privileges previously associated with Jerusalem to Jabneh[25] and decreed that he had the authority to determine the time of the beginning of the new month. His academy was more than a place of study,[26] for it served as a substitute for the law court, which had been in Jerusalem.[27] His doctrine that righteousness had the same force as a sin-offering[28] is one of the foundation stones for the diminution of the centrality of the rites of Temple sacrifice among his followers. Through him and those of his persuasion, Judaism became independent of the locus of the Temple and could survive in the Diaspora with the portability of the oral and written Torah.

The final blow to the centrality of Jerusalem came with the Second Roman War, the Bar Kochba Revolution, which also brought widespread devastation and misery in Judea. The discontent of the Jews throughout the Roman empire was a cause for considerable concern among Rome's leaders, and they employed the two-pronged policy of redress of grievances and military force to deal with the problem of a possible Jewish revolt in the Roman *oikoumene*. One area of contention between the Diaspora Jews and the Roman government was Rome's collection of a "Temple" tax, originally intended for the Temple, but after 70 C.E. directed to Rome's coffers as the unprecedented *Fiscus Judaicus*. During the course of the development of the *Fiscus Judaicus*, much of the unofficial racial hatred of the Jews became embodied in the manner in which the tax was collected, so that Jews and those with distant Jewish ancestors were subject to harsh treatment as well as this impost. Rabbinic authorities had said that the Temple tax was a duty of every Jew while the Temple was still standing, and when the Temple was destroyed, some held that it was no longer an obligation to pay the tax. This attitude was interpreted as treasonous by the Romans, who tended to see all the Jews as part of a despised ethnic unit regardless of where they might live within the empire. While the procedures for assessment and collection of this tax were "reformed," the hated tax was not abolished.[29] Persecutions of Jews, and incidentally Judeo-Christians, continued, aimed with particular intensity toward anyone with claims of descent from the house of David; and starting in 115 C.E., the emperor Trajan prosecuted a war against the Parthians, which reduced many Babylonian and Mesopotamian Jewish communities to Roman control, increasing the number of anti-Hellenistic and discontented Jews in the empire.

Jewish reaction was intense and violent. Revolts against Rome broke out throughout the empire, and Messianic hopes were awakened in those who felt that the Parthians would defeat Rome, reconquer Judea, and prepare the way for the coming of the Messiah. Both 2 Esdras and 2 Baruch bear witness to these feelings. Rabbis preached obedience to Rome but hoped for divine intervention to bring about the "New Edom's" demise.[30] Around 116 C.E. a revolt broke out in Cyrenaica, which spread to Cyprus and Egypt.[31] The revolts were put down with great loss of life and property to both Greeks and Jews, and the Alexandrian community was severely damaged. By 117 C.E. when Emperor Hadrian visited Egypt, the troubles were only barely under control, but Jewish legend credits Hadrian with an extravagant generosity to the Jews, promising them the ability to rebuild the Temple. While this legend seems unlikely, it was probably born of Hadrian's apparent liberalism. In fact, however, he was a thorough Hellenist and had a vision of the integration of all Rome's subjects into the *oikoumene*. One item from Hadrian's whole program was specially hateful to the Jews—Hadrian's ban on circumcision. When this was coupled with the foundation of Aelia Capitolina on the site of Jerusalem, linking Hadrian's own family and the Capitoline Zeus to the location of the Temple, and funding the construction with the *Fiscus Judaicus*, Judea was inflamed in the Second Roman War, beginning in 132 C.E.

The Second Roman War was actually planned well before 132 C.E. by Simon bar Kozibah, better known in history as Simon Bar Kochba, a name given him by his staunchest rabbinic supporter, Rabbi Akiba ben Joseph, at that time Judea's principal Pharisaic leader.[32] After initial success, the revolt against the Romans was ended with general slaughter at Bethar, and Simon Bar Kochba died in 135 C.E., it is alleged on the sixty-fifth anniversary of the destruction of the Temple. Thousands of Jews were sold into slavery, many others fled to other lands, and Judea was renamed Syria-Palestina to remove any reminder of Jewish nationalism. As a final blow, Jews were forbidden to visit the Temple mount or the environs of Jerusalem.

In the persecutions of remaining Jews after the revolt, Ten Martyrs, including the aged Rabbi Akiba, were executed. Rabbi Akiba was a central figure in developing the ideology of the revolt and was an active recruiter for its support. He made numerous trips throughout the Diaspora expounding the cause, and even traveled to Arabia.[33] While almost nothing is recorded of his journey to the Jewish communities in Arabia, we can safely assume that his mission was at least that of bringing the word of the revolt to potentially sympathetic Pharisaic Jews living in Arabia.[34]

Rabbi Akiba's journey to Arabia raises an issue of importance to our consideration of the existence and nature of the Jewish communities there. It is a source of some regret that we do not have more concrete information about the aims of this Pharisaic leader in Arabia, but he is not the first Pharisee to go. Paul, who had been Saul of Tarsus, spent three years in Arabia after his conversion to Christianity.[35] Paul had been a pupil of Rabbi Gamaliel I and a staunch Pharisee. He is represented as having vigorously persecuted Christians before he became one himself.

Aside from the information that Paul went to Arabia, almost nothing is known for certain about the time he spent there. It is possible to make an argument, however, that Arabia was attractive to him just as it was to the student of the next generation after his, Rabbi Akiba. But where in Arabia might Paul have gone? Because Damascus is specifically mentioned in the New Testament records of Paul's missionary activities,[36] we must assume that it was outside Damascus, possibly inside Arabia Nabataea.

Arabia Nabataea was under the rule of Aretas IV, and, according to the evidence of 2 Corinthians 11:32, his rule included Damascus at this time. As indicated above, Arabia would have been understood to extend from the environs of Petra south, through the Negev and Sinai into the Hijâz—and throughout all of these areas Jews had become settlers, farmers, and participants in the Nabataean economy. Some of these Jews dwelling in Arabia, according to contemporaneous Christian reports, were "devout men" who would return to Jerusalem to participate in Temple celebrations connected with Shabu'ôt.[37]

From a period slightly later than Paul, we have records from one of the caves above En Geddi that a Jewess, Babatha, the daughter of Simeon, retreated into the caves to try to survive the Bar Kochba Revolution.[38] The earliest document is dated to 93 C.E., taking it back to nearly the time of Paul.[39] Babatha's father, Simeon, had settled in Zoar, southeast of the Dead Sea near the lands of the Nabataean king.[40] Undoubtedly through use of Nabataean techniques of irrigation, he grew date-palms, and was guaranteed title to the land through the Nabataean legal system. During the period under documentation, there appear to have been a number of Jews moving into Nabataean areas, increasing when the area became a Roman province.[41] The documents show that the Jews in the new province did not escape Roman culture by moving to Provincia Arabia, because all the litigation in the legal documents is in the Roman tradition.[42] The combination of economic opportunities, the right to hold land legally, and the familiarity of culture probably all combined to make the transition easy for these pioneers out of Judea. Babatha's records end in 132 C.E., just as the Bar Kochba Revolt was gathering force. As Bowersock observes, Babatha probably fled to the relative security of the Judean caves to avoid reprisals and would not have been alone.[43] Others must have decided to leave their Arabian gardens for other places of safety.

We cannot be certain what kind of Jews emigrated from Judea into Arabia Nabataea, but it is a safe assumption that they were wealthy enough to purchase lands from the Nabataeans, Hellenized enough to fit within Nabataean society, and, if Babatha is any example, still strongly enough identified with Judaism to return to Judea at the outbreak of the Bar Kochba Revolution. They probably subscribed to or accepted some notion of political and/or religious Messianism, and practiced a kind of Judaism that was largely independent of the Temple cult. In other words, they were likely the kind of Pharisaic Jews who would be candidates for Rabbi Akiba's message of the new political messiah, Bar Kochba. They would also have appeared to have been likely candidates for conversion to Paul's political and religious messiah, Jesus, a generation earlier.[44]

The fact that we fail to hear of Arabian churches being formed as a result of Paul's missionary activity should not cause us to regard his sojourn as any different from his preaching among the Jews in the synagogues in Damascus or elsewhere in his early career. Paul's mission was eventually to the Gentiles, but he usually worked through the Hellenized Pharisaic Jews in the synagogues and through the "Godfearers" (phoboumenoi) and the "reverent ones" (sebomenoi), the Judaizers who were the natural links between Judaism and the Hellenistic pagan world.[45]

As we shall see below, later Jewish communities in Arabia exhibit all the features of the Pharisaic Jews known by Paul and Rabbi Akiba. They followed the Torah and subscribed to the oral law, governed themselves by rabbis, and expected the Messiah. It would seem that the Arabian traditions about the formation of the Jewish communities in the Hijâz are probably right, and that Jews did flee from Roman persecutions into Arabia. The struggles against foreign domination from the time of the Maccabees to the end of the Bar Kochba Revolt, which saw the transformation of Judaism from a Temple-centered religion to a more abstract and portable religion based on the Torah, also saw an increase in the strength and viability of Jewish communities in the Roman empire. Those who were discontent and those who found economic opportunity limited in the center of the Greco-Roman oikoumene, fled to the peripheries, Gaul, Iberia, and, of course, Arabia. While Jews were present in the peninsula prior to the events of 70 C.E. and 135 C.E., it is after this that Arabian Judaism begins to flourish.

4

THE SOUTHERN JEWISH KINGDOMS

Legends found among the Jews of southern Arabia credit the introduction of Judaism in the southern areas of Arabia to the union of King Solomon and the Queen of Sheba, named in Islamic sources as Bilqîs.[1] Sheba, Bilqîs' land, was a land of aromatics and riches, and, because of the biblical story, this land is often connected with the mysterious land of Ophir. Legend says that the union of the two monarchs produced a son. In order that he be brought up in proper Jewish fashion, Solomon sent Jews from Israel to see to his edification.[2] These Jews were the first in southern Arabia and are credited with the establishment of a fortress near San'â.[3] While there is probably a kernel of truth in associating the earliest Jewish penetration of the south of Arabia with events like Solomon's excursions into the Red Sea from Ezion-geber, there is insufficient evidence to attribute the formation of the Yemenite Jewish community that early. Some modern historians of the spice trade from Arabia, such as Nigel Groom, would dispute the presence of aromatics trade that early,[4] but it is clear that some sort of trade was carried on between the land of Israel and the countries along the Red Sea.[5]

Another legend credits some 75,000 Jews with believing Jeremiah's prophecy about the destruction of the Temple and fleeing to Arabia, taking with them their household goods.[6] As mentioned above, when Ezra called all Jews of the Diaspora to the ingathering, the Yemenite Jews refused the return in anticipation of the destruction of the Temple again. Within the community, this legend seems to have functioned as a historical explanation of the continued presence of the community outside Jerusalem and the land of Israel. The two legends taken together link the community solidly to biblical tradition and neatly account for the group's continued existence in the face of a direct command to return. This became the accepted historical explanation for those within and without the southern Arabian Jewish communities, and lent to those Jews the dignity and prestige of an antique heritage.

Procopius of Caesarea, writing about the period of Justinian (518–610 C.E.), mentions the presence of Jews in the southern part of Arabia:

> At about the time of this war Hellestheaeus, the king of the Aethiopians, who was a Christian and a most devoted adherent of this faith, discovered that a number of the Homeritae on the opposite mainland were oppressing the Christians there outrageously; many of these rascals were Jews, and many of them held in reverence the old faith which men of the present day call Hellenic. He therefore collected a fleet of ships and an army and came against them, and he conquered them in battle and slew both the king and many of the Homeritae.[7]

Procopius continues with a description of the establishment of a Christian kingdom among the Homeritae, a revolt against the Ethiopian-supported king by a certain Abramus, and the desire of Justinian that the Homeritae "establish Caisus, the fugitive, as captain over the Maddeni, and with a great army of their own people and of the Maddene Saracens make an invasion into the land of the Persians."[8] With Procopius' story, we are introduced to one of the most unusual events in Arabian Jewish history, the rise of the Jewish kingdom of the Yemen and the brief but ambitious career of its king, Yûsuf Dhû Nuwâs.

Justinian's aim was that the Ethiopians and the Homeritae

> on account of their community of religion should make common cause with the Romans in the war against the Persians; for he purposed that the Aethiopians, by purchasing silk from India and selling it among the Romans, might themselves gain much

money, while causing the Romans to profit in only one way, namely, that they be no longer compelled to pay over their money to their enemy."[9]

The two elements of religion and economics interplay in late fifth- and early sixth-century Arabia in such a manner as to draw the inhabitants of the peninsula into the conflict between the superpowers of the time, Byzantium and Persia. This was a conflict that continued the Greco-Persian hostilities dating back as far as Herodotus, but was updated by the passions of doctrinal conflict within Christianity and war between Christianity and its chief competitor in Arabia, Judaism.

Internal struggles within Christianity that pitted one Christian against another and divided countries and regions by charges of heresy and acts of persecution, the written accounts of which are so crucial to our understanding of this era of Arabian history, can be dated with the ecumenical movement from shortly before the Council of Nicaea in 325 C.E. On the theological level, the period from Nicaea until after the Council of Chalcedon in 451 C.E. was a period of defining the nature of Jesus Christ and his relationship to God. The process of definition was made particularly difficult because it required the merger of claims found in Christian Scripture, which held that Jesus was both human and divine, with Greek logical requirements that hold that an entity cannot be more than one thing at a time. Essential to the Christian scheme of salvation is the belief that Jesus was the son of God, born through a human mother, Mary, and that he lived a human existence until his death, resurrection, and ascension into heaven. The issue for many people in that period, not just academic theologians as we would find today, was how to reconcile the two "natures" of Jesus, the human and the divine, for in order for the plan of salvation "to work" Jesus had to be both at the same time.

Coupled with the theological issues of the definition of the godhead were the temporal issues of power and self-determination. Following the natural divisions of the known world by language, custom, and tradition, differing centers of power developed within the early Christian church. The bishops of Rome and Constantinople were often recognized as spiritual heads of that part of the church that occupied territories of the former Roman empire, but only because the inhabitants were used to looking to those cities as the centers of bureaucracy and judicial administration. Alexandria, Antioch, and Jerusalem also claimed jurisdiction, at least over their immediate areas, and the inhabitants of the Egyptian and Aramaic-speaking areas resisted Greek claims of superiority emanating from Constantinople. As the Roman empire after Justinian became more and more theocratic, centralized temporal control was exercised through the structure of the church. Greek was imposed as the liturgical language, and celebration of the Mass in Syriac and Coptic became the symbols for resistance to domination by Byzantium. Taxes and doctrinal conformity replaced taxes and worship of the emperor as outward signs of loyalty to the state. In the fourth-century-Mediterranean world, adoption of a particular Christological doctrine meant a declaration of loyalty to a religious ideal, a political party, a local language, and an ideal of an autonomous region. Such a coupling of theology and politics found adherents willing to kill and die for their beliefs. Theology was debated not only in the sanctity of the council chambers but also, and with more vigor, in the streets and on the battlefields.

The great church councils, starting with Nicaea in 325 C.E., were designed to produce one unified Christian world through the adoption of generally acceptable creedal statements. The process of definition, however, is exclusive as well as inclusive, and those views that were excluded from the belief set of the community were branded as heretical, and those who held excluded beliefs were expunged from the community if they could not be persuaded to change their views. Many who found themselves branded as heretics fled from persecution into the wildernesses of the desert. They were soon followed by missionaries and others intent on converting the world to their particular point of view. Arabia, which had earlier been a refuge for Jews, also became a refuge for Christians, a circumstance that destined it to play an important part in the two simultaneous conflicts, the Greco-Persian war and Christian internecine struggle. The Jews of Arabia found themselves in the middle of both these struggles.

In 428 C.E. a monk from Antioch named Nestorius became bishop of Constantinople. Famous as a preacher and popular as a melodious liturgist, Nestorius started his episcopal career as a zealous supporter of orthodoxy, expunging Constantinople of heretics. One of his fellow Antiochans, a priest named Anastasius, rejecting the notion of Mary as *Theotokos*, that is, the Bearer of God, invited Nestorius' defense.

From the ensuing debate, Nestorius and others developed the doctrine that Jesus possessed two distinct natures in one body and that the divine nature was separate from the human one. Rome and Alexandria condemned Nestorius' doctrine, holding that Jesus had only one composite nature, melded by a mystery, and the ecumenical Council of Ephesus in 431 C.E. confirmed the condemnation, and deposed and excommunicated Bishop Nestorius. After Nestorius' death, his views gained support chiefly in Syria where they often became the focal point for resistance to Byzantine Orthodoxy and Egyptian Monophysitism. Pressure from Byzantium forced Nestorianism into areas under Persian control and, when Emperor Zeno expelled all Nestorians from the empire, Nestorianism and Nestorians fled to the Persians. Nestorian Christianity, practicing its liturgy in Syriac, became the Christianity tolerated in the Persian periphery, and Arabia became one of its missionary aims.

Alexandria, the center for Hellenistic learning in the eastern Mediterranean, became a leading center of Christianity from a relatively early date. Alexandrian bishops led church councils, and Alexandrian missionaries spread Christianity into Africa and Asia. Called Copts, a form of the name that gives us the name Egypt, these missionizing Christians spread to Nubia and Ethiopia, so that by the time of the Council of Chalcedon in 451 C.E., the area from Egypt to Ethiopia was, nominally at least, under the control of the bishop of the See of Alexandria. At the Council of Chalcedon, Pope Leo I led a condemnation against the Alexandrine interpretations of the nature of Jesus, charging them with "monophysitism," that is, the belief that Jesus had but one nature, the human element subsumed into the divine in accord with their interpretation of the Nicaean Creed that Jesus was "truly God." The Egyptian Christians did not at first call themselves Monophysite, which they regarded as an insult, but they did emphasize the unity of the divine and human elements, and when they were condemned as heretics, they began to assert their independence from Constantinople. They rejected Greek as the liturgical language, changed the calendar slightly, and refused to pay taxes. The Greeks periodically invaded Egypt to try to force Orthodoxy on the Coptic population, but the attempts were unsuccessful. Coptic missionary successes in Africa, however, placed the Egyptian church in a strategic position by Arabia and, heretics or no, the Byzantine rulers saw

Monophysite Copts as preferable to Nestorian Persian clients and useful for their aims against their enemy.

By the beginning of the fifth century, Arabia was the scene of intense
missionary activity. In general, the Persian Gulf areas were under the
influence of the Persians and their Nestorians, while the Red Sea areas
were Monophysite and nominally under Byzantine control. Persia
aggressively asserted itself in both the Ḥijâz and the Yemen, acting
through local agents to collect taxes. In the Ḥijâz, the Jewish tribes of the
B. Qurayẓa and the B. an-Naḍîr were set up by the Persians as "kings" of
Medina to collect the kharâj tax.[10] The connection was through the
Lakhmid dynasty at Ḥîra, the center of Persian clientage among the
Arabs and the center of Nestorian missionary activity.[11] According to a
report from at-Tabarî, the head of the Lakhmid dynasty at Ḥîra was a
"governor" for the Persians in the areas of ʿIrâq, Jazîrah, and the Ḥijâz as
early as the last decades of the fourth century.[12] From Byzantine perspective, then, Judaism in the Ḥijâz would have been identified with Persian
interests and ambitions in Arabia.

Christianity was not the only religion to have its missionaries in
Arabia. According to Ibn Isḥâq, Judaism was introduced into south-
ern Arabia by missionary rabbis brought to the Yemen by the last
Tubbaʿ king of the Yemen, Tibân Asʿad Abû Karib.[13] While Abû
Karib was campaigning against the Jewish city of Medina, he was
deterred by two rabbis who impressed him with their knowledge.
He converted to Judaism and took the rabbis to the land of the
Himyar in the Yemen. His people refused him reentry into his land
until his rabbis bested their pagan priests in a series of ordeals
involving fire. The rabbis emerged from the fire unscathed, in the
manner of Abraham or the three in the furnace, Azariah, Hananiah,
and Mishael. The story in Ibn Isḥâq is full of legendary material and
is part of the genealogical cycle that forms the introduction to the
biography of Muhammad. Yet we know that when the Christian
missionary Theophilus came to the Yemen in the middle of the
fourth century, he found a great number of Jews.[14] By the middle of
the next century, the rulers of the Yemen are using monotheistic
formulas that appear to be Jewish or based on Judaic ideals.[15] The
adoption of Judaism by the rulers of the Yemen does not necessarily
mean that all of the native population was converted, but it does
point to the cultural and political attractiveness of Judaism, particu-

larly when it could be regarded as a statement of separation from and opposition to the Christian kingdom in Ethiopia and their distant ally, Byzantium.

In Ibn Isḥâq's chronology of the Yemen, the son of Tibân Asʿad Abû Karib, Ḥassân, was overthrown by a Lakhnîʿa Yanûf Dhû Shanatîr, a person with no connection with the royal family of the Tubbaʿ.[16] His policy for consolidation of power was either to kill the leaders of the society or to sodomize them, rendering them unfit for rule because of their shame. Ibn Isḥâq informs us:

> One day [Dhû Shanatîr] sent for Zurʿa Dhû Nuwâs son of Tibân Asʿad brother of Hassân. He was a little boy when Ḥassân was murdered and had become a fine handsome young man of character and intelligence. When the messenger came he perceived what was intended and took a fine sharp knife and hid it under the sole of his foot and went to Lakhnîʿa. As soon as they were alone he attacked him and Dhû Nuwâs rushed upon him and stabbed him to death. He then cut off his head and put it in the window which overlooked the men below. He stuck the toothpick in his mouth and went out to the guards, who in coarse language inquired what had happened. "Ask that head," he replied. They looked at the window and there was Lakhnîʿa's head cut off. So they went in pursuit of Dhû Nuwâs and said: "You must be our king and no one else, seeing that you have rid us of this disgusting fellow." They made him king and all the tribes of Himyar joined him. He was the last of the Yamanî kings. He adopted Judaism and Himyar followed him. He was called Joseph and reigned for some considerable time.[17]

For Ibn Isḥâq, Dhû Nuwâs appears to be a legitimate claimant to the throne, although his father is called the last of the Tubbaʿ, which epithet may mean only that each ruler ruled in succession without interruption. Certainly there is clear evidence of co-regency in the Himyaritic dynasties, and unbroken succession may have been a cultural desideratum. Dhû Nuwâs's conversion to Judaism, which is followed by the rest of the Himyarites, is mentioned without comment. For Ibn Isḥâq this type of conversion would not have seemed strange. Rulers of tribes converted to Islam during the lifetime of Muhammad, and the whole or the majority of the tribe was regarded as having con-

40

A History of the Jews of Arabia

verted unless specific mention was made to the contrary. Careful examination of the traditions has led us to understand that this type of conversion, whether in this instance to Judaism, or later to Islam, did not always embrace everyone, but such a situation, also, appears to have been regarded as usual enough not to warrant special mention.

Franz Altheim concludes that Medina remained the primary source of inspiration for Dhû Nuwâs's Judaism.[18] In part, his conclusions are based on the existence of a triangular relationship involving Medina, Dhû Nuwâs's Himyarite kingdom in the Yemen, and the Lakhmid dynasty in Hîra, ruled by Mundhir III. He sees an attempt to construct a Jewish client state allied with Hîra as a means of extending Lakhmid power, and, by extension, Persian power, in territory sought by the Ethiopian-Byzantine axis.[19] The one major impediment to Mundhir's plan was the center of Monophysite Christianity, the city of Najrân. Altheim's construct assumes that Medina was linked to the other cities of the Hijâz as a major political center for Arabian Judaism, that Dhû Nuwâs was in close touch with both Hîra and Medina, and that Dhû Nuwâs had a politico-religious agenda.

Medina was situated just beyond the southern end of Nabataean influence in the fourth century but was an important part of the Jewish sphere of cities in the Hijâz. The cities of Medina, Khaybar, Fadak, Hegrâ (Madâ'in Sâlih), al-'Ulâ, Taymâ, Tabûk, and the island of Yotabê sat astride the main communication and trade routes of western Arabia, and all were inhabited or dominated by Jews. From a grave inscription dated to around 355 C.E. from Hegrâ, we see the linkage between Hegrâ and Taymâ:

1. This is the stele and the grave which was constructed
2. by 'Adnôn, the son of Hny, the son of Shmw'1, the Prince
3. of Hegrâ, for Mônâh, his wife, the daughter of
4. 'Amr(w), the son of 'Adnôn, the son of Shmw'1,
5. the Prince of Taimâ [Taymâ], who died in the month
6. /7. of Ab, in the year 251
7. /8. at the age of thirty-eight.[20]

It appears that the town leadership for both Hegrâ and Taymâ in the middle of the fourth century were grandsons of the same Jewish ancestor, Samuel (Shmw'l).[21] From the nearby town of al-'Ulâ, another inscription indicates the presence of Levites.[22] The mention of

Samuel in association with Taymâ at this early date produces, of course, anticipatory resonance with another Taymân Samuel, as-Samaw'al of the castle al-Ablaq, nearly 200 years later.

We need not assume that Dhû Nuwâs had to rely only on the Jewish activists of the city of Medina for his knowledge of Judaism. According to the Chronicle of Se'ert, Yûsuf's mother was a Jewess from Nisibis, married the Ḥimyarite king, Ma'dîkarib Ya'fur, and first taught him Judaism.[23] As we have seen above, from at least the middle of the fifth century, the kings of the Ḥimyarites were using formulas that were either Jewish or strongly influenced by Judaism, and sometime after 496 C.E. the king Marthad-'ilan Yanûf left a dedicatory inscription that concluded with a Jewish formula.[24] It is unfortunate that we know so little about Dhû Nuwâs's mother, but it is striking that she is reported to have come from Nisibis. During Herodian times, this northeastern Mesopotamian town was an important center of Jewish intellectual life and the location of the school of Judah Bar Bathyra.[25] It was well within the Persian sphere of influence, and the marriage indicates the extent of Persian influence among the Jewish inhabitants of the Yemen.

It is not certain when Yûsuf assumed the role of the Ḥimyarites. Some would place it as early as 515 C.E.[26] while others would place the accession as late as 523 C.E.[27] Whichever date one chooses, Yûsuf's period of accession was a time of great pressure on the southern Arabian kingdom. Even though the great powers, Persia and Byzantium, had concluded a seven-year truce in 505, they continued their hostilities through their agents in Arabia. The Jewish trading colony on the island of Yotabê had come under Byzantine rule around 500, and by 515 Abyssinians were invading southern Arabia. The conflict had already taken on a religious character, and Yûsuf's father, Ma'dîkarib Ya'fur, had begun to persecute Christians, undoubtedly because of their role as agents of the Abyssinian Monophysite ambitions in Arabia.[28] When Justin I acceded to the Byzantine throne in 518, 'Ella 'Asbeha, the ruler of Abyssinia, was planning an invasion of the Ḥimyaritic kingdom. According to Smith's chronology, this would have been in reaction to Yûsuf's and his father's campaigns againt the Abyssinian Christians in Zafâr, Nûkhâ, and Majrân.[29]

Mundhir III b. Nu'man (505–53 C.E.) was king of Ḥîra and the vassal of the Sassanid ruler Kavad (488–530 C.E.), who had been involved in an unsuccessful plot with the Palestinian Jews. In the last quarter of the fifth century, Rabbinist Jews as well as Samaritans had revolted against Byzantine rule.[30] Their goal was independence, but the conflict between the Byzantines and the Persians provided hope for enough of a Persian victory to weaken Greek hold on Palestine.[31] To this end, the Palestinian Jews had been sending priests as missionaries and agents provocateurs to support the Jewish kingdom of Himyar and advise the king.[32] They joined the ranks of other foreign "advisers" sent by the various powers who had interests in the area. There were Byzantine and Abyssinian advisers among the Christians in Najrân and, somewhat surprisingly, Christian advisers from Persia and Hîra, Yûsuf's patrons.[33] While it appears that there was often support for the Himyarite kingdom from Persia and Hîra, Mundhir seems to have been pursuing his own course, often in conflict of Himyar. This conflict came to blows around 513 C.E. when Ma'dîkarib Ya'fur and his southern allies fought an alliance of the B. Tha'labat and troops of Mundhir.[34]

The kingdom that Yûsuf ruled appears to have been plagued by more than external pressures. Trade had been a major factor in the economy of the region, and it is likely that the hostilities disrupted the flow of goods up the western side of the peninsula. If the Muslim sources are reliable, this is the time of the ascent of the Meccans and their control of the trade, obviously at the expense of the south. Yûsuf's father had been compelled to borrow a large sum of money from a Christian in Najrân, some of which may have been a gift.[35] This did not solve his financial problems, and he had to ask for more from the same source. Ibn Ishâq's traditions report that someone from outside the royal family had seized power from Ma'dîkarib Ya'fur, and that Yûsuf's accession was a coup d'état in favor of the royal family. Subsequent events, as we shall see, support the view that there was more than one party claiming power in the kingdom.

The alliance that Yûsuf was able to bring together to fight the Abyssinians include some of the most prominent Himyaritic families, the most noted of which was the family of Dhû Yazan. From one inscription, we learn that Sharah²il Yaqbul, the son of Shurahbi²il Yakmul of the family of Yazan led the expedition against the Abyssinians in Zafâr, Mûkhâ, and Najrân, burned or destroyed the churches, and captured a tremendous booty.[36] This is an ancestor of Sayf b. Dhû Yazan, the Himyaritic hero of the saga of the expulsion of the Abys-

sinians from southern Arabia.[37] Another participant was Sumu-yafaᶜ
ʾAshwaᶜ, who was probably a Christian and would be appointed king
of the Ḥimyarites by ʾElla ʾAsbeha after Yûsuf's death.[38] Naturally this
major attack on Abyssinian interests could not go unanswered.

At some point before 523 C.E., and probably in connection with the
growing intensity of the conflict between Christians and Jews in
southern Arabia, the synagogue at Najrân was burned.[39] This had
been done by Ḥayyân b. Ḥayyân, who is said to have introduced
Christianity into Najrân, by which Monophysite Christianity must be
meant.[40] This appears to be one of the contributing causes for Yûsuf's
most fateful act, the instigation of a siege of Najrân and the persecution of its Christian population. This second persecution like the first,
invited foreign intervention, but unlike the first, the Abyssinians
destroyed the Ḥimyaritic kingdom, killed Yûsuf, and brought to an
end hopes for an expanded Jewish state.

We know about the persecution of the Christians of Najrân from the
martyrological narratives and the Islamic traditions based on the
Christian martyrologies. There are no extant Jewish records other
than the two inscriptions cited above,[41] so we are obliged to sort out
the events from narratives that have been obviously elaborated in the
hyperbolic manner of the hagiographic tradition. A recent thorough
study of the Christian and Islamic sources, prompted by the discovery
of a new document, demonstrates an essential consonance among the
variety of independent hagiographic narratives and adds to our confidence in the essential outlines of the events, even when we must distrust the number of martyrs and the manner of their individual
suffering.[42]

The surviving narrative of *The Book of the Himyarites* starts with the
events of 515 C.E. and the attack on the Abyssinian Christians in the
town of Ẓafâr. Yûsuf, who is called Masrûq, is said to have promised
with oaths that the 300 Abyssinian fighting men who were besieged in
the church could go free if they would surrender to his forces. When
they did so, he is said to have ordered their death despite the oaths,
the destruction of the church, the death of anyone not apostatizing,
and the death and destruction of the property of anyone found harboring Christians.[43] The narrative then continues with a detailed
description of the martyrdom by slow butchering of one of the inhabitants who would not deny his religion. This pattern is continued for

A HISTORY OF THE JEWS OF ARABIA

the remainder of the narrative, with Jewish untrustworthiness a recurrent topos. Yûsuf's claim, even as represented in the martyrologies, is that the towns of Zafâr, Mûkhâ, an Najrân were in revolt against his rightful and legitimate authority. He even offered to enter into litigation with the rebels in the country's courts if they were to cease hostilities.[44]

Najrân was besieged next, and it was evidently a heavily defended town, for the siege lasted for some time. One of the besieged Najrânîs, Daws Dhû Th'laban, escaped and is said to have informed the Byzantine emperor Justin, according to the Islamic version,[45] but an analysis of the Letters of Simeon of Bêth Arshan strongly indicates that knowledge of the events came through Simeon's letters, in part from refugees from Najrân and in part from information from Yûsuf himself. When some of the Najrânîs came out to Yûsuf, he treated them properly, promising them litigation and fines. These are called the "Pure Brethren of the Holy Order" and may not have represented all of the factions of the town.[46] The discovery of foreign agents in the town, and probably among the Pure Brethren, Monophysite agents from Ethiopia, Byzantium, and Persia, changed his mind about how the town should be treated.[47] He felt the need for a declaration of loyalty from the people he regarded as his subjects, and, since Christianity was identified with his enemies, the declaration took the form of a renunciation of the Christian faith.[48] The reaction was resistance by the Christians and increased rage by Yûsuf, and the bulk of the narrative of The Book of the Himyarites describes the terrible deaths of willing Monophysite martyrs.

At the completion of the siege, Yûsuf sent letters to the Lakhmid king Mundhir at Hîra and to the Persian emperor Kavad informing them of his actions, asking for their advice, and requesting that they treat the Christians among them as he had dealt with the Christians at Zafâr and Najrân.[49] Probably unknown to Yûsuf was that Mundhir was at that moment engaged in peace negotiations with the Byzantines at a conference at Ramla, a town some ten days' march from Hîra. Mundhir had successfully fought the Byzantines and had captured two Roman high officers. This prompted Justin to send Abraham, the son of Euphrasius, to negotiate the release of the soldiers and effect a peace with Mundhir. A secondary purpose for Justin was to intercede on behalf of the Diophysite Christians living in areas under Mundhir's control.[50] This was a legitimate concern both because of the strong Nestorian character of Mundhir's realm and because Mundhir apparently seriously considered acting toward the Christians as had Yûsuf. Indeed, at another time, Mundhir is reported to have sacrificed 400 Christian maidens to the goddess al-ʿUzzâ and later sacrificed the son of his Ghassânid enemy Arethas to the same goddess.[51] But his anti-Christian sentiments[52] could not overcome the political realities. Continued conflict with Byzantium would have isolated him from his Persian sovereign, since Kavad did not renew hostilities until some three years later, and a general persecution of Christians would have alienated the Christian elements in the Lakhmid army.

Even more dangerous for Yûsuf was the presence of Simeon of Bêth Arshan at the conference.[53] Simeon was a major Monophysite literary figure and an extremely effective apologist, as his letters show. When he heard of the persecutions, he publicized the events so skillfully that both the emperor Justin and eventually the Ethiopian Negus had to react. Simeon pointed out to the Byzantines the role that the Jews of Tiberias had played, probably as a way of indicating the extent and gravity of Yûsuf's rule of all the Himyaritic territory. So at Byzantine request, an invasion force of Ethiopians, ferried across the Red Sea in Byzantine ships, occupied the Yemen, and killed Yûsuf Dhû Nuwâs in 525 C.E., thus ending the hopes for a pan-Arabian Jewish federation.

It is unfortunate that the sources available to us about Yûsuf's reign are so limited. The inscriptions attest to his existence, a point denied by some until their discovery, but, like most inscriptional evidence, there is less color than one usually finds in a narrative history. The hagiographical works portray him as a pure servant of the Arch Enemy, as is befitting that genre of literature, although *The Book of the Himyarites*, while martyrological in structure, is more than that and reveals slight hints about Dhû Nuwâs's character. The Islamic sources are less hostile but are more removed than the martyrologies both in time and in their ability to engage the reader in the events. Nevertheless, it is possible to speculate fruitfully about some of the motives and circumstances that led Yûsuf to do what he did.

The Book of the Himyarites informs as that Yûsuf regarded the town of Najrân as part of his kingdom that was in rebellion. In his proclamation to the leaders of the town, he tells them that he would enter "with you a lawsuit regarding that because of which ye have rebelled against me. And if ye have been found guilty according to the sentence of the judges who rightly administer justice between us, then I will fine you."[54] This letter contained an oath sworn in the name of God, Rahmânâ in the text, and in the name of the law of Moses. Yûsuf the king apparently did not rule as an absolute tyrant, but delegated some of his power through judges who, if we are to conclude from his letter, would judge "by the Law of Moses." While it is true that Yûsuf is said to have promised safe conduct to the inhabitants of Zafâr and then broke his oaths, the case of Najrân seems different. To judge by his speech to the inhabitants of Najrân, Yûsuf is concerned with legal process as well as political and religious loyalty. His persecutions begin only after he discovers that the group is harboring foreign agents, Monophysite agitators, who represent his most dangerous enemies, and that they will not renounce the "false doctine" of the worship of "Jesus Christ, the son of Mary, because he was of mankind and a mortal as all men."[55] For Yûsuf, the obdurate resistance of the Najrânis is both a political disloyalty and a sin against his God, Adonai the Merciful. Irfan Shadîd has characterized the Abyssinian invasion of southern Arabia as a crusade, by which he means a war waged to propagate a religious faith. His apt characterization also applies to Yûsuf's campaigns, which were holy combat designed to bring his subjects back to proper monotheistic worship. The clash of politics and economics in sixth-century southern Arabia was also a clash of competing monotheisms. It should be noted on this point that the inhabitants of Najrân had probably been Nestorian, and the Nestorians at that time were able to manage a tolerant coexistence with the Jews. It is only at the arrival of the more zealous Monophysites, backed as they were by Byzantium and Abyssinia, that Najrân no longer tolerated Judaism.

The Book of the Himyarites describes "Jewish priests" from Tiberias as agents of Yûsuf's policies.[56] As noted above, they were only one group of many foreign advisers who were operating in Najrân. Most scholars have assumed that the term "priest" is a mistake based on the Christian perspectives of the author and that the term should be rendered as "rabbi."[57] Additionally, the connection with Tiberias has been explained as a device for propaganda to arouse anti-Jewish feelings in Justin's court.[58] There is reason to believe that there were Jewish priests from Tiberias, and that they were only some of a larger group of Jewish priests in Arabia.

Islamic traditions assert that the B. Quarayza and the B. Nadîr, two of the major Jewish tribes in Yathrib/Medina, were priests and descendants of Aaron.[59] They were called *al-kâhinân*, a term in the dual clearly referring to the Hebrew *kôhên*. In his book *Jews and Arabs*, S.D. Goitein writes that "towns exclusively inhabited by priests were common many centuries after the destruction of the Temple, because the elaborate laws of priestly purity could be more readily observed in compact communities. . . . Some *Midrashim* refer expressly to the flight of priests into Arabia."[60] Inscriptional evidence from south Arabia supports the notion that there were groups of priests living in communities in the Yemen.[61] When this evidence is put with the talmudic story that 80,000 children who were descendants of priests fled to "the Ishmaelites" after the destruction of the Temple, we can expect priestly activity in Arabia, even as late as the early sixth century C.E.[62] It would make sense that members of priestly descent would agitate for a cause that would create the possibility of restoring a Jewish state and rebuilding the Temple, the source of their power and status in the community, and, as we shall see in a subsequent discussion, the presence of a priestly influence in Arabia will help account for the plethora of eschatological traditions ascribed to Jews in Islamic literature or utilized by Muslim exegetes based on Jewish writings.

Yûsuf Ashʿar Dhû Nuwâs proved to be the last hope of the Jews of Himyar. His efforts to maintain a cohesive Arabian Jewish kingdom linked with the Hijâz and the land of Israel, free from Abyssinian domination, ended with the destruction of his realm and his death at the hands of the Abyssinian invading force. His followers defected to the winning side, and Sumayfaʿ Ashwâ, who had been with Yûsuf in his earlier campaigns, became the viceregent of the Negus.[63] Sumayfaʿ Ashwâ in turn was defeated by the Abyssinian general Abraha, who established his own semi-independent rule in Arabia and tried, unsuccessfully, to capture Mecca, reputedly in the year of Muhammad's birth. His rule was terminated by a wave of Arabian cultural and ethnic solidarity, and the result was a generalized feeling of strong mutual identification among the Arabic-speaking inhabitants of the peninsula and a distrust of foreigners among the Arabs. When Muhammad brought the Qur'ân in Arabic, Judaism and the various forms of Christianity were already hopelessly compromised by the strong identification with foreign domination, taxation, and warfare. Muhammad's message for the Arabs fell on receptive ears, and there were few counterforces to resist.

5

THE JEWS OF THE ḤIJÂZ

At the birth of Muḥammad in 570 C.E.,[1] the Jewish communities in Arabia were in political and economic decline. They could only look backward to a period when they enjoyed greater prestige and influence. The Ḥimyaritic kingdom of Yûsuf Dhû Nuwâs had been destroyed a half century earlier, and the Arab tribes around Mecca had risen to dominance along the Via Odorifera. The lucrative and powerful positions as Persian tax collectors had passed to Arabs, and gone except for memory was the title of "king."[2] Jews everywhere in the Ḥijâz were losing control over the best land and water.[3] Yet Judaism in Arabia, and in the Ḥijâz in particular, was a thriving and vital Diaspora culture. Jews were present in all areas of Arabian society. There were Jewish merchants, Jewish bedouin, Jewish farmers, Jewish poets, and Jewish warriors. Jews lived in castles and in tents. They spoke Arabic as well as Hebrew and Aramaic. They were in touch with the major Jewish religious centers in Babylonia and Palestine,[4] but, like many Diaspora communities, they had developed their own variations of belief and practice. And, like many Jewish communities in times of pressure and trouble, the Arabian Jews had become greatly interested in mysticism and the eschaton. The early seventh century was a rich time for Arabian Jews, a time before the fatal conflict with Islam.

When Jews came into Arabia in Roman times, Judaism had not been confined to urban centers. Jews in the land of Israel were farmers as well as merchants, craftsmen, and scholars. When the migrating Jews settled among the Nabataeans, as we have seen above, they participated in both the commercial and the agricultural life of Arabia Nabataea. This pattern was continued when Jews settled in the Ḥijâz, and Jews became integrated into the life of the peninsula. Jews lived in cities and villages and as pastoral nomads—bedouin—throughout Arabia. They were sailors, wine merchants, scribes, warriors, sculptors, and farmers.[5] On a sundial from Hegrâ, for example, we note the name Manasseh bar Nathan followed by the word *shalôm*, indicating both that the writer was a Jew and that he operated in a world where Jewish Aramaic was used for inscriptions.[6] In a funerary inscription from the same site, the tomb was made for a Jew, but the sculptor appears not to have been Jewish.[7] The onomastic evidence from such sites indicates that the Jews were integrated into the communities of northwestern Arabia at nearly all social and economic levels.

There has been considerable discussion among Western scholars about whether or not the Arabian Jews were also pastoral nomads or bedouin. This discussion is often linked to a discussion about the ethnic purity of the Jews. Israel Friedlander, for example, following Graetz, refers to the Arabian Jews as "sons of the desert, men of the sword, soldiers, warriors," and goes on to call them "nomads."[8] H. Hirschfeld says:

> It is hardly appropriate to call the Jewish tribes of the B. Kainoka, al Nadhir, and Kheibar "sons of the desert, men of the sword, soldiers, warriors" and "ignorant nomads." What we know from the early Arab sources points to the contrary. They were rather peaceful palm growers, craftsmen and traders who lived in settled habitations round Medina and further north. The quarrels of which Arab authors have so much to relate should not be taken too seriously. Anyway we never read of Jewish victories, but only of defeat and slaughter. There may have been a few warriors among them, but their pure Jewish blood is a matter of doubt. As to their alleged ignorance, such evidence as we possess does not bear out this statement.[9]

When the foregoing discussion and others like it were taking place in nineteenth- and early twentieth-century intellectual circles, the study of race and racial characteristics was in its infancy. Many scholars

were of the opinion that characteristics of language and social structure were determined by race. Images of Jews were set by the European experience or were subsumed under generally unfavorable
views of the Semites. While the issues of racial determinism versus
cultural conditioning are not settled among modern scholars, it is
much less likely that Jews today would be assumed to be of less than
"pure Jewish blood" because they are warriors, or poor, or any of
those things that go against the stereotype, particularly after the Jewish experiences in the modern state of Israel. Also, students of Judaism's history are much more ready to acknowledge the presence of
large numbers of proselytes to Judaism and to downplay the importance of putative genealogical purity, which, after all, is difficult to
trace with confidence beyond four or five generations at best.

Our understanding of the position of Jews in Arabian pastoral society has been aided by two recent outstanding studies. In an article
titled "Asad from Jâhiliyya to Islâm," Ella Landau-Tasseron has
destroyed the old notion of the cohesive nature of tribes in pre- and
early Islam.[10] She shows that it was the rule rather than the exception
that tribal subgroups operated as independent units, often at odds
with the aims of the majority of the subgroups of the larger tribe.[11]
Arabic historical writings about the pre-Islamic period have generally
tried to place all participants squarely within a genealogic context in
which "tribes" are regarded as the product of genetic descent from a
single ancestor. This fiction, a product of a "pastoral" literary topos,
masked the realilty that tribes were often formed by the association of
persons with common interests and geography.[12] In spite of a recogni-
tion of that fact, Western writers have frequently adopted the attitudes present in the Islamic historical texts. In the case of the Jews,
this has led to the misconception that Jews could not have been
bedouin because they were not Arab. The problem is exacerbated by
the fact that in Arabia, as elsewhere, sources tend to cluster around
seats of power, which are usually urban and reflect an urban bias.

The greatest amount of information about Jewish social groupings
in the Hijâz comes, naturally enough, then, from Yathrib/Medina. The
city is regarded by most authors as a cohesive, identifiable unit with a
population divided into an Arab faction and a Jewish faction. The
Arab tribes are the B. Aus and the B. Khazraj, while the three tribes
usually recognized as Jewish are the B. Qurayza, the B. an-Nadîr, and

52

the B. Qayunqâ'. The second of the two groundbreaking studies referred to above is by Michael Lecker, who, in his "Muhammad at Medina: A Geographical Approach," examines the locations and interactions of the various social groups in the city of Medina over time.[13] The results, particularly when viewed from the perspectives of E. Landau-Tasseron's study, force a reshaping of traditional ways of viewing interactions among the several Jewish groupings and between the Jews and the non-Jews.

Basing his work on a careful and detailed analysis of Samhûdî, Lecker shows, among other things, that a process of expelling Jews from their lands had predated the Hijrah (when Muhammad changed his residence from Mecca to Medina) and was part of a greater dynamic of realitively small groups moving into positions of advantage.[14] Coupled with this, we learn that groups from different tribes lived together in different localities around the greater area of Medina. The common denominator seems to have been social status, and possibly occupation regardless of tribal affiliation.[15] Medina and probably other "cities" of the northern part of Arabia were amalgamations of small villages, strongholds, keeps, and other kinds of dwellings. Some individuals and groups banded together for mutual interest and protection, like the reported 300 goldsmiths living in Zuhra, not all of whom were Jewish,[16] while some prominent families had their own fortified castles, like as-Samau'al in Taymâ or Sallâm b. Abû l-Huqayq in the heart of Medina.[17] The name Wâdî al-Qurrâ, the Valley of the Villages, seems to assume a similar settlement pattern in which groups of formerly independent areas merged into a larger urban unit. What is of particular interest for us is that the urban settlement pattern transcended other affiliations. When we examine the conflict between Muhammad and the Jews of Medina, we shall see that the "fiction" of tribal identifications obscures the real complexity of Medinese life.[18]

As would be expected, social groupings within the urban centers of Arabia were not isolated from the rural areas. Not only was there a steady commercial contact between the settled and the nomadic populations, but reports indicate that some of the pastoralists settled in the towns and assimilated to urban culture. In one instance, at least, that meant becoming Jewish. The B. Hishna b. 'Ukârima b. 'Awf asked to settle in Taymâ. The town was already dominated by a strong Jewish population who insisted that the Arabs adopt Judaism before settling. They are reported to have done so and later moved to Medina.[19] We are also told that some of the B. Aus and the B. Khazraj converted to Judaism or were converted by their mothers who "used to make a vow that if their child lived they would make it a Jew (*tahawwadathu*), since they considered the Jews to be people of knowledge and the book (*'ilmin wa-kitâbin*)."[20] The result was that there were a great number of Jewish clans in Medina. Samhûdî mentions a group of Jewish clans in Medina deriving from various parts of Arabia. The B. Marthad was a clan of the tribe of the B. Balî, while the B. Muʿâwiyah were of the B. Sulaim. The B. Thaʿlabah were part of the B. Ghassân and the B. Jadhmâʾ were from the Yemen.[21] The B. Jafna were also part of the B. Ghassân, who were described as "kings in Palestine,"[22] Being Jewish did not restrict one to a particular clan or tribe in Arabia in the fifth and sixth centuries C.E.

At this point it is probably germane to ask to what extent were the conversions made on "religious" as opposed to "social or "economic" grounds. This question has been asked of the Arabian Jews to determine whether or not they were "really Jewish." From the evidence that the tribes and individuals retained their Judaism after conversion, in the instance cited above, after they had moved from Taymâ to Medina, and by the fact that the converts were regarded as Jews by other Jews and non-Jews in the Ḥijâz, we have to assume that they were indeed "real" Jews as Judaism was understood in that context. From another perspective, we see that the process of conversion to Judaism in Arabia in the pre-Islamic period is paralleled by the patterns of conversion to Islam during Muḥammad's lifetime. Whole tribes became Muslim in connection with political and military submission to Muḥammad and, apparently, in proportion to his increasing strength and influence. While it has been argued in the Muslim case also that the conversions were not as "sincere" as individual conversions, particularly in light of the apparent apostasies after the death of Muḥammad, such an argument seems to derive from a Western overemphasis on the centrality of individual autonomy coupled with Muslim revisions of the history of that same period. What group conversions do underscore is the social and economic aspects of converting from one religious group to another without denying the spiritual and aesthetic qualities.

Conversion to Judaism in pre-Islamic Arabia, as well as conversion to either Monophysite or Nestorian Christianity, was both a rejection of the old social and spiritual order and a declaration of adoption of a completely new poliltical and social matrix. The Arabic term applied by the Qureish to Muhammad when he left his ancestral religion was ṣaba', implying not only a departure from the old but also the creation of active enmity between the old and the new.[23] When Dhû Nuwâs acceded to the throne, it is said that all of Ḥimyar joined him in his Judaism, and, as we saw above, his Judaism represented political opposition to the Ethiopian forces. And when the people of Najrân converted from Nestorian to Monophysite Christianity, they made more than just a statement about their spiritual relations to a Christological definition.

Unfortunately, we do not have an Arabian St. Augustine to detail the conversion process, so we shall never know the individual psychological dynamics, but the conversion of large groups to Judaism indicates the dominant social force that Judaism exerted in Arabia in the fifth and sixth centuries. In addition, it would appear that conversion to Judaism was a move by a liminal group into a less liminal context. Since group conversion appears to have been the norm both to pre-Islamic Judaism and to Islam in Muhammad's lifetime, I would suggest that the conversion of the group, rather than the individual, would attentuate much of the socially liminal character of being a new convert to an established religion and its social context.

Whatever the origin of the Arabian Jews, they identified with Jewish interests and concerns outside Arabia and expressed their interests in correct practice to authorities beyond their local rabbis and community leaders. From the Mishnah we know that the concerns of Arabian Jewry were sufficient to attract the attentions of the Babylonian rabbis. Issues of kosher dress, clothing, and food in the Arabian context were debated by the rabbis. Jewish women, and presumably men, wore veils when outside to protect themselves from the windborn sand,[24] a custom adopted from the Arabs and allowed by the rabbis. The nomadic existence in Arabia posed special problems, and those who dwelt as pastoral nomads in tents were exempt from many of the requirements incumbent upon someone living in a fixed abode.[25] As in other parts of the world, Judaism's dialectic between adaptation and tradition embraced the special problems of living outside the land of Israel.

Some Jews thus appeared to have been pastoral nomads around the time of the rise of Islam and, as we shall examine in a later chapter, there were Jewish bedouin in the Hijâz still existing as late as the six-teenth century C.E. But the Jews whom we encounter in the historical and literary texts are those with political, religious, and economic importance for those writing about the rise of Islam, This means that the Jews we know most about are the urban, literate, powerful Jews, many of whom opposed Islam and Muhammad. Several Jewish liter-ary figures are known, however, whose art and values reflect the pas-toral ideals of the pre-Islamic Arab poet, who, whatever his background or station, assumed the guise of a noble desert wanderer.

The most well-known of the pre-Islamic Jewish poets is as-Samaw'al b. ʿAdiyâ, who lived in the sixth century C.E. in a castle called al-'Ablaq in the Jewish city of Taymâ.[26] According to some, his mother was from the Ghassânids, the Arab tribe that served as the cli-ents of the Byzantines, protecting the settled areas of the Mediterra-nean from the incursions of the bedouin Arab. His father was a côhên, a descendant of the priests and a member of a powerful Jewish group in Arabia.[27] As-Samaw'al is best remembered for the story of his loy-alty to 'Amru' al-Qays, who had deposited his family's heirloom armaments with him while on a trip to the Byzantine emperor. As-Samaw'al gave 'Amru' al-Qays a letter of introduction to the Ghas-sânids, which helped him get to Constantinople. According to Arab legend, 'Amru' al-Qays was poisoned by the emperor's agents while on his way back to Arabia, leaving as-Samaw'al in possession of the armor and 'Amru' al-Qays's daughter, Hind. The implacable enemy of the Ghassânids and of 'Amru' al-Qays, Mundhir III b. Mâ' as-Samâ', the Lakhmid king of Hîra, sent al-Harith b. Zâlim, who arrived at the gates of al-'Ablaq demanding that as-Samaw'al turn over the armor and Hind to him. As-Samaw'al refused, even when al-Harith carried out his threat to kill as-Samaw'al's son before his eyes. Thus the name of as-Samaw'al became proverbial among the Arabs for fidelity and honor, even at great personal cost.[28]

The surviving poetry preserved in the great Arab collections con-tains some lines attributed to as-Samaw'al.[29] Except for the informa-tion and references in the scholia associated with these verses, there is nothing to indicate that they are particularly Jewish. The poems espouse the martial values of the literary topoi of pre-Islamic Arabia, and, as the example with 'Amru' al-Qays shows, run counter to Jewish ideals of the preservation of life. This has led some scholars to doubt the reliability of the transmission of these poems and even the existence of as-Samaw'al,[30] although most scholars now accept the existence and genuineness of most of the corpus of pre-Islamic poetry.[31]

One poem attributed to as-Samaw'al has survived in material from the Cairo Genizah. Hartwig Hirshfeld identifies a unique poem as a genuine product of as-Samaw'al and argues for its authenticity against the severe criticism of D. S. Margoliouth.[32] If, as appears to be the case, the bulk of the poem is genuine, we see an interesting combination of Jewish lore and sentiment combined with a pride in ancestry akin to that expressed by the pagan Arab poets of the *Ayyâm al-'Arab* genre.[33]

As-Samaw'al was not the only Jewish poet of pre-Islamic Arabia. The earliest was a woman named Sarah of the tribe of the B. Qurayza whose four surviving lines lament the ascendancy of the B. Khazraj over her people.[34] Ar-Rabî' b. Abî-l-Huqayq was also from the B. Qurayza,[35] as was 'Aws b. Danî.[36] One of 'Aws's poems speaks to his attitude toward Judaism in the face of his wife's conversion to Islam:

> She invited me to Islam on the day I encountered her,
> But I said to her, Nay, rather become a Jewess.
> Then we will live according to the Torah of Moses and
>   his religion.
> By life, what good is Muhammad's belief?
> It remains to be seen which of us has the right belief;
> He who is guided to the correct portal will be rightly guided.[37]

Most, like Abû ad-Diyâl,[38] Ka'b al-'Ahbâr,[39] and a number of unnamed Jews whose poetry survives in the various collections, espouse the secular values of pre- and early Islamic Arabia.[40] In Ka'b's case, the secular quality of his poetry belies his role in the transmission of haggadic material,[41] known in Islamic times as *tafsîr 'isrâ'îlîyât*, and indicates that the lack of religious content may be due, in part, to the selectivity of the editors and preservers of the poetry rather than a presentation of the entire intellectual spectrum of the Arabian Jewish poets themselves. It should be remembered that pre-Islamic pagan poetry displays a similar lack of religious content, and one could draw the conclusion that Arabic poetic genres were not the prefered medium for religious discourse.

We learn most about the religious climate, and hence about the beliefs of the Jews of the Ḥijâz, from the Islamic texts that preserve the controversies that surrounded Muhammad's confrontation with the Jews at the time of the rise of Islam, and the first text we can turn to is the Qurʾân. Two terms familiar to us from post-Islamic Jewish taxonomy are used in the Qurʾân to describe Jews who were known to Muhammad, and it seems that these two terms can be understood to designate a specific and identifiable community of beliefs and practices. These terms are *rabbâniyyûn* and *ʾaḥbâr*.

The word *rabbâniyyûn* occurs three times in the Qurʾân: 3:79; 5:44; 5:63. The term *ʾaḥbâr* occurs four times, twice in association with *rabbâniyyûn* in 5:44 and 5:63, and twice with a word usually applied to Christian monks, *ruhbân*, in 9:31 and 9:34. The word *rabbâniyyûn* appears to be the term "rabbinite," a term of self-description by the Geonim and the usual Karaite word used to refer to the majority group of Jews, the followers of rabbinic precepts. This is the sense in which it appears to be used in the Qurʾân: "We revealed the Torah containing a guide and a light by which the prophets judged the rightly guided, the *rabbâniyyûn* and the *ʾaḥbâr* according to what they preserved of God's Scripture . . ." (Qurʾân 5:44). The Muslim commentators are in general agreement that *rabbâniyyûn* refers to the rabbis among the Jews.

The term *ʾaḥbâr* presents difficulties, however, both for us and for the Muslim commentators. At-Ṭabarî reports that there is a difference of scholarly opinion about how to interpret the term *ʾaḥbâr*. In a tradition from Yûnus, on the authority of Ibn Wahb, who reported from Sufyân, reporting from Ibn Abî Najîh, Mujâhid said that the *rabbâniyyûn* are scholars and wise men "above the *ʾaḥbâr*."[42] The *ʾaḥbâr*, the singular of which is *ḥibr*, according to at-Ṭabarî, are people who possess knowledge [*ʿilm*] about something. At-Ṭabarî then offers the example of the famous Kaʿb al-ʾAḥbâr, whose alternate name is sometimes Kaʿb al-Ḥibr.[43] The traditionalists seem to be confused as to whether or not the *ʾaḥbâr* are to be regarded as the same group as the *rabbâniyyûn* or as a separate group of Jews who, nevertheless, possess knowledge of the Torah.

In talmudic usage, the term *haber* ranges in meaning from companion[44] to a scholar[45] to a person slightly inferior to a *hakam*.[46] This last usage would fit the tradition cited by at-Tabarî that the *'ahbâr* were beneath the *rabbâniyyûn*. Sometimes the term *haber* was used in contrast to the *'am ha-arez* where the *haber* was a member of a society who strictly observed the laws of cleanliness, separated himself from the general society, and practiced strict Levitical purity. At this point, it would be tempting to see a contrast between a group of Jews in Arabia who observed such strict Pharisaic practices and the claims of Muhammad that he was a *nabiyy 'ummiyy*,[47] usually translated as an "illiterate prophet," which appellation H. Hirschfeld sees as coming from the term *'am ha-arez*.[48] If this is the case, then Muhammad would have been a prophet *for* the *'amê ha-arez*. There is insufficient evidence to make such an assertion and, at any rate, the uses of the terms *rabbâniyyûn* and *'ahbâr* would indicate that we are seeing one large group of Rabbinite Jewish scholars who, nevertheless, may have been divided along lines we cannot at present distinguish. The distinctions in the Qur'ân in the passages cited above will, with present evidence, have to remain no more than tantalizing.[49] Nevertheless, later Muslim scholars allowed for the possibility that the Jews could have regarded Muhammad as a prophet for someone else, as in the case of at-Tahâwî who asserts that even the recitation of the testimony of faith does not constitute proof of conversion to Islam, only to the unity of God and Muhammad's role as a prophet.[50]

From the Qur'ânic evidence and from traditions associated with Muhammad, we would expect to find a "rabbinic" community in Arabia with whom Muhammad had contact. And, in addition to the Qur'ânic term *rabbâniyyûn* and the descriptions of the rabbis in the early historical literature, we can expect to find evidence of actual beliefs and practices that fit the Jews of the Hijâz into the rabbinic enviornment. While such evidence is certainly present, our definition of Rabbinic Judaism has to be stretched somewhat to accommodate what we find among the Jews of Arabia.

Sûrah 5:64, a passage immediately after a polemic against the *rabbâniyyûn* and the *'ahbâr*, asserts: "The Jews said that the Hand of Allah is fetterd; their hands are fettered and cursed be what they say . . . !"

As my colleague David Halperin has observed, the reference to God's fettered hand is found in two places in the corpus of extant rabbinic texts. Lamentations Rabbah on chapter 2, verse 3, mentions God's hand tied behind him because of the destruction of the Temple, and in 3 Enoch 48a, we read, "R. Ishmael said to me: Come and I will show you the right hand of the Omnipresent One, which has been banished behind him because of the destruction of the Temple. From it all kinds of brilliant lights shine, and by it the 955 heavens were created." As we shall see shortly, traditions associated with the pseudepigraphic Enoch play an important part in helping us define the beliefs of the Jews of the Ḥijâz.

Steven Wasserstrom has demonstrated that post-Islamic Karaite attacks on Rabbinite Judaism depict the rabbinites both as anthropomorphizing and as worshiping an angel that functions as the substitute creator of the universe. That angel is usually identified with Metatron.[51] Enoch was frequently equated with Metatron and regarded as a "lesser lord," an angel-creator. When we look to later authors who write about varieties of Jews, we find both anthropomorphizing and the belief in the creator-angel to be an essential definition of Rabbinite Judaism in the early Islamic period. The Karaite heresiograph, al-Qirqisanî, for example, defends Jews generally against the charges of anthropomorphism, but as a Karaite, he does criticize the Rabbinites for that very practice.[52] There is no evidence for the existence of an antiRabbinite precursive Karaite group in Arabia upon whom Muhammad was drawing. Rather, we ought to be able to look at the taxonomic categories of later polemicists against, in this case, the Rabbinites to find delineations of some of their beliefs. The Qur'ân, of course, is not objecting to anthropomorphism, as the latter part of 5:64 shows, for it mentions God's hands as open in bounty. It is clear, nevertheless, that the polemic against the Jews in this passage in the Qur'ân is against Rabbinite Jews who have, by way of interest for us, a passing acquaintance with magic and mysticism and are well acquainted with the Enoch traditions.

Another example of a belief that we can attribute to the *rabbâniyyûn*, or, in this case, the *'aḥbâr*, is that found in Qur'ân 9:30–31:

And the Jews say: Ezra is the son of Allâh, and the Christians say: The Messiah is the son of Allâh. That is the saying of their mouths. They imitate the saying of those who disbelieved of old. Allâh (himself) fighteth against them. How perverse are they! They have taken as lords beside Allâh their rabbis [ʾahbâr] and their monks and the Messiah son of Mary, when they were bidden to worship only One God.

Ezra is noted in the Bible as the leader of the expedition of return to Jerusalem from exile and the reestablishment of the Jewish state. For the rabbis, Ezra was the equivalent of Moses. Sanhedrin 21b contends that Ezra would have been the recipient of the Torah had it not already been given to Moses, but he was instead given the task of restoring the forgotten law.[53] He is credited with the introduction of the proper means of writing the Torah,[54] and for this activity he is given the title of Scribe.[55] In extra-rabbinic literature, this appellation is given as "Scribe of the knowledge of the Most High,"[56] a title usually given to one of several archangels,[57] Elijah,[58] and Enoch. Ezra was a disciple of Baruch, who was taken by God to heaven while alive, and Ezra himself was translated to heaven alive,[59] which represents another point of correspondence with Elijah and Enoch. The equation of Ezra the Scribe with Enoch the Scribe and their translations is most likely the solution to our problem.

Enoch was of the generation of the Flood, of those who transgressed. In the popular books of Enoch, he was taken to heaven so that he would not be destroyed when God abandoned the earth and as a sign of God's mercy that one pious man would be saved. When translated into heaven, he was stripped of his humanity and transformed into the powerful angel, Metatron, who was taught by God all the secrets, more than any other creature, indeed, and was given guardianship over the treasures of God and became a lesser God. In 3 Enoch 48C, verses 1–4 we read:

> ʾAlep: The Holy One, blessed be he, said: I made him strong. I took him, I appointed him, namely Metatron my servant, who is unique among all the denizens of the heights.
> ʾAlep: "I made him strong" in the generation of the first man. When I saw that the men of the generation of the Flood were behaving corruptly, I came and removed my Shekinah from their midst, and I brought it up with the sound of the horn and with shouting to the height above, as it is written.

God went up to the sound of horns,
the Lord went up with a fanfare of trumpets.
Lamed: "I took him"—Enoch the son of Jared, from their midst,
and brought him up with the sound of the trumpet and with
shouting to the height, to be my witness, together with the four
creatures of the chariot, to the world to come.
Peh: "I appointed him"—over all the storehouses and treasuries which I have in every heaven, and I entrusted to him the keys
of each of them. I set him as a prince over all the princes, and
made him a minister of the throne of glory. . . . I committed to
him wisdom and understanding, so that he should behold the
secrets of heaven above and earth beneath.

It is particularly interesting to find this material in 3 Enoch, because
we can deduce that the inhabitants of the Ḥijâz during Muhammad's
time knew portions, at least, of 3 Enoch in association with the Jews.[60]
The angels over which Metatron becomes chief are identified in the
Enoch traditions[61] as the sons of God, the *Bene Elohîm*, the Watchers,
the fallen ones as the causers of the flood. In 1 Enoch,[62] and 4 Ezra,[63]
the term "Son of God" can be applied to the Messiah, but most often it
is applied to righteous men, of whom Jewish tradition holds there to
be no more righteous than the ones God elected to translate to heaven
alive.[64] It is easy, then, to imagine that among the Jews of the Ḥijâz
who were apparently involved in the mystical speculations associated
with the *merkâbâh*, Ezra, because of the traditions of his translation,
because of his piety, and particularly because he was equated with
Enoch as the Scribe of God, could be termed one of the *Bene Elohîm*.
And, of course, he would fit the description of a religious leader (one
of the ʾahbâr of Qurʾân 9:31.) whom the Jews had exalted.[65]
Another example of Arabian Jewish eschatological speculation
involves Kaʿb al-ʾAhbâr, mentioned above, who was accused by the
famous traditionist and Qurʾân exegete, Ibn ʿAbbâs, of contending
that the sun and the moon would be brought to judgment on the Day
of Resurrection as if they were two castrated bulls. Ibn ʿAbbâs called
that belief Judaism and condemned him, saying, "God fight that *habr*
and befoul his *habriyya*."[66] This belief, which is a reference to an Arabian midrash on Genesis 49:6, also derived from the traditions surrounding Enoch and the story of the disobedient angels whose
intercourse with earthly women produced beasts and monsters. As

Chaim Rabin has observed, a concern with apocalypticism seems to be characteristic of at least one important strain of Arabian Jewish thought,[67] but this would not make the Arabian communities unique in Diaspora Judaism. Apocalypticism and Messianism had become a major part of the thinking of Jews in both Palestine and the Diaspora in the years of Roman domination of the eastern Mediterranean. Not only the destruction of the Temple, but also tragedies like the virtual elimination of the Egyptian Jewish communities in the time of the Egyptian revolt (114–17 C.E.) persuaded many that the messianic age was near and deliverance would soon come. It is not surprising to see Jews represented in Islamic texts as predicting the imminent coming of a prophet or a messiah.[68]

Early Muslim sources tell of a young Jewish boy named Ibn Ṣayyâd about whom prophetic and messianic claims were made.[69] Ibn Ṣayyâd, who lived at the time of Muhammad, claimed to be the Apostle of God. In one early tradition, Muḥammad said to him, "Do you bear witness that I am the Apostle of God?" Ibn Ṣayyâd replied, "Do you bear witness that I am the Apostle of God?" In some versions, Muḥammad does not reply and in others he gives a noncommittal answer.[70] In one variant, Ibn Ṣayyâd admits that Muḥammad is an Apostle to the Gentiles,[71] while in others his answers to Muḥammad's questions indicate that he possesses the right knowledge to substantiate his claim to apostleship. Included in that knowledge is information gathered from the practice of mystical contemplation in which Ibn Ṣayyâd saw the throne of God in the middle of water surrounded by the hayyôt, the Living Creatures of the book of Ezekiel who are identified later as the bearers of God's throne. Ibn Ṣayyâd's vision was induced by wrapping himself with a cloak and murmuring incantations in Hebrew, all of which features David Halperin identifies with Jewish merkâbâh mysticism.[72]

The presence of merkâbâh mysticism in the Jewish communities of Arabia allows us to understand a number of different aspects of Arabian Judaism and some of the accusations made against the Jews in Islamic texts. Metatron/Enoch, mentioned above, had a central role in mystic visions and journies into the seven heavens because he acted as the guide for the mystic travelers who saw themselves as not only seeing the seven heavens but actually visiting there. It can be assumed that they had some identification with those individuals in Jewish tradition who were translated to heaven alive, and when they returned to the earthly realm, they were bound to tell of their experiences as a didactic and cautionary warning to their fellow Jews. In other words, the mystic returned as a messenger from the heavenly realm. Looked at in this way, Ibn Ṣayyâd's claim to be an Apostle of God makes sense. From the Arabian Jewish perspective, Muhammad fitted the pattern of the Jewish mystic. He wrapped himself in a mantle,[73] recited mantic prose,[74] brought a message from the heavenly realms, and toured heaven himself.[75] Interestingly, Ibn Ṣayyâd practiced his mystical exercises in a palm-grove where Muhammad spied on him.[76] This feature of *merkâbâh* mystic practice seems to be alluded to in the story of al-Walîd b. al-Mughîra's characterization of Muhammad's speech as sweet and his "source" a palm tree whose branches are fruitful.[77] These traditions seem to imply that Muhammad was perceived by some of his contemporaries as fitting in with the Jewish mystical practice represented by Ibn Ṣayyâd. Later Muslims transformed Ibn Ṣayyâd into the anti-Messiah,[78] while interpreting Muhammad's role as quasi-messianic. These traditions still, however, preserve Muhammad and Ibn Ṣayyâd as reflexes of one another.

Muslim sources are replete with examples and references to examples of Jewish Midrashîm developed, apparently, within the Arabian Jewish communities. Some are simple, such as that associated with Qurʾân 2:80: "And they [the Jews] say: The fire will not touch us except for a certain number of days." In the *Sîrah*, the explanation is offered that the Jews contended that "the world would last for seven thousand years and that God would only punish men in hell one day in the next world for every thousand in this world. There would be only seven days and then punishment would cease."[79] In this elegant little *drôsh*, there is a symmetrical relationship made between the creation of the world in seven days and the "uncreation" of the world in seven, after which, of course, all would cease to exist. The tendency to make commentary on the basis of word and number associations, a technique that is part of Jewish Midrash-making and Muslim *Tafsîr*-making, earned the Jews in the polemical context of seventh-century Arabia the opprobrium of "Textual Corrupters." This "corruption," *tahrîf* or *tabdîl* in Arabic, is mentioned in Qurʾân 4:46:

Of those who are Jews are they who transform the words from their places and say, "We heard and disobeyed, and hear without being caused to hear and pay heed to us," twisting with their tongues, refuting the religion. If they had said, "We heard and obeyed, and hear us and look at us," it would have been better for them and more upright, but God cursed them for their ingratitude, and they did not believe, except a few.

Assuming that the Qurʾânic description of the Jews was one that would best make sense if it were based on actual Jewish ideas and practices, it appears that we have a reference to a Jewish commentary on the events of Sinai prior to the receipt of the Torah and the great sin of the worship of the Golden Calf.[80]

Both Tanhuma[81] and Tosefta Baba Qamma link Psalm 78:36–37 with Exodus 24:7 to assert that the Jews lied to God when they said they would hear and obey his commandments and keep the Covenant. Psalm 78:36–37 reads: "But they beguiled him with their mouth, and lied to Him with their tongue. For their heart was not steadfast with Him, Neither were they faithful to His covenant." Tanhuma expounds Hosea 9:10 as follows:

> Just as grapes are lovely on the outside and ugly on the inside, so were the Israelites when they stood at Mount Sinai and said, "naʿaseh v'nishma'" [We hear and obey]. That was what they uttered with their mouth; but their hearts were not steadfast. For thus said David, "They deceived him with their mouth, and with their tongue they lied to him, and their heart was not steadfast with him" (Ps. 78:36f.). Hence, "like grapes in the desert . . ." (Hos. 9:10).

Neither Tanhuma nor Tosefta state what was really in the hearts of the Israelites, but we can, with caution, reconstruct a Midrash that originated in the bilingual community of the Jews of the Hijâz in which the midrashist knew what was really meant by the Jews at Mount Sinai: "We heard and we disobeyed," an accurate portrayal of the biblical events.

In another example from the Qurʾân, there is the curious story of an extra son of Noah who drowned in the flood. It has been assumed by many that this represents confusion on the part of Muhammad, but a closer examination shows that it also is most likely derived from Jewish lore and learning in the Hijâz. Of all the portions of the Noah story in the Qur'ân that have caused commentators difficulty, few have proved more vexing than the passage Qur'ân 11:42-43:

> It [the Ark] was running with them among the waves which were like mountains, and Noah called to his son, while he was standing apart, "O my son, ride with us and do not be among the ungrateful." He said, "I will take refuge on a mountain which will protect me from the water." He [Noah] said, "There is no protector today from the decree of Allâh except for him upon whom is mercy." And the wave came between the two of them, and he was among the drowned.

On these two verses, Abû Qâsim Mahmûd b. 'Umar az-Zamakhsharî (538/1144) reports a conversation between Qatâdah b. Di'âma (118/736) and al-Hasan al-Basrî (110/728), which, along with other traditions, illustrates some of the problems that arose with this passage in the early centuries of Islam:

> [Az-Zamakhsharî said:] It is said that the name of his [Noah's] son was Kana'an, and it is said that it was Yâm, and 'Alî, May Allâh be gracious unto him, read it as "her son" *[ibnahâ]* with the pronoun referring to his wife, and Muhammad b. 'Alî [Zayn al-'Abidayn b. Al-Husayn Abû Ja'far Al-Baqîr, 114/732] and 'Urwa b. Az-Zubayr [93/712] read it *ibnaha*, with a short "a" vowel on the letter "hâ," intending it to be "her son," and the two of them did not require the 'alif, and thereby the view of al-Hasan al-Basrî was supported. Qatâdah said, "I asked him and he [al-Hasan al-Basrî] said, 'By Allâh, it was not his son.' I said, 'But Allâh quotes from him: my son is from my family, and you are saying that he was not his son, while the People of the Book do not disagree in the fact that he is his son.' He said, 'And who takes his religion from the People of the Book?!' He took his conclusion from his words, 'from my family,' and he did not say 'from me.' He can be related to the mother in two ways: one of them is that he can be a stepson just as 'Umar b. Abû Salama was for the Messenger of Allâh, may the prayers and the peace of Allâh be upon him, or he could have been an illegitimate child, but this would have been a blemish from which the prophets would have kept themselves pure."[82]

The circulation of non-Islamic materials for use as the basis for Qur'ân commentary was present during Muḥammad's lifetime and saw a considerable increase in the two generations after his death. The Companion, Abû Hurayrah, although illiterate, had extensive knowledge of the Torah, as did ʿAlî, Salmân al-Fârisî, and, of course, the "Ocean of *Tafsîr*," Ibn ʿAbbâs, who is often called the "ḥibr al-ʾumma," or "Rabbi of the [Muslim] Community," on account of his extensive knowledge of Judeo-Christian as well as Muslim Scripture and commentary acquired in Arabia.[83] Muḥammad, Abû Bakr, and ʿUmar are reported to have made several trips to the Bet Midrash in Medina, and Muḥammad's amanuensis, Zayd b. Thâbit, who was so central in matters Qurʾânic, is reported to have gone so far as to learn *al-yahûdiyyah* in a Bet Midrash at Muḥammad's behest in order to read Jewish material.[84] More to the point, converted Jews like ʾUbayy b. Kaʿb. [21/642] and Kaʿb al-ʾAhbâr [or, sometimes, *ḥibr*, the probable paradigm for Ibn ʿAbbâs's appellation], who converted to Islam under Abû Bakr, transmitted much information originally derived from rabbinic tradition.[85] Some of this material can be found in the Talmud and the Midrashîm, but some of it is preserved only in Islamic versions.

Much credit has to be given, however, to three individuals whose participation in the nascent activities of history writing and Qurʾân commentary lent respectability and sanction to the introduction of scriptural and para-scriptural material derived from the People of the Book: Abû Hurayrah; ʿAbdullâh b. ʿAmr b. al-ʿÂs, who read Syriac, engaged in theological discussions with converts, and had extensive knowledge of the Talmud; and Ibn ʿAbbâs.[86] Their names are featured over and over again in the *isnâds* (citations of authority) and, even if some of what is attributed to them can be regarded as spurious, the point still remains that their names were the touchstones of proper conduct in this field. The generation of the Followers, the next generation after Muḥammad, saw many who followed the paradigm of the Companions and actively pursued knowledge from Jews and Christians. Abû Jald of Basrah, for example, was accustomed to reading both the Torah and the Qurʾân in his daily devotionals, claiming that Divine Mercy derived from reading either one or both of them.[87] Wahb b. Munabbih was another source in this generation of the introduction of Judeo-Christian material into the Islamic mainstream, and much that was known among the early Muslims from the Talmud and the Midrashîm comes through traditions ascribed to him and whose *isnâds* go back no earlier than he does, making him the authority for the introduction of this material.[88]

Many of the individuals involved in the transmission of interpretive traditions derived ultimately from the People of the Book were *mawâlî* (clients of Arab tribes) whose family background and place of origin could have given them special knowledge of Jewish, Christian, and Zoroastrian sources. Both al-Ḥasan al-Baṣrî, who was the son of a Persian slave and who rose to preeminence in Islam as one of the greatest teachers, dogmatists, preachers, and transmitters of Qur'ânic interpretation, and Qatâdah b. Di'âmah, who was also from the city of Basrah and rivaled al-Ḥasan al-Baṣrî in Qur'ânic knowledge, were *mawâlî* who capitalized on their wide range of knowledge of outside sources for their interpretation of the Qur'ân. Both were regarded in their time as reliable interpreters of the Qur'ân, and, from the point of view of modern investigation, they show a remarkable reliability in faithfully transmitting traditions from Judaism and Christianity when commenting on figures in the Qur'ân that also appear in the Bible, and when we have extant antecedent texts to check their knowledge. They had ready access to knowledge of the Bible and its commentaries through a flood of translations that were distributed by stationers and booksellers. Works of doubtful origin were sometimes translated, copied, and marketed under the guise that they were part of the Seventy Scriptures that had been revealed to humankind.[89] One should remember the claim of Wahb b. Munabbih that he had read a large portion of the Seventy Scriptures, which had been revealed in the seventy languages of humankind.[90]

Assuming for the moment in our examination of the Noah account that there was normal and ready access to material from outside Islamic circles, it is somewhat surprising to see Qatâdah take the position that he does when he asserts that the People of the Book do not disagree that the son referred to in Qur'ân 11:42 is his, Noah's son. The usual Jewish and Christian sources indicate that both Judaism and Christianity do not hold that Noah had more than three antediluvian sons, namely Shem, Ham, and Japheth. And, those same usual Jewish and Christian sources are in agreement that the three sons survived the flood by riding on the Ark with their father, Noah. An additional problem comes when one tries to determine the name of the drowned son. In the Islamic traditions under consideration for this paper, two names are given, Canaan and Yâm. Canaan is mentioned in the Bible as the fourth son of Ham, Noah's grandson, but Yâm is nowhere mentioned in the Bible in conection with the Noah story.

When one examines the texts that comment on the biblical Noah story for clues to the identity of Canaan as an extra son, one finds that the narrative of Ham, Canaan, and the great transgression mentioned in Genesis 9:20–27 is most appropriate:

And Noah the husbandman began and planted a vineyard. And he drank of the wine and was drunken; and he was uncovered within his tent. And Ham, the father of Canaan, saw the naked-ness of his father and told his brothers without. And Shem and Japheth took a garment and laid it upon both their shoulders and went backward and covered the nakedness of their father, and their faces were backward, and they saw not their father's naked-ness. And Noah awoke from his wine and knew what his young-est son had done unto him. And he said, "Cursed be Canaan."

For the rabbis, and later for the church fathers, this passage presents several problems. What did Ham do that is implied in the verb "saw"? It is more than just a glance, they reason, because the consequences are so great. Further, why is Canaan cursed rather than Ham? Does he have a part in the crime, or might he be the real culprit and not his father, Ham?[91]

The usual opinion is that Ham could not have been cursed, no mat-ter what he might have done, because God blessed him along with all the party of the Ark upon disembarking: "And God blessed Noah and his sons, and said unto them: 'Be fruitful, and multiply, and replenish the earth'" (Genesis 9:1). For the rabbis, this verse not only estab-lishes protection for Ham, but also sets the context for the understand-ing of the interpretation. The blessing involves sexual activity and procreation. After all, that was the greatest need at the time, and so acts that would be cursed would be acts that would limit or inhibit fruitful procreation. It comes as no surprise, then, to find the follow-ing solution to the problem in the Talmud (Sanhedrin 70a):[92]

[With respect to the last verse] Rab and Samuel differ, one main-taining that he castrated him whilst the other says that he [Ham] sexually abused him. He who maintains that he castrated him [reasons] thus: Since he cursed him by his fourth son, he must have injured him with respect to a fourth son. But he who says that he sexually abused him draws an analogy between "and he saw" written twice. Here it is written, and Ham the father of Canaan saw the nakedness of his father, whilst elsewhere it is written, And when Shechem the son of Hamor saw her [he took her and lay with her and defiled her]. Now, on the view that he emasculated him, it is right that he cursed him by his fourth son; but on the view that he abused him, why did he curse his fourth son; he should have cursed him himself?—Both indignities were perpetrated.

Following from this line of reasoning, it was then maintained that Canaan was both alive and involved in the crime. Late Jewish sources, reflecting attitudes expressed among some of the church fathers, hold that it was, in reality, Canaan and not Ham who committed the major abuse of Noah, thus fully earning the curse.[93]

Another text which is of some interest in this matter is a passage in the Ethiopic version of the book of Jubilees [7:10]:[94] "And Noah awoke from his sleep and knew all that his younger son had done unto him, and he cursed his son and said: 'Cursed be Canaan.' " The Ethiopic reads: wa-ragamo la-waldu wa yebe Kanaʿan. The noted scholar of this text, J. C. Vanderkam, dates this material about a century before our era, with the Ethiopic text redacted about a century before the time of Muḥammad and the Qurʾân. A literal reading of this text gives Noah a son named Canaan whom he curses. We can make several observations about the possibility of a connection between this tradition and the Islamic material. One line of possible connection is to assume that the Ethiopic text reflects a tradition of interpretation that preserves material not found in extant "rabbinic" material. That this is the case with other material has been amply demonstrated by L. Ginzberg in his Legends of the Jews, particularly the material concerning the figure of Enoch, of which more shortly. Another possible connection is through the south Arabian Jewish communities from which transmitters like Wahb b. Munabbih draw so heavily. And, while the certain nexus cannot be made at this point, the parallelism is striking.

The intellectual life of the Arabian Jews is far better known than their communal structures and their everyday religious practices, because it was at the level of belief and ideas that Islam and Judaism clashed most seriously. We do, however, get hints of the structure of the community, how they educated themselves, how they earned their living, and how they observed their festivals. Religious practices in Islam are often compared or contrasted with pre-Islamic Arabian customs which include references to Judaism. But the social history of Arabian Jewry must remain, compared with other times, a speculative and fragmentary picture.

We get hints of Jewish religious practices most clearly in those texts that mention them as a background for the subject at hand. One clear example is the Arabian Jewish observance of Passover. In the story of a Muslim guerrilla raid on a prominent Jewish leader in Khaybar, we discover that the Jews there roistered during the festive meal, a practice forbidden in the Talmud.[95] ʿAbdullâh b. ʿAtîk, the chosen leader of the raid, a speaker of al-yahûdiyyah, the dialect of Judeo-Arabic, and the son of a Khaybar Jewess, was informed that he and his assassination party could enter the heavily fortified city at night "during the *khamr* of the people. . . . The Jews do not lock their doors fearing lest a guest will knock at it and one of them will wake up in the morning in the guest chamber and not have offered hospitality. So he [the guest] will find the door open, and he can enter and sup."[96]

Now this was a time of great trouble in the Ḥijâz, with frequent Muslim raids, and it seems most unlikely that open-door hospitality was a regular feature of Khaybar Jewish life. The reason given for the doors to be open was that there was a possibility of a guest who would come and who should be offered a meal. Of all the major and minor Jewish holidays in which hospitality has become a major feature, Passover is the one that best fits the details of our story. Now, of course, the custom is that, at the drinking of the third cup, the door is opened for the eschatological guest, Elijah, who has a cup of wine waiting for him. Presumably this is timed for the last possible minute so as not to violate the rule that a guest should not enter after the third course.[97] The opening of the door for Elijah seems, however, to be a late development, and possibly later than the early seventh century C.E. Earlier customs were tied to the introductory section of the Haggadah, *kôl dîkfîn yêtê* . . . , which invites all hungry and needy to participate in the Passover celebrations.[98] Even though some practiced a more generalized form of hospitality, as did Saʿd b. ʿUbâda of the

Ansâr, who imitated R. Huna by welcoming all the indigent with the cry of "All who are poor should come and partake of the meal," the mention of wine seems to confirm that this story is about Passover.[99]

When the assassins entered the fortified castle of their target, the prominent Jewish leader of the opposition to Muhammad, Abû Râfiᶜ, they found him reclining full of wine, most likely following the injunction of the Mishnah that "Even the poorest man in Israel must not eat until he reclines, and they should not give him less than four cups."[100] The raiders had entered on the pretext of being guests, and this leads to the conclusion that it would not have been unusual for guests to go from house to house on the night of Seder. The rabbis of the Talmud are careful to explain, in the context of explaining the *apikoman*, that the festive meal must be eaten in one spot.[101] Apparently this is in reaction to the Hellenistic practice of roistering as part of the celebration of the Passover meal.[102] While it is not entirely clear from this account, apparently the Jews of Khaybar did go from house to house, drinking wine, and this was the time that the assassins entered. Bernard Heller mentions in his analysis of sections of the *Antar Romance* that the Jews of Khaybar ate their unleavened bread without fat and drank an abundance of wine during Pesah.[103] Again, this practice fits with our notions of Passover where the matzah is eaten without the usual spreads. Apparently the festival anticipated the arrival of the Messiah Joshua,[104] paralleling later practice of expecting another eschatological figure, Elijah.

Yôm Kippûr was observed on the tenth day of Tishri as we know from the later Muslim designation of it as the Fast of ᶜAshûrâ, "tenth." It was a total-abstinence fast, called the Ṣawm al-ʾAkbar. During the public services, a confession of sins was recited, probably similar to the modern ᶜAl Ḥêt.[105] As S. D. Goitein has previously observed, the Muslim explanation for the institution of the fasting month of Ramadân rests on a polemical claim that Islam had taken over the institution of the fast of Yôm Kippûr. Those Muslim traditions tell us that it was celebrated as a solemn festival associated with Moses. As Goitein says:

Now any Jew of the seventh century A.D. asked about the meaning of the Day of Atonement would have answered: "This is the day on which Moses completed his second stay of forty days on

Mount Sinai and descended, bringing with him the new tables, after having been granted remission and forgiveness for his people in a special manifestation of God. In commemoration of this day, the Fast of the Tenth was instituted."[106]

In Islamic interpretation, the fast was also regarded as a remembrance of the exodus, a physical deliverance of the Jews as the Day of Atonement was a spiritual one. The discussion hinges on the variety of meanings in Arabic of the root *frq*. The Qur'ân is called *al-furqân* in Qur'ân 2:185, while in Qur'ân 2:50, God is described as having divided, *frq*, the waters of the sea to save the Jews from Pharaoh. Within the dialogue between Muslims and Arabian Jews, the Hebrew/ Aramaic word *purqân* took on an added dimension and, while it is impossible to say whether or not this interpretation was invented by a Muslim or a Jew, it is clear that it was understood by both, and would not have been outside the Jewish spirit of interpretation as the modern *Mahzôr* describes Yôm Kippûr: *miqra' qodesh zêker lîsî' at misrayîm*, "a holy convocation as a remembrance of the departure from Egypt."[107]

Arabian Jews seem to have observed the Sabbath in many familiar ways. They observed the law of *Tehûm*, the law of the Sabbath limit, for even if they were riding, they would dismount on the Sabbath and trace a limit beyond which it was not permissible to walk.[108] Also, they would not fight on the Sabbath but made arrangements with non-Jews to take over their fighting. They, nevertheless, kept themselves at the ready, so that they could commence fighting just as soon as the Sabbath was over.[109] From the perspective of the Qur'ân, the breaking of the Sabbath was one of the major sins that the Jews had committed against God and was a cause for his anger and punishment of them.[110]

One of the accusations made in the Qur'ân against the Jews was that they were practitioners of magic instead of proper Judaism. One example concerns the group who are accused of abandoning Scripture and following a practice of magic, which they attributed to Solomon. The Qur'ân (2:101–2) has:

And when there cometh unto them a messenger from Allâh, confirming that which they possess, a party of those who have received the Scripture fling the Scripture of Allâh behind their backs as if they knew not, and follow that which the devils falsely related against the kingdom of Solomon. Solomon disbelieved not; but the devils disbelieved, teaching mankind magic and that which was revealed to the two angels in Babel, Harut and Marut.

This passage presents a picture of preoccupation with magic that we know to have been the case among Jews and Christians in the period immediately prior to the advent of Islam. For example, the Sefer HaRazim opens with:

And when he [Noah] came forth from the ark, he used (the book [of mystery given to Noah by the angel Raziel]) all the days of his life, and at the time of his death he handed it down to Shem, and Shem to Abraham, and Abraham to Isaac, and Isaac to Jacob, and Jacob to Levi, and Levi to Kohath, and Kohath to Amram, and Amram to Moses, and Moses to Joshua, and Joshua to the elders, and the elders to the prophets, and the prophets to the sages, and thus generation by generation until Solomon the king arose. And the Books of the Mysteries were disclosed to him and he became very learned in books of understanding and so ruled over everything he desired, over all the spirits and demons that wander in the world, and from the wisdom of this book he imprisoned and released, and sent and brought in, and built and prospered.[111]

And within the praxis of magic bowls, which continued into Islamic times, Solomon and his seal ring appear a number of times in prophylactic incantations designed for maintaining good health.[112] In spite of the mixed population using the bowls, there is a strong Jewish element when God is conjured; the usually Aramaic text gives way to Hebrew and Hebrew formulas for the supplication. When the Solomon of the magic texts of the Sefer HaRazim and the Testament of Solomon are compared with the Solomon of the Bible, which lends only the faintest support to the notion that Solomon possessed esoteric wisdom, it is easy to understand the Qur'ânic objections to Solomon as a magician. During Muhammad's lifetime, Jewish magicians are supposed to have cast a spell on Muhammad, rendering him impotent for a period of time. Many of the spells required a knowledge of potions and herbs as well as the ability to conjure God by the use of his secret Name, and we read of one Jew, a certain Aaron (Hârûn), characterized as a scholar "who knew the commandments and prohibi-

74

A History of the Jews of Arabia

tions of the Torah and the plants, herbs and roots," who makes use of an Indian plant as a soporific. One is reminded of the use of frankincense as a reliever of pain for those about to be executed.[113]

Throughout all the sources that mention Jews in the immediate pre-Islamic period of Arabia, the names of the Jews have presented scholars with difficulties in identifying both who was a Jew and to what extent these people had assimilated into Arabian culture.[114] It is difficult to draw much religious evidence from names, as a glance at "Jewish" names in our own society will attest, but names are often an indication of interaction with local culture.[115] As we have seen, most of the names from the earliest inscriptional onomasticon are similar to biblical names, like Manasseh, Nathan, Samuel, and so forth. But already in the earliest period after the destruction of the Temple, some of the names exhibit a linguistic assimilation toward Arabic, as in the famous Nabataean inscription of Hani bar Samawʾal resh Hijra dedicated to his wife Mûnâ bat ʿAmru bar Samawʾal resh Taymâ. By the time that we encounter the Jews mentioned in the Sîrah, the naming pattern reflects almost complete linguistic assimilation. For example, we find names like Mukhayrîq, Huyay, Sallâm, Finhâṣ, Nuʿmân, and Kaʿb. This last name, Kaʿb, is assumed to be a hypocoristic formation from the name Jacob, Yaʿqôb/Yaʿqûb. It is not a mere excision of the first syllable, which at any rate would look like an inflectional preformative in both Arabic and Hebrew, because the palatalized stops are different. Rather, Kaʿb is a translation into Arabic from the story of Jacob, because the word kaʿb means "heel" in Arabic, and obvious reference in the name to the aetiology of the name "Jacob" in Genesis 25:26. And finally, such a name as ʿAbdullâh is immediately understood as a translation of ʿObadyah. We have no evidence that there was an "inside-outside" pattern of dual names, as in our culture, but it must be remembered that our evidence is reported from outside the community. In all other respects, though, the naming patterns of the Arabian Jews seem to conform to what we would expect of a culturally assimilated Diaspora community.

We can derive very little sense of the internal organization of the Jewish communities in Arabia other than that they were led by men who were called "rabbis." In Heller's observations, however, Khaybar seemed to have been stratified within its leadership.[116] The head of the community was called a qarnâṣ, which equates with the

Hebrew *parnas*. The terms *khaber* and *khazân* were also used as terms of rank. *Khaber*, in the form *Ḥibr*, was discussed above. The *khazân*, "treasurer and/or cantor," was a member of a group headed by the *al-Khazân al-Kabîir*, the chief *khazân*. There was also a *jûqâr*, equaling the Hebrew *khaqar*, "an examiner." Except for the most obvious meanings of these terms, we have little sense of how they interacted within the community. They do not seem to be strictly religious terms, indicating the function of the individuals within the liturgical environment, because they are described in military terms within the text examined by Heller.

We are at a similar disadvantage when we try to ascertain anything about the status of women in the Arabian Jewish communities of the Ḥijâz. They seldom show up in the predominantly androcentric literature except as occasional references. We know that Abû Râfiʿ, the Jewish leader in Khaybar, had a wife, but we know little else about her. We know that Muḥammad married a Jewish captive, but we learn little of her former life from the Muslim sources. Marriage preparations are, by accident, mentioned in the *Antar Romance*, so we do learn some from there.[117] In the rites for the preparation for marriage, the Jews are described as sending the girl, presumably non-Jewish, to the house of the chief *khazân* where she would reside for three nights and be purified of her impurities so that she could be married according to the laws of Israel. This appears to be a version of the regulation pertaining to captives in Deuteronom;y 21:10–14, but with the twist that it is to the house of the chief *khazân*.[118]

Trade and agriculture had first sustained the Jews when they came into Arabia, and those two professions sustained many in Arabia into Islamic times. The city of Medina, and most of the other Jewish communities in the Ḥijâz, were at base agricultural communities, unlike Mecca, which was based on trade and religion. The chief crop was dates, which required intensive and trained human effort to grow and maintain. The Jews had brought Nabataean techniques of irrigation to the oases of western Arabia, and they employed the techniques of hand pollination of the date flowers to ensure more than a spotty yield. Dates were a major source of nourishment in the Arabian diet, and provided the basis for fermented drink.[119] Wine made by Jews was regarded by most in pre-Islamic Arabia as the best available, and as Ignaz Goldziher observes, "the designation 'Jewish' of a wine

76

meant that it was of the best sort."[120] In Medina, Taymâ, and Khaybar, the date fields were dominated by the Jews, and one of the sources of conflict between the Arab tribes of the B. Aus and the B. Khazraj of Medina and the Jews was the control that the Jews exercised over the fields. When Muhammad came to Medina, displacement of the Jews provided a source of revenue for the new community, but, as will be discussed more extensively in the next chapter, the nonagricultural Muslims were limited in their ability to derive benefit from an agricultural technology in which they were not trained. The practical realities of exploiting agricultural lands is part of the basis for the establishing of the Jews on their lands in Muhammad's treaty with the defeated Jews of Khaybar.[121]

In some cities, the Jews appear to have controlled the trade and markets. In Medina, the market was under the jurisdiction of the B. Qaynuqâ'. It was in their quarter of the city, and they were able to levy an impost on the transactions there. Muhammad's attempt to establish a rival market, free from taxes and thereby offering the possibility of lower prices, was one of the major points of conflict between him and the B. Qaynuqâ'.[122] Jewish control of the markets in the Hijâz also meant that market day for the week was on Friday, the time just before Shabbat. This day, called 'arûba in the Old Arabic sources, a word from Aramaic meaning "eve," was a time not only for purchasing supplies before the holiday, but also for legal cases to be decided and for entertainment.[123] This institution apparently influenced the selection of Friday as Islam's day of congregational prayer, called yawm al-jum'a in Arabic, parallel to the Hebrew and Aramaic yôm hak-kenîsa. S. D. Goitein draws parallels between the Friday rural market and the urban markets of other Jewish cities held on Mondays and Thursdays, observing that this was a time for religious education, fasting, reading of the Torah, and the holding of rabbinical courts.[124] When everyone had gathered together for the market, Muhammad would preach his message, competing with other storytellers, preachers, and entertainers. Preaching, prayer, and the recitation of the Qur'an, which formed the core of the Muslim Friday congregational worship, grew out of the social institutions associated with the Jewish market on the eve of the Sabbath. Judges in this setting could be drawn from any group in the community, and evidently exercised their power according to the degree of personal prestige they wielded.

We have already seen how ʿAmir b. Zarib, a non-Jew, used Jewish material for his decision-making process, and we know that Jews would act as judges for both Jews and non-Jews.[125] Muhammad's position in Medina was also as a judge for the community, again for both Jews and non-Jews, as the evidence of the Qurʾân and the ʾumma agreement of Medina both demonstrate.[126] If we are to judge from the role that Muhammad played, the function of the judge was not only to render the wise decision, but also actually to negotiate with the two parties as an intermediary [Arab. wasît] to effect a settlement.

Arabs and Jews traded in the market of the B. Qaynuqâʾ, but the Jews were known for certain items. Wine has already been mentioned, but Jews were also manufacturers and traders of arms, jewelry, and clothing. As Goldziher observed, pre-Islamic poetry indicates that Jews not only purveyed fine imported cloth, they also acted as tailors. The story is told that ʿAʾisha bought two suits of silk from a Syrian Jew because Muhammad was too uncomfortable wearing homespun in the summer heat.[127] Jews were also manufacturers and traders of eye makeup, kuhl, worn by men as well as women.[128] Absent from the lists of commodities sold by Jews in the Hijâz are the aromatic spices from the south. While it is not out of the realm of possibility that there were Jews involved in that trade, it seems more likely that they functioned in an indirect way as suppliers of ancillary products. And while it may be just a bias of the pro-Makkan texts, the usual explanation is that the Qureish of Makka had formed a tight economic control over that trade through the Hijâz. Thus on the eve of the rise of Muhammad and Islam, political and economic circumstances had reduced the Jews of the Hijâz to a marginal role in the society. Their legacy remained, however, in the profound influence they had on the ideas of Muhammad and Islam.

6

MUHAMMAD AND
THE JEWS

The story of the Arabian Jewish communities' encounters with
Muhammad begins with the time of Muhammad's move from the city of
Mecca to Medina, the Hijrah of 622 C.E., or slightly before. Islamic literature is filled with descriptions of Jewish sages who "knew" of Muhammad's advent or were aware of the miraculous portents that were said to
have surrounded his birth. From our vantage, those tales are part of the
collection of biographical traditions that fit Muhammad into the models
of previous holy men, making the collection of traditions more of a hagiography than a history.[1] History in our sense begins when Muhammad
moves his mission and community to the major Jewish town in the
Hijâz, Yathrib, known as al-Madînah, "the City."[2]

Muhammad's Hijrah was necessitated by the increasing hostility
toward him among his fellow Meccans, resulting in their attempts to
kill him.[3] Before this, one or more groups of early converts to Islam
had gone to live in Abyssinia, and Muhammad had made attempts to
negotiate support at at-Tâ'if, the sister city to Mecca. While there is
some debate about all the reasons for Muhammad's sending his followers to Abyssinia, there is clear indication by this act and the negotiations with at-Tâ'if that Muhammad had put Islam into the Byzantine-
Abyssinian axis. It is probable that Muhammad was attempting to
exploit Meccan neutrality and, to judge by later events, the Qureish's
association with the Jews, as well as their willingness to trade with the
Persians, which cast them in a bad light with the Abyssinians. Cer-

tainly the Abyssinians would have welcomed an opportunity to regain the foothold in Arabia that they had lost, and they probably felt that supporting Mecca's enemy, the nascent Islamic community, would weaken the Meccan military alliance that dominated the Ḥijâz.

Muhammad had negotiated his coming to Medina with a few members of the pagan Arab tribe, the Banû Qaylah, more commonly known by the two branch names, the Banû Aus and the Banû Khazraj, when they had come to Mecca for the annual fair. Traditions indicate that the Banû Qaylah had come to Medina from the Yemen sometime in the middle of the sixth century C.E. and settled among the inhabitants, the majority of whom were already Jewish.[4] Originally they were under the domination of the Jewish tribes and had settled on the least good agricultural land. Competition over the limited natural resources of the oasis put them at odds with the Jewish inhabitants, and in the ensuing conflicts they gained some measure of independence from the Jews, if not always domination. For the Aus and the Khazraj, linking their fate with Muhammad's rising fortunes would have been seen as a means toward further independence from the Jewish control of the city of Medina. It would also have been perceived as striking out at Arabia's biggest power. For our purposes, the success of Muhammad's negotiations with the ʾAnṣâr, or "Helpers" as the Aus and the Khazraj are called in Islamic sources, is an indication of the weakness of the Jews of Medina to control their destiny.

As we have already seen, the social structure of Medina was extremely complicated. Not only were there a greater number of clans in Medina than in Mecca, for example, but the clans were also hostile to one another. The long war of Ḥâtib, which had ended in the Battle of Buʿâth shortly before the Hijrah, had left everyone exhausted but not at peace. Clans were armed camps, and agricultural lands were jealously guarded against raids by hostile neighbors. Tribal affiliations were not strong enough, if they were not totally fictitious, to override the hostilities, and the cramped space of the oasis probably exacerbated the hatreds. Jews and non-Jews formed alliances that were abandoned when they proved unable to meet the needs of the groups, and new groups were formed. Treaties were apparently signed, and later abrogated, leading to new treaties.[5] As has already been mentioned, factors of location and occupation were apparently as important as religion and tribal heritage in some of the alliances. Still, there appear to be remnants of older relationships. In a tradition cited by at-Tabarî, a subgroup of the Khazraj are identified as in a client relationship with the Jews.[6]

The agreement that Muhammad had made with the Aus and the Khazraj had allowed some seventy of his followers to go to Medina before him. These were accommodated in the homes of the Medinans who had, apparently, accepted Muhammad on both religious and political grounds, although it is not clear to what extent religion played a part in the acceptance of Muhammad by the majority of the Aus and Khazraj. It appears most likely that Muhammad's appeal was as an arbiter among the warring factions in the town, which would fit perceptions that some had of him in Mecca.[7] The Arabic sources do not tell of a document that survived from this agreement, and it seems assumed that whatever treaty there might have been was subsumed under conversion to Islam.

After Muhammad's arrival, however, the sources do tell us of a treaty, or several treaties, known in Western scholarship as the "Constitution of Medina," that established Muhammad in a central role within Medinan society. Ibn Ishâq reports that Muhammad made an agreement with the *Muhâjirûn*, the ones who had come from Mecca with Muhammad on the Hijrah, and the *'Ansâr*, the "Helpers" of Medina who supported them. Included in this agreement in the form reported by Ibn Ishâq, were the Jews of the city, although, as we shall see, there are serious questions about which Jews and when the agreement was made. In part it states:

> This is a document from Muhammad the Prophet between the believers and the Muslims of the Qureish and Yathrib, and those who followed them and adhered to them and struggled (Arab. *jihâd*) with them. They are one community (Arab. *'ummah*) to the exclusion of others. The Emigrants from the Qureish shall pay the wergeld in accord with their former custom among them, and they will ransom their captives with the kindness and fairness customary among the believers.
>
> And the Banû ʿAuf shall pay the wergeld as was their former custom. . . .
>
> A believer shall not enter into an alliance with the associate of a believer against him. The devout believers shall be against him

who rebels among them or tries to spread injustice or crime or
enmity or corruption among the believers. All hands shall be
against him even if he is the son of one of them. A believer shall
not kill a believer for the sake of an unbeliever nor help an unbeliever against a believer. God's protecting covenant is indivisi-
ble. The lowliest of them may grant asylum on their behalf.
Believers are associates to one another to the exclusion of
others.

The Jews who follow us get help and equality and shall not be
wronged. Nor will their enemies be aided. . . .

It shall not be permitted to a believer who agrees to what is in
this document and believes in God and the Last Day to aid an
evil-doer or give him shelter, for on him who helps and gives
shelter will be God's curse and anger on the Day of Resurrection
and neither repentance nor restitution will be accepted from him.

Whenever you disagree about something, it must be referred to
God and to Muhammad.

The Jews shall contribute to the cost as long as they are fighting
along with the believers. The Jews of the Banû ʿAuf are one community [ʾummah] with the believers. The Jews have their laws
[dîn] and the Muslims have their laws [dîn]. [This includes both]
their associates and themselves except those who act unjustly and
sinfully, for they only destroy themselves and the people of their
households. To the Jews of the Banû an-Najjâr belongs what
belongs to the Jews of the Banû ʿAuf, and to the Jews of the Banû
al-Hârith, the Banû Sâʿida, the Banû Jusham, the Banû Aus, the
Banû Thaʿlaba, and the Banû ash-Shutayba.

Reverent duty wards off sin.

The associates of the Thaʿlaba are like themselves. The relatives
of the Jews are like themselves. None of them shall go out except
with Muhammad's permission, but he will not be prevented from
taking revenge for a wound. . . .

The Jews must bear their expenses and the Muslims must bear
their expenses. They shall help each other against anyone who
attacks the people of this document. They must mutually consult.

Reverent duty wards off sin. . . .

The Jews shall bear expenses along with the believers as long as
the fighting lasts. Yathrib shall be a sanctuary for the people of
this document. . . .

The Jews of the Aus, their associates and themselves, have
equal standing with the people of this document. . . .[8]

A HISTORY OF THE JEWS OF ARABIA

Ibn Isḥâq dates the agreement at the beginning of Muhammad's stay in Medina, and later Muslim historians agreed. In al-Wâqidî, for example, he states:

> ʿAbdullâh b. Jaʿfar told me on the authority of al-Ḥârith b. al-Fudayl, from Ibn Kaʿb al-Qurazî, "When the Prophet of God, may the prayers and peace of God be upon him, came to Medina, all its Jews concluded peace with him, and a document was written between him and them. And the Prophet of God, may the prayers and peace of God be upon him, bound all the people together as allies of one another and made peace among them."[9]

By dating a general agreement with all of the Jews of Medina early, Muhammad is credited early with the honor and power he acquired later,[10] but more important, subsequent Jewish opposition to Muhammad is explained as a violation of the agreement, thus justifying the retaliations we shall examine below.

A question that is prior to the dating is the authenticity of the document. Western scholars have spent considerable energy trying to determine the nature of the document, whether or not it is genuine, and, if so, whether the version we have is a composite of several versions or separate documents. The best summary of this scholarship can be found in Moshe Gil's article, "The Constitution of Medina: A Reconsideration."[11] Gil argues convincingly for the essential unity and authenticity of the document, citing facts that others had observed previously, that non-Muslims are included in the ʾummah, that Ibn Isḥâq does not appear to make any corrections or interpolations, and that Muhammad holds a relatively minor position within the document.[12] But, if this is so, scholars have asked, why then are not all the Jews and Arabs mentioned in the document, and what is the relationship between this document and the tradition cited by al-Wâqidî that Muhammad had made a pact with all the Jews, which they are alleged to have subsequently broken? The answers appear to be found in the chain of events that eventually eliminate the major Jewish political groupings from Medina.

When Muhammad was in Mecca, he seems to have entertained notions that Jews and possibly Christians would embrace his message. While it is difficult to sort out completely those later readings of nascent Islam that make Islam subsume all that had gone before, there appear to be quite clear examples of Muḥammad's feelings that he was of the line of Jewish prophets. More important, when he came to Medina, Muḥammad seems to have taken it upon himself to legislate both for his community of Muslims and for the Jews. In the first portion of the fifth chapter of the Qurʾân, for example, we find the rudimentary outlines of dietary laws, laws of interconfessional marriage, and ritual hygiene. In verse 5 we read, "Today the good things are made lawful for you. The food of those who have been given Scripture is lawful for you, and your food is lawful for them." That this is said with the Jews in mind is confirmed by verse 7, where the hearers are told, "Remember the kindness of God to you and His covenant by which He bound you and you said, 'We hear and we obey.' " Dietary practices have bound Jews together and separated them from the rest of the world, and it is reasonable to expect that Muḥammad's motives are to use the same device to weld together his new community. From the perspective of this legislation, Jews could be included in the ʾummah if they were to accept Muḥammad's definition of kashrût.

Another early consonance between Islam and Judaism was the common observance of the fast on the tenth of Tishri, the Yôm Kippûr fast. As we saw above, this was replaced by the fasting month of Ramaḍân, but not abrogated. Also, Mondays and Thursdays became fast days in Islam as they had been in Judaism.[13] Early Muslims prayed toward Jerusalem along with the Jews, and some Muslims persisted in reading the Torah along with the Qurʾân in their devotionals.[14] And, Muslim ideas about the sanctuary at Mecca, which includes more than just the Kaʿbah, seem to have arisen in a Jewish environment. In an article published in 1982, Gerald Hawting raises the old issue of the origins of the Muslim sanctuary at Mecca and challenges the notions concerning the similarities between Muslim sanctuary ideas and those of Judaism.[15] He finds neither the explanations put forth by Dozy in his *Die Israeliten zu Mekka* nor those by Snouck Hurgronje in his *Het mekkaansche Feest* adequate to account for the wide variety of traditions about the formation of the sanctuary. Dozy's explanation that argued for successive migrations of Jews into Arabia from a time even before the establishment of Jerusalem as a Jewish sanctuary was successfully replaced by Snouck Hurgronje's arguments that held that the acceptance of the Meccan sanctuary was a result of Muhammad's rejection by the Jews. Hawting argues, instead:

> It seems that the Muslim sanctuary at Mecca is the result of a sort of compromise between a pre-existing pagan sanctuary and sanctuary ideas which had developed first in a Jewish milieu. I envisage [Hawting says] that Muslim sanctuary ideas originated first in a Jewish matrix, as did Islam itself. . . . It seems likely that the Meccan sanctuary was chosen only after the elimination of other possibilities—that in the early Islamic period a number of possible sanctuary sites gained adherents until finally Mecca became established as the Muslim sanctuary. And it also seems likely that one reason for the adoption of the Meccan sanctuary was that it did approximate to the sanctuary ideas which had already been formed—although they had to be reformulated, the physical facts of the Meccan sanctuary did not mean that already existing notions and terminology had to be abandoned. . . . The Muslim sanctuary at Mecca should no longer be regarded as simply a remnant of Arab paganism.[16]

Hawting then cites numerous traditions, which cannot be easily interpreted except by accepting the thesis that the notion of the sanctuary at Mecca cannot be dated to the time of Muhammad's "break" with the Jews.

For our considerations, the implications of Hawting's work fall into two general categories. First, from his evidence, it can be argued that Muhammad's reactions to Jewish rejection of his message in Medina did not persuade him to turn toward an accommodation of pre-Islamic paganism or to adopt a general condemnation of Jews and Judaism. Second, following from that, Muhammad appears to have operated within categories shared with the Jews of the Hijâz, even when he and his message were under attack by them. I see this as fundamental in Muhammad's message: Muhammad appeared to himself and to some others as a genuine continuation of the process of divine revelation; he was not crassly "accommodating" to the Jews to try to win them over, only to abandon them in the face of opposition. Such cynicism falls short when it comes to explaining Muhammad's appeal and successes. Islam and Judaism in Arabia during Muhammad's lifetime were operating in the same sphere of religious discourse: the same fundamental questions were discussed from similar perspectives; moral and ethical values were similar; and both religions shared the same religious characters, stories, and anecdotes. We can see this when we look at the implied context of the Qur'ânic message. There is no expectation that the stories we call biblical are anything but familiar to the Arabian listeners, whether they are pagan, Jewish, or Christian.[17] And to this argument we must also add the element of paganism. Not only is there the implication from the Qur'ân that pagans knew the Jewish, Christian, and Muslim stories, but it is also implied that Jews, Christians, and Muslims knew the pagan stories. When there was disagreement, as between Muhammad and the Jews, the disagreement was over interpretation of shared topics, not over two mutually exclusive views of the world.

Muhammad's expectations that he might convert the Jews to his view were not unreasonable. It is clear that Muhammad did not think that he was starting a "new" religion but, rather, restoring and reforming the Abrahamic heritage among the Jews and Christians of Arabia. From that perspective, it is not surprising that we are told that one of the "learned *haberîm*," ʿAbdullâh b. Salâm, joined Muhammad, albeit in the face of community opposition:

He [ʿAbdullâh b. Salâm] said, I kept my Islam secret from the Jews, and then I went to the Apostle of God, may the prayers and peace of God be upon him, and said to him, O Messenger of God, the Jews are a bad people, so I want you to put me in one of your houses and hide me from them. Then ask them about me so that they will tell you how I am with them before they know about my Islam, for if they know about my Islam, they will slander me. So the Apostle of God, may the prayers and peace of God be upon him, put me in one of his houses. They came to him and disputed with him, and he said to them, What sort of person is al-Ḥusayn b. Salâm among you? He is our chief and the son of our chief, a *haber* of ours and one of our learned men. When they had finished their words, I came out to them and said to them: O company of Jews, fear God and accept what has come to you from Him, for, by God, you know that he is the Messenger of God. You will find him written about in the Torah by his name and his description. Indeed, I testify that he is the Messenger of God; I believe in him, regard him as truthful, and acknowledge him. So they said, You lie! And they reviled me. . . . I revealed my Islam and the Islam of the people of my household, and my aunt Khâlidah bt. al-Hârith adopted Islam, and her submission was beautiful.[18]

The number of Jews who accepted Muhammad were very few and probably only served to raise the level of anxiety among the rest.[19] Some of the *Ahbâr* are said to have joined Islam falsely and to have slandered Muhammad among those Arabs of Medina (called *munâfiqûn*) who also had not fully adopted Islam.[20] The *Sîrah* reports that the debate was carried on in public with both sides trying to win the uncommitted to their side. Sometimes the arguments seem *ad hominem*, as in the example of the Jews saying that Muhammad was receiving his messages from Gabriel, an angel who was an enemy of the Jews,[21] and sometimes they were trivial jibes, when Huyayy b. *Akhtab counted up the mysterious letters at the beginning of the second chapter of the Qur*ân—*Alif, Lâm, Mîm*—according to their numerical value in Hebrew—one, thirty, forty—and concluded that Islam would last only for seventy-one years. In questioning Muhammad about other mysterious letters, they found other numbers, the sums of which are said to have made 734 years.[22] Most of the arguments are set forth in a brief form in the second chapter of the Qur*ân.

Jewish opposition to Muhammad appears from our vantage to be a combination of religious and political motives, which were not separated in the minds of the Jews and Arabs of sixth-century Arabia. Regardless of whether the so-called Constitution of Medina is dated early or not, Muhammad's position as an effective political leader whose movement would triumph over both the Qureish and the status quo must have seemed tenuous, particularly before the first major battle between Muslims and Meccans at Badr in the second year after the Hijrah. After the "miraculous" victory by the Muslims, Muhammad gained considerable prestige in Medina and among the surrounding bedouin tribes, and that prestige represented real political power. Muslim historians and Western writers see Badr as the turning point in Muhammad's attitudes toward his enemies, the coalition of the Jews and the *Munâfiqûn*. Watt would see this as the time of the rejection of the fast of *'Ashûrâ* and the adoption of Abraham as a pre-Jewish and pre-Christian monotheist and the first Muslim.[23]

The great event of Badr was followed by a raid on the Muslims by Abû Sufyân, the Meccan general, who had vowed to abstain from women and other normal activities until he made a retaliatory raid against Muhammad.[24] Abû Sufyân and the raiders were hosted by Sal-lâm b. Mishkam, described as the chief of the B. an-Nadîr at that time as well as their treasurer. He supplied the raiding party with up-to-date intelligence about the Muslims and then served them a fermented drink made from wheat and barley, which gave the raid its name as the Raid of as-Sawîq, "the Barley Raid."[25] The raiders then left, burned some fields, killed two Medinans, and fled before Muhammad, who had warning of their coming, could engage them. While the raid itself was insignificant from a military standpoint, it did serve to point out the relationship between the Jewish tribe of an-Nadîr and Muhammad's Meccan enemy. Muhammad's intelligence not only let him know about the raid in time to prevent serious damage, but also made the secret meeting between Abû Sufyân and Sal-lâm b. Mishkam a matter of public knowledge.

The combination of Jewish public rhetoric against Muhammad and secret dealings with his enemies demanded that Muhammad respond in a decisive manner. Some of Muhammad's appeal in the Hijâz was undoubtedly that he was defying the rich and the powerful. In order to continue gaining the respect and ultimate loyalty of those attracted to him, he had to show that he was not weakened by these attacks. The time after Badr was ideal for him to make his first move because his prestige was at a high point. The redoubtable Meccan army had been defeated by the Muslim upstarts. Ibn Ishâq, who dated the Constitution of Medina to the first few months after the Hijrah, tells us that "The B. Qaynuqâ' were the first to abrogate what was between them and the Messenger of God, may the prayers and peace of God be upon him, and they went to war between [the times of] Badr and Uhud."[26] Ibn Ishâq does not tell us the causes for this breach, but Ibn Hishâm adds the story that some Jews of the B. Qaynuqâ' pinned the skirt of an Arab woman while she was seated in their market so that when she stood up, her pudendum was exposed. A Muslim who was present took revenge on the Jew who played the trick and killed him. The Jews immediately killed the Muslim.[27]

Watt asserts that the B. Qaynuqâ' were besieged in their strongholds and then expelled after being allowed to collect their

A HISTORY OF THE JEWS OF ARABIA

debts. They had to leave behind "their arms and perhaps some of
their other goods, such as their goldsmith tools (though one might
conjecture that by the latter are meant the tools used in making weapons and armor). The usual account is that they went to the Jewish colony at Wâdî 'l-Qurâ, and after a month proceeded to ʿAdhraʿât in
Syria."[28] Barakat Ahmad contends that the expulsion of the B.
Qaynuqâʾ never took place during Muhammad's lifetime.[29] Following
Ibn Ishâq and Ibn Hishâm, he observes that it was only al-Wâqidî who
introduced this feature of the story. He points out that stories in the
two famous collections of Traditions by al-Bukhârî and Muslim date
the expulsion after Muhammad's death. The defeat of the Qaynuqâʾ
and the confiscation of their arms seem to have been sufficient for
Muhammad, because he succeeded in separating them from their
allies. Not only did none of the other Jews come to their defense, but
ʿUbâda b. as-Sâmit of the B. ʿAwf publicly renounced his *hilf* relationship with the B. Qaynuqâʾ.[30] Ahmad's argument is further strength-
ened by the traditions which hold that the needy *Muhâjirûn* were not
given confiscated land until after the expulsion of the B. an-Nadîr.[31]
Ibn Ishâq informs that after an altercation between Muhammad and
ʿAbdullâh b. 'Ubayy b. Salûl of the Khazraj, with whom the B.
Qaynuqâʾ had a *hilf* agreement, the B. Qaynuqâʾ were given to
ʿAbdullâh b. 'Ubayy.[32] The once mighty Qaynuqâʾ who had been able
to boast of their prowess in war[33] were now humiliated, disarmed, and
cut off from their allies, and Muhammad had shown all the groups in
Medina that previous treaty arrangements would not necessarily
guarantee support in a fight with the growing Muslim coalition.

The Jews continued their resistance to Muhammad, and one of their
leaders, Kaʿb b. al-Ashraf, who was of the B. Tayyiʾ and whose mother
was from the B. an-Nadîr, began a propaganda campaign against
Muhammad, the Muslims, and, in particular, the Muslim women. As
has been observed before, poetry served the function of journalism in
Arabia, informing, inciting, and molding public opinion.[34] The poetic
word was often thought to have magical powers and certainly served
as the opening shots in any battle. Kaʿb's poetry was intended to be
vulgar and insulting, as when he spoke of 'Umm al-Fadl:

Are you leaving and not stopping in the pass,
Leaving Umm al-Fadl in Mecca. . . .

What lies between ankle and elbow is in motion
When she tries to stand and does not
Like Umm Hakîm when she was with us
The rope between us firm and not to be cut
She is one of the B. ʿAmir who bewitches the heart,
And if she wished she could cure my sickness. . . .
Never did I see the sun rise at night untill I saw her
Display herself to us in the darkness of the night!

The vulgar nature of these verses ensured that they would travel
quickly to the greatest number of people, and Muhammad's reaction
was predictable anger when he asked, "Who will rid me of Ibn al-
ʾAshraf?"[36] Muhammad b. Maslama of the B. ʿAbd al-Ashhal volun-
teered and became one of the first secret agents for assassination in
the Muslim force. Muhammad b. Maslama was evidently urged to his
role by Saʿd b. Muʿadh, the leader of the B. ʿAbd al-Ashhal.[37] Saʿd had
effected the conversion of the B. ʿAbd al-Ashhal to Islam,[38] served as
Muhammad's personal bodyguard at Badr, and urged the slaying of
all the Qureish.[39] Described as a man of hasty temper,[40] we shall see
that he plays a crucial role in the elimination of the Jewish tribe of the
B. Qurayza. So with the backing of his tribe, Maslama devised a plot,
gained permission from Muhammad to tell lies to gain entry to Kaʿb,
and killed him. He is reported to have said, "Our attack upon God's
enemy cast terror among the Jews, and there was no Jew in Medina
who did not fear for his life."[41] And according to Ibn Ishâq, Muhammad followed this by a blanket order to "Kill any Jew that falls into
your power."[42] The Muslims had begun a campaign of terror against
the Jewish opposition.

Muhammad's next major military encounter was the famous battle
of Uhud, which took place in the third year after the Hijrah. The earlier battle of Badr, which had surprised everyone by the Muslim victory, had evidently set expectations in the minds of some that the
Muslims would always be victorious because God was on their side.
Muhammad even rejected Jewish military assistance, although the
reports assume that the Jews were allied to the Muslims in an obligation to assist in the fighting.[43] In the battle outside Medina around the
hill of Uhud, the Muslims were routed when they thought that
Muhammad had been killed, but they regrouped and were able to

hold off the Meccan army, who left without achieving their aim of defeating and killing Muḥammad. The sources for the battle are confused and devoted to glorifying the actions of one or another Muslim in the face of what was perceived as a defeat. It was not a defeat, however, and Muhammad and the Muslims emerged having shown that they could not be eliminated by the largest regular army the Meccans could muster. Still, in order to show that he was still a potent force, Muḥammad needed a demonstration, and the target was the Jewish tribe of the B. an-Nadîr.

The B. an-Nadîr had shown that they were willing to support Muhammad's enemies when they hosted Abû Sufyân in the Barley Raid. According to Ahmad, when Muḥammad approached the tribes of B. Qurayza and B. an-Nadîr for a renewal of the mutual nonaggression pact, the B. an-Nadîr refused.[44] Ibn Isḥâq reports that Muḥammad asked the B. an-Nadîr to pay the bloodwit due under the existing agreement, which they refused. Further, he informs us, they plotted to drop a rock on Muhammad's head, but he was divinely forewarned and was able to avoid assassination.[45] The number of conjectures found in the sources leads one to the conclusion that the explanations are after-the-fact justifications for Muḥammad's move against the tribe. But whatever the cause, Muslim hostility forced the B. an-Nadîr into their strongholds where they were besieged by Muḥammad's troops. The Jewish tribe was promised support by members of the B. ʿAwf, a subsection of the B. Khazraj, but the help never came, and they were forced to surrender.[46] The terms of the capitulation meant that they would be expelled from Medina. They were allowed to take only those goods that they could carry on camelback, except weapons of war. It is reported that they dismantled their houses and carried away even portions of the doors.[47] They departed with great pomp, dressed in finery, some for the Jewish military town of Khaybar and the rest for Syria. Three leaders of the B. an-Nadîr, Sallâm b. Abû al-Huqayq, Kinâna b. ar-Rabîʿ b. Abû al-Huqayq and Huyayy b. ʾAkhtab settled in Khaybar "where its people became subject to their rule."[48] The tribe's real property was distributed to the Muhâjirûn, making them independent from the ʾAnsâr. So, by the fourth year after the Hijrah, Muhammad had neutralized the B. Qaynuqâʾ and deported the B. an-Nadîr. That left only the B. Qurayza as a major block of Jewish opposition.

In the fifth year after the Hijrah, the Meccans gathered all of their military strength not only from their allies close at hand but also from the great bedouin tribes of the B. Ghatafân and the B. Sulaim. Watt estimates that the combined Meccan army was around 10,000 men when it marched out to meet Muhammad's force of about 3,000.[49] Muhammad's forces were without the assistance of the B. Qurayza, who did not send troops for the conflict. The Muslim stratagem of constructing a trench around the unprotected areas of the city coupled with Muhammad's adroit political maneuvering among the B. Ghatafân and the B. Sulaim led to a Muslim victory. But, even though the B. Qurayza contributed shovels and baskets to the effort of digging the trench,[50] they also negotiated with the besieging Meccans and would have probably joined them if they had been able to trust that they would not be left isolated when Muhammad attacked them.[51]

As the Meccan military alliance crumbled significantly as word spread of Muhammad's success, Muhammad decided to remove the last block of resistance to his control of Medina, the B. Qurayza. According to Ibn Ishâq:

> Gabriel came to the apostle wearing an embroidered turban and riding on a mule with a saddle covered with a piece of brocade. He asked the apostle if he had abandoned fighting, and when he said that he had he said that the angels had not yet laid aside their arms and that he had just come from pursuing the enemy. "God commands you, Muhammad, to go to B. Qurayza. I am about to go to them to shake their stronghold."[52]

With divine sanction, according to Ibn Ishâq, Muhammad massed the recently victorious Muslim army around the strongholds of the B. Qurayza and forced them to surrender unconditionally. They had sought the terms given the B. an-Nadîr, but were denied, and, because they were in such an impossible situation, outnumbered and without allies, they had to submit to whatever Muhammad wished.[53]

We are told that the B. 'Aws made entreaties to Muhammad that he deal with the B. Qurayza as he had with the B. Qaynuqâ', allies of the B. Khazraj.[54] Tribal pride and tribal rivalry demanded that each section of the 'Ansâr be treated equally, and they did not want it said that they were less able to protect their allies than their rivals. So Muhammad persuaded them to agree to his appointing a *ḥakam*, a judge, from among them. When they so agreed, he appointed Saʿd b. Muʿâdh to the post. From Saʿd's past involvements, Muhammad must have been certain that Saʿd's judgment would be harsh and in line with his wishes. And, since Saʿd was not only one of the ʾAws but had been wounded at Uhud, there was little that anyone could do to speak against the choice. They could only urge him to treat their allies with kindness. Saʿd replied, "The time has come for Saʿd in the cause of God not to care for any man's censure."[55] After obtaining the explicit permission that they would abide by his decision, Saʿd ordered that the men should be killed, the property divided, and the women and children taken as captives. Muhammad supported the judgment by saying that it had come from God "above the seven heavens."[56] It is reported that anywhere from 400 to over 900 adult males were killed and buried in trenches in the market of Medina. Some accounts indicate that ʿAlî and az-Zubayr were involved in the executions, and Watt speculates that most of the Companions were involved.[57] The women and children were sold as slaves to obtain horses and weapons for the Muslims, although some were distributed to the Muslims, and Muhammad chose one woman, Rayhâna bt. ʿAmr b. Khunâfa, who is said to have remained with him until she died. Some of the women and children were bought by Jews in Medina, Khaybar, Taymâ, and Wâdî al-Qurâ.[58] The tribe of the B. Qurayza was thus eliminated, breaking all organized Jewish opposition to Muhammad in Medina, but by no means eliminating all the Jews from the city. Muhammad and the Muslims, having secured the city from Islam, could take on other Jewish enclaves in the Hijâz.

The execution of the B. Qurayza has been strongly criticized by Western scholars, who see this as a barbarous act unworthy of someone with claims to religious leadership.[59] This has prompted some recent revisionist examinations of the topic by two Muslims, W. N. Arafat[60] and Barakat Ahmad.[61] Both works attack the integrity of the sources, and Barakat Ahmad attempts to show how the story as presented by Ibn Ishâq could not have been possible. In a penetrating and thorough survey of the sources, M. J. Kister presents a convincing argument that the main outline of the events as presented in the *Sîrah* is correct, even if there has been some embellishment by later authors.[62] It should not come as a surprise that the massacre of the B. Qurayza took place as it did. The escalating tension between Muḥammad and the Jews was bound to force a military confrontation. It is clear, however, that the underlying policy was not totally anti-Jewish, because Jews remained in the city of Medina and in the teritories under Muhammad's control until after his death.

Returning to the question of the dating of the Constitution of Medina, the greatest problem remains the question of why only some of the Jews of Medina are mentioned in the agreement. All of the collateral traditions concerning the Jews assume that there was an agreement or a series of agreements with the Jews which were essentially in accord with the terms of the Constitution. In his discussion of the fate of the B. Qurayza, Kister outlines the essential details of the process of concluding "a crude, not elaborated agreement of peaceful co-existence. It was probably of the *muwâdaʿa* kind granting assurances of mutual safety."[63] In other words, some of the agreements between Muhammad and the Jews would have been unwritten and/or unelaborated at various stages. If we read what Ibn Isḥâq has to say about the Constitution, he characterizes it as follows: "The Messenger of God, may the prayers and peace of God be upon him, wrote a document concerning the *Muhâjirûn* and the *ʾAnṣâr* in which he concluded a pact with them, confirmed for them [their rights to] their religion and their property and stipulated the following conditions for them [the *Muhâjirûn*, the *ʾAnṣâr*, and the Jews]."[64] The Constitution as we have it from Ibn Isḥâq appears to be the agreement between Muḥammad, the Muslims who were *Muhâjirûn*, and the tribes of the *ʾAnṣâr*, who, according to this agreement, would have retained their former alliances insofar as those did not conflict with Islam.

As we have seen above, clans of Jews were allied to clans of Arabs, just as clans of Arabs were allied with clans of Jews. Those Jews who were in treaty relations with the *ʾAnṣâr* were included in the treaty process. But those Jewish political units who were not in a *ḥilf* relationship with the *ʾAnṣâr* would have had separate agreements with Muhammad of the sort outlined by Kister. It is interesting to note that the Jews of the B. Thaʿlaba and the B. Jafna are included in the Constitution. As we have seen, both the B. Jafna and the B. Thaʿlaba were counted by Samhûdî as related to the B. Ghassân, the "kings" who were clients of the Byzantines. Given the complexity of the political alignments in Medina, it would not be surprising to see a pro-Byzan-tine faction among the Jews, particularly among those who were not members of Medina's Jewish elite, the Persian-sponsored B. Qurayza and the B. an-Nadîr, the two tribes who receive the full force of Muhammad's wrath. Viewed in this manner, it would help explain why the many groups of Yathrib's Jews do not act in concord against Muhammad at any time in his Medinan stay.

With the massacre of the B. Qurayza, serious opposition in Medina was eliminated, but Jewish resistance in the Hijâz continued from the strongly fortified Jewish city of Khaybar. The Jewish leader of the coa-lition of tribes that had besieged Muhammad during the Battle of the Trench was Abû Râfiʿ Sallâm b. Abû al-Huqayq. As we saw above, Muhammad authorized a raid against him by a small band of guerril-las headed by the Judeo-Arabic speaking ʿAbdullâh b. ʿAtîk. Isn Ishâq represents the reason for this raid as competition between the B. ʾAws and the B. Khazraj, the latter wishing to do a deed as "glorious" as the killing of Kaʿb b. al-ʾAshraf by the B. ʾAws.[65] This raid, too, was to be a terrorist raid, for it appears that Muhammad was not ready at this point to invest the most heavily fortified city in the Hijâz.

In the sixth year, Muhammad concluded the agreement of al-Hudaybiyya. Muhammad had marched to the outskirts of Mecca with a large force with the intention of making an ʿumra, a "lesser pilgrim-age." He was stopped at the borders of the sacred territory that sur-rounded Mecca and there negotiated that he would withdraw from Mecca for a year so that the Meccans would not lose face. But, in the following year, Muhammad and his followers would be allowed to enter the city, which the Qureish would abandon, for a space of three nights.[66] Despite the face-saving clause of immediate withdrawal, the Treaty of al-Hudaybiyya showed that Muhammad had won and that there was no longer any serious Meccan opposition possible.

Several months later, in the seventh year, Muhammad invested Khaybar. He did not fear that the Meccans would come to the aid of their onetime allies, and he had no need to worry about a force at his back from Medina.[67] The only possible allies that the Khaybarî Jews had were the bedouin tribe of the B. Ghatafân, but Muhammad neu-tralized them by feigning an attack on their families and property. The siege was tightly held, and the Jews were forced to capitulate after a period of negotiation. The main wealth of Khaybar, as with the other oasis towns in the Hijâz, was agriculture, particularly dates. This required considerable expertise in hydraulic engineering, horticulture, and all the other skills required of a successful farmer in a desert climate. Because the Jews had the skill, they were able to negotiate terms that allowed them to remain in their homes and on their land for the payment of half of the annual harvest.[69] The town of Fadak capitulated on similar terms, although, because it was not besieged or taken in warfare, it did not come under the stipulations of the division of booty, and Muhammad was able to keep the proceeds for himself and not divide them among the Muslims.[69]

The notion of capitulation became a regular feature of "submission" agreements mentioned in the Sîrah. For example, when the deputation comes from the Himyaritic kings to inform Muhammad that they had submitted to Islam, the agreement reads, in part:

> If a Jew or a Christian becomes a Muslim he is a believer with his rights and obligations. And he who remains in his Judaism or Christianity is not to be seduced from it, and he is obligated for the capitulation tax [Arab. jizyah]. On each adult, male or female, free or slave, a full dînâr, the value of a Yemenite garment, or its equivalent in clothes. He who pays that to the Messenger of God, may the prayers and peace of God be upon him, has God's guarantee of protection of life and property [Arab. dhimmah] and that of His messenger.[70]

In a large sense, Muhammad's actions became the paradigm for the later Muslim community and, when Islamic society is established outside Arabia with hegemony over large numbers of Jews and Christians, the models of capitulation in Arabia are used to regulate non-Muslim communal life. There is the charge that many of the capitulation traditions have been tendentiously shaped by later transmitters to reflect their desires for how things ought to be, but in the main it seems that Muhammad was willing to tolerate a non-Muslim population in his ʾummah as long as it was willing to submit to the Muslim will.

The Sîrah's attention to the Jews stops after the story of the capitulation of Fadak, except to mention the tradition that during Muhammad's last illness he is supposed to have said that "two religions shall not remain together in the peninsula of the Arabs."[71] This is the supposed basis of the legendary expulsion of the Jews by ʿUmar when he was caliph, a subject to be treated in the next chapter. Muhammad went on to conquer the rest of the Hijâz and obtain the capitulation of most of the major political and tribal groups in Arabia. By the time of his death in 632 C.E., the promise of a grand pan-Arabian Jewish state, which had seemed so alive a century and a quarter earlier, was completely gone, and the once powerful Jews of the Hijâz ceased to be a major political or cultural force anywhere in Arabia except in the Yemen.

7

ARABIAN JUDAISM
AFTER MUHAMMAD

The death of Muhammad produced a profound crisis in the Muslim
community. There were many who had anticipated the coming of the
Day of Judgment during Muhammad's lifetime and were surprised by
his apparently sudden demise. There were others, primarily from
Medina, who saw Muhammad's death as an opportunity to break
from the direction that Muhammad had taken during his lifetime in
favoring the newly converted Meccans over the 'Ansâr. Potential splits
were exacerbated in large part because Muhammad had made no pro-
vision for a political heir.[1] Three of Muhammad's closest Companions,
Abû Bakr, 'Umar, and Abû 'Ubaydah, acting swiftly on the day of
Muhammad's death, managed to persuade an assembled crowd that
Abû Bakr should be Muhammad's successor, and the first caliph was
chosen.[2]

When Abû Bakr assumed the leadership of the Muslim community,
he was faced with a serious rebellion. Not only did some factions of
the Muslims, including Companions of Muhammad, refuse to
acknowledge Abû Bakr's leadership, but tribes that had submitted to
Muhammad now broke away in what has become known as *ar-Riddah*,
the Apostasy. Jews and Christians apparently followed the lead of
some of the Muslim's, saw Muhammad's death as an opportunity to
return to former freedoms, and moved away from Islam's domination. In at-Tabarî's report derived from az-Zubayr b. al-'Awwâm, we
learn:

When Abû Bakr was given allegiance, and he had united the 'Ansâr over their differences, he said, "Let the expedition of 'Usâmah [to Syria] be carried out." So the Arabs apostatized as complete tribes or in part, and the Jews and Christians rose up. The Muslims were like sheep on a rainy night on account of the loss of their prophet, may the prayers and peace of God be upon him, and because of their small number and because of the great number of their enemies. People then said to him [Abû Bakr], "They [the expeditionary force] are the bulk of the Muslims. The Arabs, as you have seen, have revolted against you, and it is not necessary that you send off the bulk of the Muslims." Abû Bakr replied, "By Him who has Abû Bakr's soul in His hand, even if I thought I would be torn apart by wild beasts, I would still send forth the expedition of 'Usâmah as the Messenger of God commanded. Even if no one were left in the villages but me, I would send it."[3]

While the Syrian expedition left the city of Medina and the new caliph relatively undefended, the Arabian tribes sent delegations to Medina to negotiate new terms for their association with Islam now that Muhammad was dead and their agreements with him broken. Some, apparently, even tried to take advantage of the situation to attack Abû Bakr. But the caliph was able to hold off all resistance, and when the Syrian expeditionary forces returned, he sent out some eleven different armies throughout Arabia to bring the Arabs into line with his expansionist vision of Islam. Using techniques that had proved successful for the Romans, Abû Bakr's forces incorporated the energies of the reconquered tribes to subdue the next areas of resistance, and soon Islam was challenging Byzantium in Syria and Persia in Babylon.[4]

Abû Bakr ruled for only two years, until 634 C.E., but during that time he managed to change the nature of Arabian society more profoundly than Muhammad had been able to do. Following his vision of Muhammad's precedent, he did much to unite the various tribal factions into one Islamic force, although, to be sure, he neither eliminated all political divisions nor solved the basic problem of succession. But his reorganization seems to have quieted rebellion in Arabia sufficiently to eliminate any opportunity for Jews and Christians to throw off the dominion of Islam. They no longer had any allies among the

Arabs, and they were too weakened and few in number to resist on their own.

Muslim sources fall silent about any further resistance of Jews in Arabia, just as they turn almost all attention away from the peninsula, and it is not until the reign of the next caliph, ʿUmar, that the community is mentioned again. Some Muslim sources contend that, as caliph, ʿUmar I "expelled the Jews from the Ḥijâz and banished them from the Arabian peninsula into Syria, and he expelled the people of Najrân and settled them in the area of al-Kûfah."[5] ʿUmar was supposed to be acting on Muhammad's dying statement that two religions could not exist together in Arabia. We know, however, that Jews did continue to live in Arabia after the time of Caliph ʿUmar, and another source limits the terms of the order of expulsion. According to at-Ṭabarî, in the year 20 A.H., "ʿUmar divided Khaybar among the Muslims and removed the Jews from there. He sent Abû Ḥabîbah to Fadak, and he set for them half [of the dates and half of the land to be paid in gold]. And he granted [that] to them, and went on to Wâdî al-Qurâ and divided it. And in [that year] he removed the Jews of Najrân to al-Kûfah according to al-Wâqidî."[6] At-Ṭabarî is apparently using al-Wâqidî as his source, as was al-Wâqidî's "secretary," Ibn Saʿd, but at-Ṭabarî's reports appear more "primitive," less smoothed over into a running narrative, and, to judge by his use of other material, more reflective of the original. At-Ṭabarî does not indicate that all the Jews were expelled from Arabia.

The process described by at-Ṭabarî is one of gradual expropriation of Jewish land holdings and driving them from their land. Kister observes:

> The changes which the redistribution of land by the rulers in the Arabian peninsula introduced were considerable: vast areas of pasture land were expropriated and turned into *himâ* territory[7]; lands of expelled Jews and Christians in Najrân were divided and leased out on terms now fixed by the Caliph and exacted by his governors. . . . Muʿâwiya's grasp of the economic importance of real estate led him to acquire lands in the area of Mecca and Medina, where he also purchased buildings and courts. He did the same in al-Ṭâʾif, buying land from Jews and Christians who had settled there as merchants after being expelled from al-Yaman and Medina."[8]

A HISTORY OF THE JEWS OF ARABIA

This means that as late as twenty years or more after the supposed order of 'Umar to expel all the Jews from Arabia, Jews were still living in areas of the Ḥijâz. Just as the Ḥijâzî Jews had ceased to be a major political force earlier, they now ceased to be a major force in the Arabian economy, but they did persist as Jews.

Taymâ and Wâdî al-Qûrâ were places of refuge for some of the Jews from Khaybar and elsewhere, where there is evidence of Jewish communal existence beyond the twelfth century. From the eleventh century, there are letters to R. Sharîrâ Gaôn and his son, R. Hai Gaôn of Pumbedita from Jews of Wâdî al-Qûrâ, asking about problems of real estate, showing not only that there was an active community in the Ḥijâz, but also that they regarded themselves as "rabbinic" in orientation.[9] We also know that

"In a Geniza document dating from the eleventh century reference is made to two letters addressed from Tyre containing an inquiry about a certain Isaac of Wadi al Kurah who, some four years previously, had abandoned his wife in Rabbat-Ammon. Such correspondence gives point to the belief that in the days immediately preceding the Crusades there were constant contacts between the Jews of Wadi al Kurah and those of Transjordania and Palestine."[10]

This may be the community that the famous traveling Jewish merchant, Benjamin ben Jonah of Tudela, who lived in the last half of the twelfth century, mentions:

Here is the habitat of the Jewish tribes of the Rechabites and of those roaming around Taimâ'. They have a Jewish governor of their own in Taimâ', known as Hanan the *Nasi*. It is a large town, and the distance from one end of the country to another is 16 days. There are several fortified cities in it, and Jews are independent of any gentile yoke. They are all valiant warriors who go out in raiding parties against their neighbors, the Arabian tent-dwellers. They have no houses and live on brigandage. All their neighbors are afraid of them. Many of them are workers of the soil and cattle breeders. Their land is vast; they give a tithe of the yield of their land to their scholars who dedicate themselves to study as well as to the poor of Israel and to all who mourn the fall of Jerusalem. They eat no meat, drink no wine and are attired in black clothes. . . . They address their inquiries on points of Jewish law to the *Rosh Golah* in Baghdad. They sit in torn clothes, lamenting the fate of all the Jews throughout the dispersion and fast 40 days in the year for the welfare of the Jews of the Diaspora.[11]

Benjamin did not personally visit the sites, so he cannot be said to be totally trustworthy about what he reports, but his stories do correspond to the material confirmed elsewhere.

In addition to Taymâ and Wâdî al-Qûrâ, Benjamin mentions a thriving Jewish community in Khaybar, the place from which ʿUmar was said to have expelled the Jews. He informs us:

> "Its people claim to be descendants of the tribes of Reuben, Gad and half the tribe of Manasseh, who were carried as captives by King Shalmaneser of Assyria, and it is the descendants of these captives, who built the large town, who now go to war against many kingdoms. . . . Hubar [Khaybar] is a very large town with a community of 50,000 Jews, including many scholars and skilled warriors who are not afraid to go to war both against the northerners of Babylon and against the southerners of al-Yemen."[12]

This story is reminiscent of the sojourn of Nabonidus in Arabia and is most likely embellished in the telling. But there are a continuous stream of reports about Khaybar, its fierce Jews, and their bellicose relations with their neighbors. There are also reports of surviving treaties between the Jews of Khaybar and Muhammad. One of these, typical of the rest, is discussed by Israel Wolfensohn (Ben-Zeev), who concludes that the plethora of anachronistic material in the version indicates that the whole treaty is false.[13] Such "documents" were used by the Jewish and Muslim communities, however, as legal precedents to establish customary conduct in the context of Islamic legal praxis. As in other instances, the historical fiction becomes the operative reality.

Around 1488, Obadiah ben Abraham of Bertinoro arrived in Jerusalem from where he sent his travel impressions of the state of the Jewish communities in the eastern Mediterranean. Among his stories, we find a fantastic elaboration on the fierce Jewish tribes of Arabia:

> It is known throughout these territories that the Ishmaelites (Moslems), going from Egypt to their holy shrine in Mecca, have

A History of the Jews of Arabia

to traverse a vast and terrifying desert. They always go in caravans of 4,000 camels. Sometimes they are attacked by a tribe of
formidable giants who spread terror in the land, one of whom can
pursue a thousand. The Ishmaelites call them "Arabians of Shad-
dai" that is, Arabian Sons of God, seeing that when they go to
battle they pronounce the name of God. Ishmaelites say of them
that each can carry a whole camel on one shoulder and can use his
other hand to carry a dagger with which to fight the enemy. It is
well known that their religion is the Jewish religion and it is said
that they are descendants of the Rechabites.[14]

From this same period are other accounts that corroborate the existence of bedouin Jews in the Hijâz. An Italian traveler, Ludovico di
Varthema of Bologna toured Khaybar around the beginning of the
16th century and reported that there were some 4,000 to 5,000 Jews
living in and around Khaybar. Three decades later, David de Rossi of
Safed records evidence he had gathered about the existence of Jewish
tent-dwellers in the Hijâz.[15]

By the eighteenth century, the Jews still survived in intact communities in the Hijâz, according to the Danish traveler Carsten Niebuhr.
He observed isolated Jews living under Muslim rule as well as "whole
tribes in the Hejaz hills, adjacent to Khaibar, who are governed by
Independent Sheikhs of their own. . . . There live to this day free Jews
ruled by governors of their own exactly like Arabs".[16] Niebuhr goes on
to comment on the fact that there is only slight contact between the
Arabian Jews and those of Damascus and Aleppo, and is told by the
Jews of those communities that the Jews of Arabia cannot be true
Jews, thus accounting for their lack of contact. One has the sense that
the process of assimilation may be taking over the Arabian Jews; that
they are no longer the independent and fierce Rabbinite Jewish warriors of Obadiah of Bertinoro's description, but are becoming indistin-
guishable from their desert neighbors. We know from the time of the
ʾUmayyid caliph Muʿâwiyya that Arabian Jews were converting and
assimilating to Islam, as is shown in the story of the Kitâb al-Aghânî,
where Muʿâwiyya observes a Jew from Taymâ praying in the sacred
mosque in Mecca during the pilgrimage season, properly garbed in
two white cloths.[17]

But even into the nineteenth century, reports, often third-hand,
assert the continued existence of the Arabian Jews of the Hijâz. The

Jerusalemite David de-Beth-Hillel reports in 1832 in his memoirs that he had heard from a European Jew, Jacob Taylor, two years earlier, saying:

> In 1828, a Jewish trader from Africa visited the Hauran on business. One day, while he was engaged in prayer, a Bedouin approached him, kneeled and kissed his phylacteries. The Bedouin said that he was a Jew of the tribe of Dan, and that his family would be happy to offer the guest hospitality. Asked by the merchant how far his place was from there, he replied that it was a distance of ten days by ordinary march, but that he could be carried on the back of speedy camels in three days. The merchant asked further how long he could stay with them, to which he replied that all depended on their king and chieftain, as all were anxious to see one of their brothers from Palestine. The merchant said: "Come with me to Safed where I will take leave of my wife and children and join you," but the Bedouin replied, "We dare not cross the Jordan until the appropriate day arrives," whereupon they parted. Their conversation was in Hebrew."[18]

From the same period, 1833, a French traveler, Baron Bois le Comte, reports that the "people of Arabia are Wahhâbîs or Moslems; many tribes are Shi'ites, as are the Arabs of Bahrein. The Jewish tribe of the Rechabites, estimated to number 60,000, lead a patriarchal nomad existence, exactly like all other Bedouins, and, like them, engage in pillage and warfare."[19]

Three decades later, the Jewish explorer of the Yemen, Jacob Sappir, traveling on a commission from Jerusalem to the Jews of the "Southern countries" to collect contributions for the poor of Jerusalem, reports about bedouin Jews:

> I saw some of them going on the *Haj* pilgrimage and spoke to them. Twice a year these Arabian Jews attend the great fair and market day. They are known to be observant Jews, yet no one has traced their descent exactly or studied their customs and their faith or established their tribal descent. It may well be that it is of them that the Moslem *Haj* pilgrims say that they must pay the "infidels' tribute" whenever they cross these routes."[20]

Unfortunately, when we get the report of a generally reliable witness, the famous Charles Doughty, whose *Travels in Arabia Deserta* remains important for anyone studying the peninsula, we find precious little to corroborate these late accounts. Doughty speaks of a certain chief named Aly es-Sweysy the Yahûdy,[21] and persistently follows leads about descendants of the Jews of Khaybar,[22] but fails to produce any real evidence that independent Jews continued to exist in Arabia outside the well-known communities in the Yemen.

Ben-Zvi speculates that "the sovereign Jewish tribes in northern Arabia must have completely disappeared as Jews by the middle of the eighteenth century, at the same time that the Wahhâbî forces made their appearance in the arena of Arab history."[23] While he cannot show a link between the rise of the Wahhâbîs and the decline in the reports of north Arabian Jewry, he postulates the development of a secretive pattern of social survival, a kind of "Arab-marrano" Judaism similar to that of the Iberian peninsula or the Meshhed Jews. To substantiate his hypothesis, Ben-Zvi reports a conversation he had in 1930 with an eyewitness to Khaybar Judaism in which his informant asserted that the inhabitants of Khaybar, claiming to be descendants of the Israelites, refused to intermarry with those outside the tribe. And from another informant, we learn that the Khaybar Jews "observe the Sabbath, but rob and raid."[24] In addition, on the Sabbath, the Khaybar Jews did not take their cattle out to graze.

Both the persistence and number of reports leads one to conclude that the Jews of northern Arabia probably did survive in some form for a long period after the rise of Islam, but how long and to what extent is impossible to say at this time. It is clear that more archaeological investigation in the Hijâz is needed, not only for this question but also for the history of the region in general. It is also evident that time is running out if any answers are to be found about the survival of Jewish elements in bedouin society, since the bedouin are being settled and educated at a very great rate. The present political climate in the region does not bode well, however, for the intense scholarly efforts that would be needed to preserve what vanishing heritage may be there.

Bernard Lewis observes in his book *The Jews of Islam* that the Jews of Arabia "were of no great importance in Jewish history and are virtually unknown to Jewish historiography."[25] He correctly observes that "Of far greater significance were the large and active Jewish communities in Southwest Asia and North Africa—countries into which the

Arabs came in a great wave of conquest in the seventh and eighth centuries, and which constituted the core of the Islamic caliphate."[26] Arabian Jewry, destroyed, dispersed, or disguised, failed to claim a place in the revised memories of the great Jewish communities dominated by Islam. One can only speculate about the reasons, but some aspects are clear. The period of the Himyaritic Jewish kings, particularly that of Dhû Nuwâs, did not fit the historiographico-literary topos of Judaism as moral exemplar. Here was a case of Jews "persecuting" Christians, and, however justified the reasons, however limited the actions, the story did not mesh with the pattern of sin, punishment, and redemption that characterizes the sojourn in Egypt and God's deliverance through Moses and the Exodus, the story that is nearly paradigmatic for Jewish historical writings in pre-modern times. Jewish encounters with Muhammad were equally inappropriate as part of the collective memories of Jews under the domination of Islamicate culture, and besides, Muslims had appropriated that past for their polemic against the Jews.

The Arabian Jews left no advocates to argue for their importance in history's court, but one cannot agree with Bernard Lewis that they were of "no great importance in Jewish history." As we have seen, Islam developed against the background of an Arabia strongly under the influence of Judaism. The very words and stories that form the fabric of religious discourse in Arabia are part of the stock of Jewish lore and legal speculation. The Qur'ân cannot be understood, as the early Muslim exegetes showed, without recourse and reference to rabbinic haggadic and midrashic material, even if only to reject it.

To grant this relationship between Judaism and nascent Islam, one does not have to go to the extreme that scholars did in the beginning of Western investigation about the relationship between Judaism and Islam and adopt the polemical stance of Abraham Geiger and his followers. In 1833 the famous Reform rabbi, Abraham Geiger, published the German version of a prize-winning essay prepared under the tutelage of the Arabist G. Freytag. That essay, titled *Was hat Muhammad auf dem Judenthume aufgenommen? [What Did Muhammad Receive from Judaism?]* marks the formal beginning in Western scholarship of a discussion of pre-Islamic history and the Jews of Arabia in particular.[27] Geiger assumed that Judaism was a fixed system with a standard against which all Jews could be measured and against which religious ideas found in Islamic writings could be judged for their origins within Judaism. Deviations from his theoretical standard were regarded as mistakes and errors, either on the part of Muḥammad and his fellow Muslims for not getting the story straight, or on the part of the Arabian Jews, Muhammad's supposed teachers, who were themselves thought to be at such a low level of religious and intellectual development that they taught perverted and false doctrines. The myth of the existence of a normative Judaism obscured the investigation of the unique character of the several Arabian Jewish communities.

Geiger's attitudes were adopted by both Jewish and Christian scholars, who began to write apologies for which religion had more "influence" on early Islam. The perspectives were determined by the religious confession of the author. These attitudes ultimately reduced the importance of the Arabian Jewish communities because Arabian Jews were held to be either ʿamê ha-ʾarets, ignorant bumpkins, or merely irrelevant to the understanding of the cultural interaction. For many Western writers, it became enough to prove that Muḥammad had "taken" his ideas from Judaism or Christianity. This typological approach solved a number of serious historiographic problems. The difficulties in identifying Arabian Jews and Christians, determining their social and religious settings, and demonstrating their participation in the formation of Islam were greatly simplified. One merely had to demonstrate the similarities between Judaism or Christianity and Islam, assume that the Jewish and Christian material was older and prior to the Islamic material, and, remarkably, Islam was shown to be derivative. Not only did the history of Islam suffer from this approach, so did the history of pre-Islamic Arabia. In many historical texts, Arabian Jews, for example, assumed a function similar to the function Muslims have served in Western medieval history texts. Muslims often appear merely to provide the Crusaders with someone to fight. Arabian Jews appear only when one needs to explain certain passages in the Qurʾân and its collateral texts.

At the practical level, both the common discourse and the shared historical experience determined the fate of future Jewish communities under Islam, the majority of the world's Jews in pre-modern times. Islam, in its reaction to the political strivings of Judaism and Christianity as instruments of foreign domination, naturally regarded Judaism with suspicion, confirmed by Muḥammad's experiences in

Medina. Yet, in spite of all the hostility, outlined above and set forth as the core of the second chapter of the Qur'ân, the suspicions do not produce a totally negative reaction. Muhammad's vision of a poly-confessional community shows through, and Jews are tolerated within the larger construct of the Islamicate 'ummah. This is in contrast, of course, to the status of Jews and Muslims in medieval kingdoms in the West that were identified as Christian. There, no one but Christians of the type recognized by the ruling powers held legal status, forcing the Jewish population to exist only at the sufferance of the kings, who often confined them to a limited number of occupations and severely circumscribed places to live. So Jewish life flourished under Islam, and as S. D. Goitein has spelled out:

> The Jews took their full share in this great Middle-Eastern mercantile civilization, in particular from the tenth to the thirteenth centuries, and it was at that time and in that part of the world that Judaism itself received its final shape. There, under Arab-Muslim influence, Jewish thought and philosophy and even Jewish law and religious practice were systematized and finally formulated. Even the Hebrew language developed its grammar and vocabulary on the model of the Arab language. The revival of Hebrew in our own times would be entirely unthinkable without the services rendered to it by Arabic in various ways a thousand years ago. Arabic itself became a Jewish language and, unlike Latin in Europe, was employed by Jews for all secular and religious purposes, with the sole exception of the synagogue service.[28]

Because Islamicate society was history- and tradition-minded, its dominant cultural attitudes and forms were erected on the real and imagined records of, among other experiences, encounters between Jews and Muslims. The net result was that Arabian Judaism continued to live in paradigmatic form, as a kind of *sunnah*, just as Muhammad's Companions continued to exert their influences through the ages by their *sunnahs*. Even today, some of the attitudes of opposition to the state of Israel among Muslims is formed by the rhetoric presented as the historical record of Jewish opposition to Islam drawn from both the Qur'ân and tradition. This fact alone is sufficient to count Arabian Judaism as central to the determination of the fate of future Judaism.

A HISTORY OF THE JEWS OF ARABIA

The last word about the Jews of Arabia is not in. More archaeology is certain to yield new texts, artifacts, and data, and the continuing reexamination of the literary and archaeological remains is bringing about greater understanding both of Judaism and of the early development of Islam. It is unlikely that this new understanding will do much to change current attitudes of confrontation, but where goodwill does exist, the clarified historical record of the shared experiences of Jews and Muslims can only strengthen the resolve for peaceful coexistence. The contributions of the Jews of Arabia have helped shape both Judaism and Islam, and the history of Arabian Judaism, as a facet of the shared heritage of Judaism, Christianity, and Islam, helps illumine our common past.[29]

8

AFTERWORD ON HISTORIOGRAPHY

Recent critics have challenged the possibilities not only of solving the puzzle of historical reconstruction, but even of the validity of the pieces, particularly when those pieces are derived from traditional religious and literary or quasi-literary sources. In particular, there has been unease about the reliability of the histories, traditions, poems, and stories from the earliest periods of Islam,[1] and some modern historians of Islam have called for changes in approach to Islamic texts that would take the problems into account. For those of us interested in the history of the Jews of Arabia, we are often dependent on Islamic texts as the only sources of our knowledge of that important Jewish community. While we are forced to come to terms with the problems presented by those texts, we are also in a position to offer assistance to the general Islamicist and to the general historian of religion in assessing the value of early Islamic materials.

Patricia Crone and Michael Cook, in their provocative book *Hagarism*, reject the view that early Islamic sources can, of themselves, be used to reconstruct the Islamic past.[2] They argue that "what purport to be accounts of religious events in the seventh century are utilisable only for the study of religious ideas in the eighth. . . . The only way out of the dilemma is thus to step outside the Islamic tradition altogether and start again."[3] Patricia Crone continues this view in her *Slaves on Horses*: "For over a century the landscape of the Muslim past was thus exposed to a weathering so violent that its shapes were reduced to dust and rubble and deposited in secondary patterns, mixed with foreign debris and shifting in the wind."[4] For Crone, there are very few examples of rocks in this landscape, the so-called Constitution of Medina a monolithic exception.[5] These rocks only serve to point up for her the contrast between them and the bleak waste of the knowable Muslim past.[6] The reconstructable past as presented in *Hagarism* relies only on sources outside Islam, and constructs a view of a past so at odds with conventional views that it has been almost universally rejected. This has been particularly so because the authors' criticisms of the possibilities of understanding the earliest periods of Islam would seem, if applied as a general method to the sources used by historians of religion, to lead toward a kind of historical solipsism.

If Cook and Crone were alone in their efforts to change the way we view early Islamic history, and if their arguments did not appear to be so persuasive and cogent, they could be dismissed. But such a historiographical stance has been present in literary and anthropological studies in the West for a long time, bringing strong attacks on historicism in those fields.[7] In the field of classics, for example, just as in the field of Islamic studies, literary texts are often used as historical sources. A traditional approach to these texts has been to decide what is "literary" and what is "historical." The literary portions of a work, even a historical work, are analyzed for any aesthetic content, while the historical portions are mined (to keep Patricia Crone's geological image) for gems of historical truths. But herein lie the very difficulties mentioned above. Before we can proceed to divide what is literary from what is historical, we have to determine to what extent our modern divisions between the "objective, immutable, or quantifiable facts" of history and the "fiction" of literature are really useful categories in the analysis of work written before modern times.

Douglas J. Stewart, commenting on recent trends in anthropological analysis of literary texts, effectively demonstrates that a factor of "mythomorphism" operates throughout the Greco-Roman historical writings, even in places that seem unlikely. He contends, for example, that Marcus Antonius saw himself as more than just a human participant in the events of his time. He was, in his own regard, "a mythical figure. As a self proclaimed descendant of Heracles, he saw himself as the new Heracles with a divinely sanctioned mission to father an innumerable brood of dynasts throughout the world."[8] Plutarch, the biographer or hagiographer, can be seen as the mere reporter of a mythic biography already formed by the central character himself, or as the creator of a characterization of Marcus Antonius that justifies the myth-making process. Either way, when we, as moderns, view Antonius' affair with Cleopatra, we are in a quandary in our search for the "historical" Antonius; we have to doubt not only the transmitter of our information but also the central figure himself:

> First, in such cases, one must speculate to what extent we can trust our witnesses and records, if indeed they *are* invincibly prone to assimilate to mythical patterns what they see or transmit as supposedly historical actions. And second, we must also ask how we can "trust" historical agents themselves. Can we be so very sure that they are acting with *some* sense of the particularity of their own situations, which is to say that they are both conscious and self-conscious individuals, in the sense that "history" assumes? In order to have history at all—we think—we need not assume that men always act wisely or decently, but we must assume that they are at least *awake*, and in sufficient command of their free will to make personal choices of the actions—at least among a range of mistakes and blunders. Now, even that minimal and modest assumption may be threatened for long and important stretches of history.[9]

If the foregoing thesis is to be accepted for Islamic traditions as well as for the Greco-Roman period, one of our tasks is to pursue the influences of "mythomorphisms" in early Islamic texts. It will not do merely to identify the "fictional" elements and discard them in favor of the assumed "facts" about the times of Muhammad and his contemporaries, for example, because the set of facts at our disposal would seem to be preselected by the operation of the myth(s) on both the historian(s) and the actor(s).

What has now become almost the classic formulation of the structuralist analytic method applied to early Islamic texts is set forth in John Wansbrough's two works, *Quranic Studies: Sources and Methods of Scriptural Interpretation*,[10] and *The Sectarian Milieu: Content and Composition of Islamic Salvation History*.[11] In these two studies, particularly in the second, Wansbrough analyzes the historiographical styles of the *sîrah-maghâzî* literature, the biographical literature purporting to tell the story of Muhammad and his Companions during the rise of Islam and their relationship to Muslim Scripture. He regards the *sîrah-maghâzî* literature as an example of "salvation history" *(Heilsge-schichte)*, characterized by two narrative techniques: "exegetical, in which extracts (serial and isolated) from scripture provided the framework for extended *narratio*; and parabolic, in which the *narratio* was itself the framework for frequent if not continuous allusion to scripture."[12] He contrasts his approach with previous studies, which he disparages as "distinctly positivist,"[13] and states that his "purpose in these chapters is not historical reconstruction, but rather, source analysis . . . to plot the position of Islamic salvation history along that literary spectrum."[14] He maintains that the historicist character of early Islamic writings is part of the structure of the presentation of the message of salvation:

> Now, in the corpus of Islamic salvation history, of which scripture is only a part, the quality of "revelation" remains unchanged. Indeed, emphasis upon its historicity is achieved by the various devices of reification. . . . The past (genesis: *mubtada*ʾ), constructed round Biblical and South Arabian genealogies, is there retailed as *praeparatio evangelica*; the present (exodus: *mabʿath*) as fulfillment of the prognosis. The future is hardly mentioned . . . . [Salvation history] in order to be "salvic" must be "historical," that is, composed with a view to its eventual resolution in time. In the Judaeo-Christian tradition the "once for all time" revelation of the Law was transposed by the prophetic and apocalyptic acknowledgement of change into a concept of linear progression towards a stated (for Christianity already "revealed") end. The past is proleptically interpreted as simultaneous promise and fulfillment. . . . Transposed into historical description: the theological definition of Islam was posterior to the fact of a sociopolitical community. The interpretation implied is one of recasting: a process of conscious "exemplification" in terms of which the origins of the community were adapted to the circumstances of the "sectarian milieu." . . . The underlying motive *(Geistes-beschäftigung)* of Islamic salvation history, or "election" history, might be formulated not as "eschatology" but as "protology": a reaffirmation and restoration of original purity. The course of Biblical salvation history, essentially proleptic and teleological, was thus reversed to produce a *restitutio principii*.[15]

Historical presentation of early Islamic history is seen by Wansbrough as the literary vehicle to comment on the fundamental message of revealed Scripture:

> The end product may well be "l'histoire vraie," but from an epis-temological point of view it is nostalgia. Salvation history may thus be envisaged not only as an exercise in legitimation, but as an experiment in language foundation: "the isolation of a semio-logical space" into which may be inserted a selection of themes and symbols intended to recall the event of revelation.[16]

Wansbrough's analysis of early Islamic historical texts has impor-tant implications for a reconstruction of a history of the Jews of Arabia. As one example, he identifies a literary pattern that casts the Jews of Muhammad's time into a stereotypic adversarial position. The Jews are the rejectors of Muhammad's message from God, even though they are the ones who also foretell his coming.[17] The presentation, he would contend, is polemical, and the content is selected to further that polemic. This same perspective, although without the explicit theoret-ical underpinnings and overt polemic, is adopted by Barakat Ahmad in his treatment of Muhammad's encounter with the Arabian Jews.[18]

Marilyn R. Waldman, in her book *Toward a Theory of Historical Narra-tive*, has proposed a method of analyzing Islamic historical texts. Through a careful dissection of the Persian *Ta'rīkh-i Bayhaqī*, she comes to the conclusion that there is a range of material that one can confront in a text, which extends from a point of more certain knowledge (in which one regards the text as an example of language use and a source of information about the author) to the point of least certain knowl-edge (the traditional view of the text as a source of information about the past). She argues for "the use of historical narratives principally in writing the history of that for which they are events in and of them-selves—the history of images and representations of the past, and a corresponding deemphasis of extracting or mining presumed histori-cal realities from them."[19] She calls for considering the work as a whole, as a context and within its larger context.[20]

My own research with early Islamic texts supports the directions in which Marilyn Waldman and others would take our analysis of histor-ical texts. I have worked on the reconstruction of the lost first portion of the earliest complete biography of Muhammad, the *Sîrah Rasûl Allâh*, written by Muhammad b. Ishâq about a century after the death of Muhammed; it is, we shall see, one of the major texts for the history of the Arabian Jews. The *Sîrah* appears to have been written as a text-book for the prince al-Mahdî, the son of the Abbasid caliph al-Mansûr. It presents itself as a grand scheme of a universal history beginning with the Creation and proceeding through the lives of Jewish prophets and Christian holy men down to the life of Muhammad. This first portion, known as the *Kitâb al-Mubtada'* and derived mainly from Jewish sources, lays the ground for the second portion of the biography, the portion that sets forth the details of Muhammad's life and is the portion that survives in an epitome by the ninth-century scholar Ibn Hishâm.

The grand scheme of the *Sîrah* can be analogized to the Christian view of Scripture. The first portion corresponds to the Old Testament and describes the previous dispensation up through Christianity. The second portion is like the New Testament, describing the new dispensation of Islam. As would be expected, it is easy to find literary topoi designed to fit Muhammad into the paradigm of holy men current in the eastern Mediterranean world at the time. The mythic process depicts Muhammad in Christomorphic guise, but also in the guise of the *new* Adam, Abraham, Jacob, Moses, and so on through the lists of Jewish prophets. From this point of view, the *Sîrah* is easily read as a document through which we can understand Abbasid inclinations toward Islamic universalism and by which we can see how religious ideas served the ends of the newly forming state. It was a work of conquest in which the Jewish and Christian past was textualized in Islamic modes, reducing the historiographic perspectives of the two older religions to the dependent and servile mode of handmaidens to the Muslim views of history.[21]

A case in point of the mythic process is the tale of Muhammad's mother's pregnancy. When Muhammad's father, ʿAbdullâh, was going to marry Âminah bt. Wahb, described as the "most excellent woman among the Qureysh in birth and position at that time," the sister of Waraqah b. Nawfal, the Christian [?] savant who predicted Muhammad's advent, propositioned ʿAbdullâh because, as she later explained, there was a "white blaze" between his eyes, and she had hoped to be the bearer of his child because she knew of her brother's prophecy. When the marriage between ʿAbdullâh and Âminah was consummated, the blaze passed to Âminah's womb, and she heard a voice say to her, "You are pregnant with the lord of this people, and when he is born say, 'I put him in the care of the One from the evil of every envier'; then call him Muhammad."[22] This is obviously a paraphrase of both Luke 1:31 and Matthew 1:21. The blaze is the traditional nimbus, the mark of a holy person, which was bright enough, according to one report, to shine from inside Aminah's womb far enough to light up the castles in Syria![23]

The previous example could be construed as hagiographic hyperbole, the traditionist's drawing with words what an artist in an iconographic tradition would have done with paint and color. But in another version, Muhammad is represented as participating himself in the mythomorphic process. In the story of Muhammad's early childhood, Ibn Ishâq quotes, "The Apostle of God used to say, 'There is no prophet but has shepherded a flock.' When they said, 'You, too, Apostle of God?', he said, 'Yes.' . . . The Apostle of God used to say to his companions, 'I am the most Arab of you all. I am of the Quraysh, and I was suckled among the Banû Saʿd b. Bakr.' "[24] Here Muhammad is made to fit into the mold of the pagan Arab pastoral hero—a model much like the American cowboy and with as much reality—as well as the model of the religious figure as pastor.

Not only is Muhammad's representation defined within the mythomorphic process, but so are members of his family, and here the problem becomes even more complex. One of the claims of Islam is that Muhammad is the last in a line of prophets from God all of whom have been given the mission by being selected. Prophethood is an office; prophets and messengers are bound by certain parameters, which determine who they are and how they act. It is not surprising that we find elements of the mythic shape of the prophets interacting with all the figures of the biography. So we see a story of Muhammad's grandfather, ʿAbdu-l-Muttalib, in which he is represented in an Abraham-Isaac isomorph: ʿAbdu-l-Muttalib, in preparation for the restoration of the well of Zamzam, the well in Mecca dug for Abraham's son, Ishmael, sleeps one night in the Hijr, the area containing the graves of Hagar and Ishmael. He receives a vision, which commands him to dig the well, and, in the midst of the restoration, he determines to sacrifice his son, ʿAbdullâh, Muhammad's father.[25] In the *Sîrah*, these events are placed within a larger frame, which is designed to make Mecca the new Jerusalem and the Ka'bah the new Temple.[26] In Jewish tradition, it had been long understood that the Temple was the location for the Binding of Isaac, so 'Abdu-l-Muttalib's intended sacrifice would have been understood to be evocative of the earlier Abrahamic intention.[27] As in the ur-story, God intervenes and accepts alternate sacrifice.[28] Muhammad and his followers agree on a view of Abraham and of the historical past. And this view is not based on just faith. In general, they also share this view with Jews and Christians, however much they may disagree with them on details of the role of Muhammad and Islam.

The current trends in historical criticism of Islamic texts are paralleled by developments in biblical criticism and history in general. Starting with the criticisms of Jean Astruc, Johann Eichhorn, and Wilhelm De Wette, which lead to the creation of the Graf-Wellhausen hypothesis, biblical scholarship accepted the notion of an essential literary character to the sacred text. But the approach inherent in this type of "literary" analysis was positivistic. That is, there was the underlying assumption that real documents reflecting a real period in history were the underpinnings of the Bible. The task of the scriptural critic was to date the documents and extract the historical truth. This was followed by a reaction that rejected any notion of historicity in the text. These "form-critics" saw the text exclusively in literary terms and were content to analyze only the literary typologies. This was a period when ancient historians were identifying the "mythic" elements in traditional histories of Greece and Rome. The more anthropologically based critics of the "traditionist" school sought to identify patterning derived from the techniques of transmission and questioned the written character of the Graf-Wellhausen documentary hypothesists. The Homeric poetry was subjected to similar scrutiny by the followers of Albert Lord, and ancient historians began to recognize the influences of "oral" transmissions.

From the study of anthropological linguistics, scholars—often grouped under the polemical term "structuralists"—are engaged in "a mode of analysis of cultural artifacts which originates in the methods of cultural linguistics."[29] Scholars like Roland Barthes, Claude Lévi-Strauss, Jacques Derrida, and Phillipe Sollers see patterns and structures of meaning underlying all acts, including or especially acts of speech, which are culture specific and, for some, entirely isolate the investigator from "objective reality."[30] "The analysis of cultural phenomena must always take place in some context, and at any one time the production of meaning in a culture is governed by conventions."[31] That is, we are bound by the meaning conventions of the culture we are analyzing, which are both relative and abstract and do not function as certain indicators of objective reality. Experience and the reporting of an experience have meaning only within the confines of a cultural context. The observer from outside a culture, unless provided with a semantic, culturally specific lexicon, can describe actions, but they will be without meaning for that person or, more usually, the observer will describe only those actions that connect with meanings that the person brings to the observation. In addition, the very act of observation and reporting is itself bound within the cultural matrix and is a culturally defined act, further distancing the observer from attaining the chimerical reality. For the structuralist, histories, particularly the histories of religions, are literary forms that bear the mythic interpretations of society. For Wansbrough, "The motive of all salvation history is interpretation, and to that extent salvation history is always mythic. . . . The material of which myth represents an interpretation is seldom fictive; it is equally seldom that one can convincingly separate that material from its interpretation."[32] Even when the material appears to be an accurate reporting of an event or series of events, this is an effect given meaning by its literary form. "Authenticity can be as much a result of (successful) narrative technique as of veracity."[33]

The problems of historical reconstruction facing the student of religious history are part of the larger intellectual questions of epistemology that have been a feature of Western thought since David Hume and René Descartes, if, indeed, the questions cannot be traced back to Plato. In recent times, the issues of epistemology have become the central points of discussion among philosophers of science. With the generally accepted demise of the dominance of Newtonian physics, belief in the existence of "theory-neutral" observational data has diminished. Science is no longer thought to base its theories on observations. History is, of course, not a science if by science we mean physics or chemistry, although there have been recent attempts to make it "like" a science, using more mathematical models and statistical analysis. The structuralists' critique of history is a literary and linguistic critique, not mathematical or "scientific." Yet both the scientific and the humanistic disciplines share the same epistemological problem: "Science apparently is a body of knowledge about the sensible world, yet if observation plays no central role either in the production or in establishing the logical status of knowledge, how can science be about the real world?"[34] And so for history, if the content of history is not about the "real" world, if it does not have an empirical base, is it not merely fictive? Karl Popper's *Logik der Forschung* and Thomas Kuhn's *Structure of Scientific Revolutions* have turned the question of scientific epistemology toward the workings of "normal" science, that is, an investigation of how scientists actually have operated in their disciplines. This debate, sparked also by the writings of Imre Lakatos and Paul K. Feyerabend, has begun to produce a new foundation for scientific claims that seem appropriate for the historian to consider, because it revives a role for experiential data, while at the same time abandoning the problems of classical positivism.

Thomas Kuhn summarizes his views and those of Karl Popper as:

> ... united in opposition to a number of classical positivism's most characteristic theses. We both emphasize, for example, the intimate and inevitable entanglement of scientific observation with scientific theory; we are correspondingly skeptical of efforts to produce any neutral observation language; and we both insist that scientists may properly aim to invent theories that *explain* observed phenomena and that do so in terms of *real* objects, whatever the latter phrase may mean.[35]

While some writers have begun to question the extent to which the psychological experiments that have been used to underpin the fallibility of sensate experience can be relied on,[36] few would claim that old empiricism can be resuscitated. But claims to knowledge can, at least according to writers like Israel Scheffler, be based on empirical foundations.

> There is no evidence for a general incapacity to learn from contrary observations, no proof of a pre-established harmony between what we believe and what we see. In the disharmony between them, indeed, lies the source of observational control

over belief. . . . The genius of science is to capitalize upon such disharmony for the sake of a systematic learning from experience.[37]

This is not to say, of course, that observations of the sort that Scheffler mentions are free from bias or from the influences of theoretical preconceptions. Indeed, as Popper and Kuhn point out, theoretical considerations are prior to observation and thereby affect the observation, but these are not absolute barriers to changes in perspective. Popper states:

> I do admit that at any moment we are prisoners caught in the framework of our theories; our expectations; our past experiences; our language. But we are prisoners in a Pickwickian sense: if we try, we can break out of our framework at any time. Admittedly, we shall find ourselves again in a framework, but it will be a better and roomier one; and we can at any moment break out of it again. . . . The Myth of Framework is, in our time, the central bulwark of irrationalism.[38]

The conclusion that one can draw from Popper's analysis of "framework" or perspective is that all observations are "theory-laden." Further, as Phillips points out, our theories are "underdetermined" by observations.[39] That means that "observations," and here I mean any data acquired by sensory means, either directly or indirectly, will not necessitate a modification or abandonment of a theory, framework, or paradigm, to use Kuhn's preferred term; rather, our observations *combined* with our paradigms, intuitions, and so forth move us to a different perspective, to what Kuhn would call a *gestalt* transition.[40] The same set of observational data will support a plurality of paradigms, justified (but not "proved" in either the classic or the analytic sense) by the rational construction of the paradigm(s):

> Knowledge claims must be defended, to be sure; however, the defense of such a claim is not an attempt to prove it, but rather the marshaling of "good reasons" in its behalf. . . . The only way to defend fallible knowledge claims is by marshaling other fallible knowledge claims—such as the best contingent theories that we

possess. There are no "ultimate" sources of knowledge or epistemological authorities.[41]

The relativity of paradigms has led some, including Kuhn at one
point, to hold the view that competing theories are "incommensurable," although even Kuhn backs away from a literal definition of that
word and speaks of the difficulties of translation from one theory to
the next.[42] In line with his *gestalt* approach, it would be difficult for an
individual to move from one theoretical perspective to another in the
same manner that it is difficult to move from one culture to another,
but it is usually the case that two competing paradigms have enough
in common that they are not truly incommensurable. Logically, if they
were, it would be possible to hold both of them simultaneously, and
they would not be competing paradigms about the same data.

In a critique of Popper's views on history, chiefly those set forth in
his *The Poverty of Historicism*, B. T. Wilkins demonstrates that "Popper's claim that history does not exist should, I believe, be regarded as
an ontological expression—or corruption—of his epistemological doctrine that 'it is not possible for us to observe or to describe a whole
piece of the world, or a whole piece of nature; in fact, not even the
smallest whole piece may be so described, since all description is necessarily selective.' "[43] While the same argument could be applied to
science or any branch of knowledge, since it is impossible for finite
creatures to possess infinite knowledge, and such a claim would be a
mystical claim relying on a belief set, Wilkins points out that one of
two possible definitions of the use of "whole" admits knowledge of a
whole, namely, when "whole" is used to mean "certain special
properties or aspects of the thing in question, namely those which
make it an organized structure rather than a 'mere heap.' "[44]

For the historian, this "heap-whole" distinction is useful because it
allows the application of a paradigm to an aggregate of data to make a
whole out of a heap. This is the nature of historical *and* scientific explanation. Historians explain specific events in terms of general paradigms, often called Laws of History by older historians, and they
assess individual actions in terms of standards of rational adequacy or
appropriateness.[45] The paradigms derive from our theoretical stance
and are confirmed by the degree to which they include the available
data into the paradigm of explanation. Often we prefer one explana-

tion over another because of the degree to which it "covers" the evidence. When new evidence is brought to our attention, we might change our point of view or, in concert with our fellow scientists, we might modify our theory just enough to accommodate the new data.[46] We do not need "ultimate" authority for our paradigms, just as the physicist does not need "ultimate" knowledge of the universe when, preferring Einstein over Newton, the physicist uses tensors as descriptions of local conditions in special cases of relativity.

Where does that leave the historian who uses religious texts and is interested in the history of religions. Most every historically minded individual would agree that in religions that have had an extended life, the practitioners have edited and reshaped the accounts of the origins and developments of the religion to conform to current doctrine. Many have argued that it cannot be otherwise for the faithful believer, because the believer cannot imagine that his or her beliefs differ from those of the religion's founder. Thus we find the anomalies in traditional Jewish circles of some holding that the dress of eighteenth-century Eastern Europe is the *correct* dress for a traditional Jew, which view is seen by others as arbitrary and at variance with other possible models. Waldman is correct when she asserts that the historical text yields its surest knowledge about the linguistic and literary character of that text, but that need not deter us from using more powerful critical tools to investigate the past that the text purports to describe.

From the theoretical considerations, it will be seen that I choose to apply a different perspective or paradigm than that offered by Wansbrough or Waldman to "cover" more of the presented data. The paradigm, as I view it, must be

> . . . a complex spatial network: its terms are represented by the knots, while the threads connecting the latter correspond, in part, to the fundamental and derivative hypotheses included in the theory. The whole system floats, as it were, above the plane of observation and is anchored to it by rules of interpretation. These might be viewed as strings which are not part of the network but link certain points of the latter with specific places in the plane of observation.[47]

This study is a beginning at constructing a matrix of explanation for the data available to us about the history of the Jews of Arabia. In dialogue with my critics, and in concert with those who share my optimism about the enterprise of coming closer to an approximation of a recoverable past, I hope I have offered those "explanations" and "judgments" that will elucidate not only a long-forgotten community but also how we can, in part, view the Jewish past.

ABBREVIATIONS IN NOTES AND BIBLIOGRAPHY

B.A.S.O.R.	Bulletin of the American Schools of Oriental Research
B.S.O.A.S.	Bulletin of the School of Oriental and African Studies
E.J.	Encyclopaedia Judaica
I.C.	Islamic Culture
J.A.O.S.	Journal of the American Oriental Society
J.N.E.S.	Journal of Near Eastern Studies
J.Q.R.	Jewish Quarterly Review
J.R.A.S.	Journal of the Royal Asiatic Society
J.S.A.I.	Jerusalem Studies in Arabic and Islam
M.W.	Muslim World
R.E.J.	Revue des etudes juives
Z.A.	Zeitschrift für Assyriologie
Z.D.M.G.	Zeitschrift der deutschen morgandländischen Gesellschaft

NOTES

Chapter 1

1. G. W. Bowersock, *Roman Arabia* (Cambridge, Mass.: Harvard University Press, 1983), pp. 1–2.

2. Ibid., p. 122.

3. Two recent works should be recommended for viewing the general problem of Rome and the Arabs, both by Prof. Irfan Shahîd: *Rome and the Arabs: A Prolegomenon to the Study of Byzantium and the Arabs* (Washington, D.C., Dumbarton Oaks, 1984), and *Byzantium and the Arabs in the Fourth Century* (Washington, D. C. Dumbarton Oaks, 1984). Shahîd's writings strongly support the ideas that the Arabs were major actors in the ancient Mediterranean political and cultural dramas, and he gathers a wide variety of new information to support his claims.

4. This gulf is also referred to as the Arabian Gulf.

5. For a readable summary of the histories of the several Eastern Christian churches written from the perspective of a Western-trained Copt, see Aziz Suryal Atiya, *History of Eastern Christianity* (Notre Dame, Ind.: University of Notre Dame Press, 1968). Irfan Shahîd, in his article "Pre-Islamic Arabia," in the Cambridge History of Islam, vol. 1, *The Central Islamic Lands*, pp. 3–29, presents a lucid summary in which he terms Arabia as *Arabia haeresium ferax* (Arabia, the producer of heresies). As we shall see with the history of Judaism in Arabia, the religious ferment that ultimately produced Islam also affected the Jews, encouraging several heterodox beliefs and practices.

6. Frankincense is found in India and elsewhere in Asia in addition to Arabia and Africa, but the consensus in the ancient world was that the best frankincense came from Arabia, as did the best myrrh. The most complete modern study of frankincense and myrrh is Nigel Groom, *Frankincense and Myrrh* (London: Longman, 1981).

7. Pliny, *Natural History*, trans., H. Rackham, Loeb Classical Library (Cambridge, Mass.: Harvard University Press, 1945), Bk. 12, chap. 41, sec. 83.
8. Groom, *Frankincense*, p. 12.
9. Kerithoth 6a–b, following Exodus 30:34.
10. Avodah Zarah 13b.
11. Sanhedrin 43a; cf. the association of frankincense and myrrh with the story of the crucifixion of Jesus, Mark 15:23 and John 19:39.
12. Cf. *The Periplus of the Erythrean Sea*, Ed. and trans., G. W. B. Huntingford (London: Hakluyt Society, 1980).
13. Richard Bulliet, *The Camel and the Wheel* (Cambridge, Mass.: Harvard University Press, 1975).
14. It is true that the horse became a major military animal among the pre-Islamic Arabs, but it was a luxury animal. It was faster than a camel, but it could not traverse the harsh terrain as easily and it required more water and fodder to maintain. The Arabian pony was highly prized in part because it was such a luxury item, but its use did allow Arabs to serve in the cavalries of the Romans and the Persians.
15. W. Caskel, "The Bedouinization of Arabia," *Studies in Islamic Cultural History*, ed. G. E. von Grunebaum, in series Memoirs of the American Anthropological Association, 76 (Menshasha, Wis.: George Banta, 1954), pp. 36–46.
16. See articles "Arabia" and "Semites" in *E.J.*
17. N. Groom, *Frankincense*, pp. 214–28.
18. P. K. Hitti, *A History of the Arabs* (London: Macmillan, 1964 p. 103, attributes this to a Sabaean word meaning "sanctuary." N. Groom, *Frankincense*, p. 257, n. 8, points out that there is no known Sabaean word with that meaning, and, from a private communication from A.F.L. Beeston, proposes *mikrab*, "synagogue," as the root of the name. A. Dilman, *Lexicon Linguae Aethiopicae* (New York: Frederick Unger, 1955), gives two roots, the conflation of which probably underlies the name *Macoraba*. The first is *meqrâb*, col. 427, defined as *locus ubi conveniunt*, with a reference to 1 Esdras 3:14. This root is cognate to the Hebrew and Arabic *qurbân*, "sacrifice." At cols. 836–37, he gives the word *mek^{w}râb*, meaning "temple" or "synagogue." This root, with the bilabial immediately following the palatalized stop, would easily yield the form *macoraba* given by Ptolemy. According to my colleague J. Vanderkam, with whom I discussed this problem, it is likely that we see a conflation of the two roots, *QRB and *KRB in this as in other words in Ethiopic that are related to Arabic and Hebrew. The connection of the name of Mecca to an Ethiopic word is another indication of the close relationship between the Hijâz and the inhabitants of the incense-producing areas of Africa.

Chapter 2

1. Abû-l-Faraj al-Isfahânî, *Kitâb al-ʾAghânî*, Cairo: Bûlâq edition reprint, 1970), vol. 19, pp. 94–98.
2. One is reminded of the Roman foundation legend that links Aeneas to Troy by, for example, Virgil's paean to Roman victories over Greek territory set as a kind of Trojan revenge. One of the obvious purposes of the Roman legend was to give the

"upstart" Mediterranean power the same claims to antique nobility proffered by the defeated Greeks.

3. L. Ginzberg, *Legends of the Jews* (Philadelphia: Jewish Publication Society, 1967), vol. 6, p. 233.
4. Ibid., pp. 47 et passim.
5. Also known as Thamad ar-Rûm; see *Kitâb al-ʾAghânî*, p. 101 and index.
6. The Arabic word *tamr* means a sun-dried date, the image being that the Romans were left in the desert to shrivel like dates in the sun.
7. Muhammad b. ʿUmar b. Wâqid [al-Wâqidî], *Kitâb al-Maghâzî*, ed. Marsden Jones (London: Oxford University Press, 1966), vol. 2, p. 480.
8. This confirms, of course, the views expressed by numerous scholars that the Hijâz was in a period of transition toward urban, settled life and that the values of the pastoral nomad were, when expressed, a kind of desert pastoralism longingly retrospective as it viewed an ideal past that most certainly never existed in anywhere near the manner it is depicted. The idealization of the bedouin and rampant pastoral nomadism are found throughout Arabic literature. For a discussion of this theme, see G. Newby, "Ibn Khaldun and Frederick Jackson Turner: Islam and the Frontier Experience," *Journal of Asian and African Studies* 18, nos. 3–4 (1983): 274–85.
9. The use of the biblical genealogy becomes, of course, a literary convention. Thus we see in Ibn Ishâq's *Sîrah* that Muhammad is provided with the double genealogy on the model of Jesus so that his followers, too, could make messianic claims for him. Because it is literary, and so embedded in the consciousness of eastern Mediterranean religious thinking, I feel that the literary claims reflect a social reality. That is, when the Arabian Jews claim to be more noble than the Arab and offer biblical ancestry as a "proof," they are tendering evidence that would have been current in the minds of their hearers.
10. Al-Isfahânî, *Kitâb al-Aghânî*, p. 101 and index.
11. Krauss in his "Talmudische Nachrichten über Arabien," *Z.D.M.G.* 70, nos. 3–4 (1916): 330; but Herzberg, "Arabia," *E.J.*, vol. 1, pp. 232–36, evidently does not read Nebuchadnezzar as a substitute for the Roman emperor Titus, and so places the migration after the destruction of the First Temple. The Arab legends assume Krauss's interpretation, although a case can be made for either reading.
12. L. Ginzberg, *Legends of the Jews*, vol. 6, pp. 431–32.
13. Haim Schwarzbaum, *Biblical and Extra-Biblical Legends in Islamic Folk-Literature*, vol. 30 of *Beiträge zur Sprach- und Kulturgeschichte des Orients*, ed. O. Spies (Walldorf-Hessen: Verlag für Orientkunde Dr. H. Vorndran, 1982), pp. 103–4.
14. Ezra 10:8.
15. H. Schwarzbaum, *Biblical and Extra-Biblical Legends*, p. 104; B. Heller, "Ezra Legends," *J.Q.R.* 24 (1934), p. 398; L. Ginzberg, *Legends of the Jews*, vol. 6, p. 432.
16. See Jacop Sapir, *Eben Sapir* (Lyck: I. Sibermann), 1866, vol. 1, sec. 20ff. From internal evidence, it is clear that the legend should be dated after the destruction of the Second Temple, but it is not necessary to date the origin of the story after the time of the Qurʾân as some would because of the Qurʾân's assertion (9:30) that the Jews regard Ezra as the "Son of God." As we know from numerous other examples, it is entirely possible that two contradictory traditions could exist within the same com-

munity. In this case, the Qur'ân refers to a conflation among Ezra, Enoch, and Metatron, all of whom are God's "Scribes."

17. Bilqîs is the name for the Queen of Sheba in Arabic sources. The name does not occur in the Qur'ân, but only in later commentary. Some have speculated that it is a corruption of the name Naukalis, the name Josephus uses for the Queen of Sheba. B. Carra de Vaux in the article "Bilkîs" in the *Shorter Encyclopedia of Islam*, ed. H. A. R. Gibb and J. Kramers (Leiden: E. J. Brill, 1961), p. 63, indicates that the story of the marriage of Solomon and the Queen of Sheba was "widespread among the Jews at an early period . . . ."

18. R. Dozy, *Die Israeliten zu Mekka von David's Zeit.* translated from Dutch original (Leipzig: W. Engelmann, 1864).

19. D. S. Margoliouth, *Relations between Arabs and Israelites Prior to the Rise of Islam*, the 1921 Schweich Lectures (London: Oxford University Press, 1924).

20. Ibid., p. 27.

21. Underlying this is, of course, a linguistic observation, felt by all who have studied more than one Semitic language, that there is an underlying structural similarity among Arabic, Hebrew, Ethiopic, Akkadian, Ugaritic, Aramaic, etc. We classify these languages together, after all, because we stress their similarities. And, because we are human and have learned our language from our progenitors, we assume a genetic model for the transmission of similar languages, as exemplified by the relations list in Genesis 10. For the purposes of identifying the historical context of the development of Arabian Judaism, the linguistic features that are more important are those that are "borrowed" from Hebrew and Aramaic into Arabic and vice versa, when we are able to control the context of the transmission. We shall examine this issue further, below, in the discussion of the development of Judeo-Arabic.

22. C. J. Gadd, "The Harran Inscription of Nabonidus," *Anatolian Studies* 8 (1958): 80.

23. Ibid., p. 85.

24. Ibid., p. 86.

25. The texts mention that Nabonidus fought and killed some of the local rulers, called *malku* , a term that would mean "king" in Arabic. This is possibly important in our understanding of the social organization of Arabia at a later period. During Persian domination, there appear to be "kings" in the Ḥijâz who are, nevertheless, subjects of more powerful distant suzerains.

26. The biblical Qedar is associated with Tema and Dedan in Isaiah 21:13ff., Ezekiel 27:20ff., and Jeremiah 49:28ff.

27. Aram. *gazar* as in the book of Daniel. See J. T. Milik, "Priere de Nabonide," *Revue Biblique* 63 (1956):407 ff.; D. N. Freedman, "The Prayer of Nabonidus," *B.A.S.O.R.* 145 (1957): 31 ff.

28. Israel Eph'al, *The Ancient Arabs* (Jerusalem: Magnes Press, 1982), pp. 179–91; Ronald H. Sack, "The Nabonidus Legend," *Revue d'Assgriologie* 77 (1983): 59–67.

29. The beginnings of this Judeo-Arabic must remain undated unless the fortunes of archaeology change, as is hoped with a recent increase in scientific expeditions investigating the antiquities of Arabia.

30. See Arthur Jeffery, *The Foreign Vocabulary of the Qurân* (Baroda: Oriental Institute, 1938).
31. Arab. *mubîn*, as in the first verse of "Sûrat Yûsûf" et passim.
32. See Bukhârî, *Tafsîr Sûrat al-Baqarah: yaqra'ûna-t-tawrâta bi-l-'ibrâniyyati wa-yufas-sirûnahâ li-'ahli-'islâmi.* This is a much more likely explanation than that advanced by C. C. Torrey, who asserts in his *The Jewish Foundations of Islam* (New York: Jewish Institute of Religion 1933), p. 40, that Hebrew and Arabic are are closely enough related to allow someone knowing one of them to be able to learn the other easily. While this may be so for the linguistically talented, and be an argument for Muhammad's having a Jewish teacher, it does not account for the presence in Arabic of words whose origins are to be found in Jewish technical religious vocabulary.
33. Muhammad b. 'Umar b. al-Wâqid al-Wâqidî, *Kitâb al-Maghâzî*, ed. Marsden Jones (London: Oxford University Press, 1966), vol. 1, pp. 391–95. Note the use of "modern" guerrilla tactics against a more powerful foe.
34. See G. Newby, "Observations about an Early Judaeo-Arabic," *J.Q.R.*, New Series 61 (1971): 214–21. We shall return to this tradition later when we discuss Jewish religious practices. Moshe Gil, "The Origins of the Jews of Yathrib," *J.S.A.I.* 4(1984):206, mentions this same tradition as well as the report by Khawwât b. Jubayr that he heard the sentries of the B. Qurayza talking among themselves in al-yahûdiyyah.
35. Newby, "Observations."

Chapter 3

1. Diodorus Siculus, *The Library of History*, trans. C. H. Oldfather, (Loeb Classical Library (Cambridge, Mass.: Harvard University Press, 1939) sec. 19. Two recent studies now serve as benchmarks for Arabia during the period of the Romans and should be consulted for the wealth of detailed scholarship that they contain. The first, G. W. Bowersock, *Roman Arabia* (Cambridge, Mass.: Harvard University Press, 1983), details Roman presence from Pompey to the death of Diocletian. The second, Irfan Shahîd, *Rome and the Arabs: A Prolegomenon to the Study of Byzantium and the Arabs* (Washington D.C.: Dumbarton Oaks, 1984), while cast as an introduction to his study of the later period, contains much insightful discussion of the sources for Arabian history in the Roman period. Shahîd has a skillful eye for identifying Arabs in the ancient world, even when they are disguised by assimilation to Hellenic and Roman customs. While some may argue that he sometimes overstates his case, it is clear that the Arabs played a larger role in Roman life than the prejudiced classical texts would have us believe. Insofar as the Arabian Jews are associated with the Arabs, they share the benefits and fate of their Arab cousins.
2. Diodorus, *Library of History*, sec. 19.
3. Bowersock, *Roman Arabia*, p. 15.
4. Ibid., pp. 12f.
5. For a thorough treatment of the nature of the Sabaean kingdom during this period, see Herman von Wissmann, "Die Geschichte des Sabaeerreichs und der Feldzug

des Aelius Gallus," *Aufstieg und Niedergang der römischen Welt,* 2. 9.1, ed. Hildegard Temporini (Berlin: Walter de Gruyter, 1976), pp. 308–544.

6. Strabo, *Geography,* trans. Horace Leonard Jones (Cambridge, Mass.: Harvard University Press, 1930), 16.4.22.

7. Ibid.

8. Bowersock, *Roman Arabia,* pp. 46–49, summarizes this expedition and makes a strong case for Syllaeus' innocence of the charges leveled against him by Strabo. Syllaeus appears to have been a perfect villain on which to hang the failure, however, and he eventually lost his life for his alleged crimes. What is clear from Bowersock's argument is that the Nabataeans acted in good faith and with considerable cooperation. This is importatnt to remember when viewing the events surrounding the annexation of Arabia Nabataea as a Roman province. It would appear that, even at this point, the Nabataean policy of accommodation to greater forces but reliance on the desert for ultimate safety was in effect.

9. Strabo, 16.4.24.

10. Ibid., 16.4.23.

11. Josephus, *Antiquities of the Jews,* 15.9.3.

12. F. E. Peters, *The Harvest of Hellenism* (New York: Simon & Schuster, 1970), p. 282.

13. Nelson Glueck, *Rivers in the Desert: A History of the Negev* (New York: Farrar, Straus & Cudahy, 1959), pp. 197–98, 211–18.

14. Theodor Mommsen, *The Provinces of the Roman Empire from Caesar to Diocletian,* trans. W. P. Dickson (New York: Chas. Scribner's Sons, 1887), vol. 2, p. 169.

15. Bowersock, *Roman Arabia,* p. 41; Diodorus Siculus, *Library of History,* 2:48.

16. Ibid., p. 26n. The legend used by Aretas is Basileos Areton Philhellenos. This issue continued down to the year 72 when Damascus, the city of issue, was captured by Tigranes, king of Armenia and a claimant to the Seleucid succession.

17. Shahîd, *Rome and the Arabs,* p. 9.

18. Ibid., p. 11.

19. 2 Maccabees 5:8; 1 Maccabees 5:25–26. See the discussion in Bowersock, *Roman Arabia,* pp. 18f., in which he argues for a harmonization between the term "king" for Aretas from the Elusa inscription and the term "tryant" in 2 Maccabees 5:8.

20. Josephus, *Antiquities of the Jews,* 13:375–82.

21. For the intellectual reaction of the Jews to the increasing pressures from Hellenism set in a lucid explication of the political intricacies, I recommend F. E. Peters, *The Harvest of Hellenism.*

22. Some Jewish males sought to undo the mark of the Covenant and submit to one of two types of plastic surgery to erase the stigma of circumcision before participating in the games, one of the central features in the life of the Hellenic *polis.* While we have reports that such medical procedures took place, we have no idea how frequent or successful the operations were. Peters, *The Harvest of Hellenism,* speculates that the Pharisees of Josephus were the likely spiritual descendants of the earlier pietists who had separated from the extremely anti-Hellenic Maccabees over the issue of Alcimus as high priest.

23. Peters, *The Harvest of Hellenism,* p. 298. For those familiar with the currents of Islamic modernism and reform (*ijtihâd*), this tendency will strike a familiar note. It

was easier for the Jews of the Diaspora to focus on the more general text of the Torah in their accommodations to Greek culture than it was when they accepted the increasingly restrictive oral law as it was being explicated in the Mishnah and the Gemarah, just as Islamic modernists always preach a return to the Qur'ân and "primitive" Islam in order more easily to secure adoption of their innovations. The level of specificity in the Talmuds certainly reflects that the rabbis knew that verses of Scripture can be interpreted in a variety of ways.

24. See W. Bacher, "Johanan b. Zakkai," *The Jewish Encyclopedia* (New York: Funk & Wagnalls, 1912), vol. 7, pp. 214–17. The sources for Johanan b. Zakkai's life in the Mishnah and later tradition depict him in almost superhuman and messianic terms, as would be fitting for the person credited with such a major role in the history of Pharisaic Judaism, and must be taken cautiously. If the sources are to be believed, he is the transmitter of all esoteric as well as exoteric knowledge, yet there appears to be an element of truth in the organizing efforts, at least, associated with his academy at Jabneh.

25. Rosh Hashanah 4:1,3.

26. *Bêt ha-midrash.*

27. *Sanhedrin.*

28. *Hesed,* Baba Batra 10b.

29. The inscription *Fisci Iudaici Calumnia Sublata* on a special-issue brass coin from the reign of Nerva did not mean anything more than a token amelioration of deviations from customary Roman law in the prosecution of evaders of the tax, mentioned by Suetonius and satirized by Martial. The presence of the coin itself bears witness to the continuation of the impost.

30. See Abodah Zarah 18a.

31. Memories of the destruction of the Temple were strong motives in the revolts. Another reaction to the destruction of the Temple was a turn toward eschatological and mystical speculations centered on a deliverance or redemption of Israel. This had already been a strong theme in the biblical view of the world, and the speculations can be viewed as merely a logical extension of the sin-punishment (usually by the evil of the earth)-repentance-redemption cycle that was reiterated as a central part of the history of Israel. But if it is an extension of biblical themes, the rabbis found it to their advantage to stress the pattern to promote obedience to Rome and offer the hope, through their program of adherence to their interpretations of Torah, of an ultimate salvation for the Jewish people. Judaism's greatest Pharisaic historian, Josephus, offers an apology for Roman domination of the world and a justification of continued accommodation. As this became a prevailing view in many areas, it left the field open to those with messianic claims, on the one hand, and those with a revolutionary political agenda, on the other.

32. See Yigael Yadin. *Bar Kochba* (New York: Random House, 1971).

33. Louis Ginzberg, "Akiba Ben Joseph," *The Jewish Encyclopedia* (New York: Funk & Wagnalls, 1901), vol. 1, pp. 304–8. Ginzberg doubts the political nature of Akiba's journey, but, as we know not only from Roman times but also from Jewish activities in the Soviet Union, the mere preaching of religious ideas can be viewed by the state as seditious politics.

34. See *Midrash Tanhuma*, ed. Naso, 13. Josef Horovitz, "Judaeo-Arabic Relations in Pre-Islamic Times," *Islamic Culture*, 3 (1929): 190, observes that "If we could be certain that Rabbi Aqiba's aim in his journeys was to visit the Jewish settlements, their existence in South Arabia would be proved for the second century A.D., but we do not know anything about the object of his travels. . . . The earliest definite information about Jewish settlements in the empire of the Himyarites, is met with in Philostorgius who tells us, that when Theophilus, in the reign of the Emperor Constantius (337–61), came there to preach Christianity 'he found there not a small number of Jews' " Philostorgius, *Historia ecclesiastica* 3.5 in J.P. Migne, *Patrologiae cursus completus*, series graeca 165 vols., Paris: 1857–86).
35. Galatians 1:17.
36. Acts 9:23–25; 2 Corinthians 11:32–33.
37. Acts 2:5,11. Paul would certainly have known of these Arabian Jewish worshipers in Jerusalem.
38. See Y. Yadin, "Expedition D—The Cave of Letters" *Israel Exploration Journal* 12 (1962): 227–57; "The Nabataean Kingdom, Petra and En-Geddi in the Documents from Nahal Hever," *Ex Orientis Lux* 17 (1963): 227–41; "The Life and Trials of Babata," *Bar Kochba*, pp. 222–53; Bowersock, *Roman Arabia*, pp. 75–79, 85–90 et passim.
39. Assuming that Paul died sometime around 70 C.E.
40. Bowersock, *Roman Arabia*, p. 77n., where he mentions several possible locations based on Josephus and Ptolemy but concludes "A Hebrew document discovered in the same cave as Babatha's material mentions 'ha-Luhît in the district of ʿAgaltain,' and this serves to confirm the location of Maḥoza [mentioned in the Greek document of Simeon's property] southeast of the Dead Sea. . . Zoar would be modern Sâfî."
41. Y. Yadin, "The Nabataean Kingdom. . . .," p. 232. Note that it was possible for Babatha's mother to own property under the conditions of both Nabataean and Roman laws.
42. See H. J. Wolff, "Roemisches Provinzialrecht in der Proving Arabia," *Aufstieg und Niedergang der römischen Welt*, ed. Hildegard Temporini and Wolfgang Haase (Berlin), 2, no. 13 (1980): 763–806. The thoroughness of the Romanization of the province at so early a date indicates that the "Philhellene" character of the Nabataeans had now embraced Rome as well. When the province of Arabia is created by annexation in 106 C.E., rather than by conquest, so that it is *Arabia Adquisita* on the coins, one must conclude that trade interests had linked Nabataea and Rome so closely that the annexation was merely a confirmation of what had preceded. In addition, the presence of large numbers of Roman troops in the area were probably sufficient to persuade the Nabataeans that they could not profit by resistance.
43. Bowersock, *Roman Arabia*, p. 89.
44. Jesus' assurances that he came to fulfill the law and not overturn it have to be taken seriously. His political program of accommodation to the existence of temporal Roman authority was certainly within the bounds of Pharisaic thought, particularly among those who saw patient acceptance of Rome's superior force as a temporary state until the imminent eschaton.

45. Peters, *The Harvest of Hellenism*, p. 307.

Chapter 4

1. 1 Kings 10; Arabic sources name the Queen of Sheba as Bilqîs. Josephus calls her Naukalis, the Queen of Egypt and Ethiopia, B. Carra de Vaux, "Bilkîs," *Shorter Encyclopaedia of Islam*, eds. H. A. R. Gibb and S. Kramers (Leiden:E. J. Brill, 1961):63, suggests that there is an association with the Greek *pallaxis*, meaning "concubine." Amid all this confusion, it is possible to see a Jewish origin to her name and the legend of a union between Solomon and the Queen. L. Ginzberg, *Legends of the Jews* (Philadelphia: Jewish Publication Society, 1967), vol. 6, p. 289, suggests an association with the Arabic name and the Hebrew *pîlegesh*, "concubine," and points out that since she was supposed to have been half demonic, her association with magic and demons would lead to Josephus' conflation of her origin with Egypt, the land of magic par excellence. For our considerations, the antiquity of the legend of the Queen of Sheba as ruler of Arabia, Egypt, and/or Ethiopia indicates that it predates the Islamic period and likely derives from midrashic considerations among the Arabian Jews.
2. Erich Brauer, *Ethnologie der jemenitischen Juden* (Heidelberg: Carl Winters, 1934), p. 19: and in another version, the Queen brought the Jews with her when she returned from her sojourn with Solomon.
3. Joseph Halevy, "Voyage au Nedjran," *Bulletin de la Société de Geographie de Paris* 6 (1873): 22.
4. Nigel Groom, *Frankincense and Myrrh*, (London: Longman, 1981).
5. Indeed, if Punt is to be located in the southern area of Arabia, the Egyptians were traveling that far to obtain aromatics, spices, and other rare products as early as the period of the Old Kingdom.
6. Jeremiah 21:9: "He that abideth in this city shall die by the sword, and by the famine, and by the pestilence; but he that goeth out, and falleth away to the Chaldeans that besiege you, he shall live, and his life shall be unto him for a prey."
7. Procopius, *History of the Wars*, trans., H. B. Dewing, (Cambridge, Mass.: Harvard University Press, 1961), vol. 1, b.20.
8. Ibid.
9. Ibid., 1.20. 9–10.
10. F. Altheim and R. Stiehl, *Die Araber in der alten Welt* (Berlin:Walter de Gruytor, 1968), vol. 5, part 1, pp. 363–64. The Arabic term *malik*, "king," indicates that these agents of the Persian authority were empowered with a certain amount of autonomy as well as royal license to operate within their limited spheres.
11. Ibid., pp. 359ff.
12. At-Ṭabarî, *Ta'rîkh*, ed. M. J. DeGoeje (Leiden: E. J. Brill, 1879), Vol 1, p. 823, where Imru'ulqais is listed as one of the ʿummâl (sing. ʿâmil). According to the chronology given by S. Smith, "Events in Arabia in the 6th Century A.D.," *B.S.O.A.S.* 16, no. 3 (1954): 430, this would be during the reign of Ardashir II through Bahram IV. But it appears that there was more than one Imru'ulqais. G. W. Bowersock, in his *Roman Arabia* (Cambridge, Mass.: Harvard University Press, 1983), pp. 138–47, argues that

at-Ṭabrî confused the two homonymous rulers of Hîra. The first, the ruler "of all the Arabs" as he is designated in the epitaph inscription found at Namâra in the Roman province of Arabia, dating from 328 C.E., was the Lakhmid king of Hîra mentioned by Hishâm al-Kalbî. He was Imruʾulqais b. ʿAmr b. ʿAdî and, from the evidence of the inscription, he provided support to the Romans. Irfan Shhîd, in his *Byzantium and the Arabs in the Fourth Century*, (Washington, D.C.: Dumbarton Oaks, 1984) pp. 31–53, skillfully analyzes the much discussed Namâra inscription, and concludes that the evidence in at-Ṭabarî refers to the Imruʾulqais of 328 C.E. and not to the Imruʾulqais of 380–404 C.E. On the basis of at-Ṭabarî's statement that Imruʾulqais was the first of the governors of Persia to become Christian, he concludes that he not only converted but defected to the Romans, hence the location of his grave in Roman territory. Bowersock strongly disagrees in his review of Shahîd's book, in *Classical Review* 36 (1986): pp. 111–117, but does admit in his *Roman Arabia*, p. 141, that "it remains possible that the first Imruʾulqais was a Christian, and that Ṭabarî's confusion goes deeper than the simple misattribution of an epithet." For our purposes, the evidence seems clear that the kings of Hîra were acting as Persian agents by the end of the fourth century. One must agree with Bowersock that their conversion to or interest in Christianity would not be a surprise, particularly because this corresponds to the time of Queen Mavia, about whom Irfan Shahîd has written so clearly in his *Byzantium and the Arabs in the Fourth Century*. The fact that two such skilled scholars can disagree about this problem not only illustrates the difficulties of the sources, but also underscores an important aspect of the position of the clients of the two "super powers." All the "civilized" ancient historians held the prejudice that the Arabs were untrustworthy, capable of betraying a trust in a moment. Then, as now, there must have been a great temptation to move from alliance to alliance to gain advantage and to maintain independence. Each move would yield, at the best, a little more territory, income, and prestige. Titles for offices become more grandiloquent in such circumstances, and if the Jews of the Ḥijâz were "kings" (see above), then the Persian ruler was "King of kings." As we shall shortly see, the Jews in Israel looked fervently for Persian successes to rid them of the Roman yoke at a time when they were under the political control of the Byzantines. These sentiments earned them the epithet of "untrustworthy."

13. Muhammad b. Ishâq, *The Life of Muhammad*, trans. A. Guillaume Oxford and Lahore: Oxford University Press, 1955, pp. 6ff.

14. As reported by Philostorgius, *Ecclesiastical History*, 3. 5.

15. D. S. Margoliouth, *The Relations between Arabs and Israelites Prior to the Rise of Islam* (London: Oxford University Press, 1924), p. 63, and J. Horovitz, "Judaeo-Arabic Relations in Pre-Islamic Times," *Islamic Culture* 3 (1929): 191, discuss the inscription of Sharahbʾîl Yaʿfur found in association with the dam at Maʾrib where he uses the formula, "By the help and assistance of God, Lord of Heaven and Earth." Horovitz, following the objections of Margoliouth, assumes that this could not be a Jewish formula because of the use of the word *bʿl*, meaning "Lord," which, he contends, would be anathema to Jews. While it is true that the root can refer to the Canaanite deity, it has a long history in the Semitic languages as a common noun and appears to be used that way in this inscription where it follows the proper name for God,

ʾlhn. In the absence of other evidence in the inscriptions that would indicate that the rulers of the Yemen are under Canaanite pagan influence, it seems unwarranted to read the word bʾl in a manner other than as a common noun. Further, there is no inclusion in the inscription of south Arabian pagan deities, nor is there any Trinitarian formulae, which would be expected if this were a Christian inscription. It seems to be a more difficult interpretation of the evidence to assume an unaffiliated monotheism among the Ḥimyarite rulers than it does to assume Jewish influence, given the known presence of Judaism.

16. Ibn Isḥâq, *Life of Muhfammad*, pp. 13ff.

17. Ibid., pp. 13–14. At-Ṭabarî, *Taʾrîkh*, vol. 1, p. 919, is the source for Guillaume's reconstruction of the Ibn Isḥâq text, and is probably an accurate reflection of the original material used by Muḥammad's first biographer. At-Ṭabarî is known to have relied heavily on Ibn Isḥâq for his own history. Later editions of Ibn Isḥâq omit the mention of Dhû Nuwâs's adoption of Judaism, although the traditions assume it for the sense of the narrative.

18. F. Altheim and R. Stiehl, *Die Araber in der alten Welt.* vol. 5, part 1, p. 361. Altheim and Stiehl rely on Ḥamza al-Isfahânî (ed. Gottwald, pp. 133, 1112ff.) who asserts that Dhû Nuwâs learned his Judaism in Medina. It may be, of course, that this is an anachronism reflecting the views of Islamic historians and their inclination to assign importance to the "City of the Prophet." Even if this is so, the area of Jewish cities in the northern Hijâz can certainly be viewed as a locus for Jewish activity and interests in Arabia. We can note that in Numbers Rabbah 13, Hegrâ is referred to as *Galût Hegrâ*, and from al-ʿÜlâ there is an inscription showing a dromedary with the name "Levi" on a household wall.

19. Ibid., p. 365.

20. Ibid, p. 306, whose Altheim gives a transliteration of the text from the original Nabataean script, a translation into German, and a proposed date.

21. It is also interesting to note that even at this early date the Jewish naming patterns, which are so well known from Islamic texts, are present in the Nabataean inscriptions. Shmwʾl will yield Shᵉmûʾêl, and Hny will yield Hônî, a name famous from legend and associated with the Hasmonean civil war as well as with the name of several high priests. ʿAdnôn is the familiar Arabic ʾAdnân, but exhibiting the shift between *â* and *ô* found in *salâm* and *shalôm*. Since one cannot assume that these two forms of the same name are cognate, thus giving rise to the "Canaanite shift" of the long vowel, we must assume that this is the result of (1) a dialect that pronounced *â* as *ô*, (2) an orthographic convention, or (3) conscious philological distinction on the part of the Jews in their onomastic conventions. ʾAmr(w) is spelled as in Arabic with the terminal *w* to distinguish it from the name ʾUmar, spelled with the same root consonants.

22. Another inscription consistently uses the word *ben* for son as opposed to the Nabataean *bar* and gives the name *bn ḥbrʾ*, "Son of the Scholar[?]" (F. Altheim, in *Die Araber*, p. 310.

23. F. Altheim and R. Stiehl, *Geschichte der Hunnen* (Berlin: Walter de Gruyter & Co., 1960), vol. 3, p. 52.

24. S. Smith, "Events in Arabia in the 6th Century A.D.," *B.S.O.A.S.* 16, no. 3 (1954): 461–62: "May the Merciful be favourable. (Thou art L)ord."

25. See Sanhedrin 32b. The city had been destroyed by Lucius Quietus, Trajan's general, but, according to Arab traditions, it was restored by the Persians and again became a major center of Jewish intellectual activity. See Yâqût, *Mu'jam al-Buldân*, ed. F. Wüstenfeld, (Leipzig: F. A. Brockhaus, 1866–73) vol. 4. p. 787. It is evident that there was Jewish activity and settlement in Nisibis during the period between Trajan and the "restoration" by Khusrau Anushirwan, and Yâqût's ascription of the rebuilding appears to be to that of pre-Islamic Iran's most noted and active ruler.

26. S. Smith, "Events in Arabia in the 6th Century A.D.," *B.S.O.A.S.*, 16, no. 3 (1954): 464.

27. M. R. Al-Assouad, "Dhû Nuwâs," *Encyclopaedia of Islam*, 2nd edition, vol. 2, p. 244. The issue of the dating is a combination of when the Sabaean era starts and how one orders the events mentioned in the paucity of inscriptions available to use.

28. This is the conclusion reached by Al-Assouad following I. Guidi's analysis of a letter of James of Sarug to the Himyarites.

29. S. Smith, "Events," p. 464.

30. The most important of the Samaritan revolts took place in 476 with an attack on Caesarea and the establishment of an abortive Samaritan kingdom.

31. It should not be assumed that the Persians were regarded as potential saviors for Jews and Judaism, since the exilarch Mar Zutra II had been executed by the Persian ruler Kavad in 520 C.E., and his family had fled to Palestine. As we shall see below, King Joseph may well have had the fate of the Persian Jews in mind when he launched his military and diplomatic offensives.

32. Axel Moberg, ed., *The Book of the Himyarites*, Skrifter Kungliga Humanistika Vetenskapssamfundet i Lund, vol. 7 (Lund, Sweden: Gleerup, 1924), p. cv. They are described as "priests" from Tiberias. The issues raised by this are discussed below.

33. Ibid., pp. cvii–cviii.

34. The inscription Ryckmans 510 is cited in W. Caskel, *Entdeckungen in Arabien, Arbeitsgemeinschaft für Forschung des Landes Nordhein-Westfalen (Geisteswissenschaften)*, vol. 30 (Cologne: Westdeutscher Verlag, 1954), p. 11.

35. Moberg, ed., *Book of the Himyarites*, p. cxxxiii.

36. Ryckmans 508 in W. Caskel, *Entdeckungen*, p. 14; S. Smith, "Events," p. 458. The inscription reports 13,000 slain, 9,500 prisoners, and 280,000 camel, oxen, and goats as booty. Even if this number is discounted by the usual half for hyperbole, it is clear that the inscription recounts a major military expedition and not just a bedouin raid.

37. See, for example, Ibn Ishâq, *The Life of Muhammad*, trans. A. Guillaume (Lahore: Oxford University Press, 1955), pp. 30ff. In this account, as in others, there is much that is fanciful and "literary," but this is not a reason to reject its basic accuracy. Islamic historians felt a need to tell a tale as well as report facts, and they were not always as scrupulous as we try to be with the details. The other side of Islamic reports is, however, that they are seldom tainted by ideological preconceptions and preconditions. Someone like Ibn Ishâq or at-Tabarî reported the facts as he knew

them, interpreted the facts, but would not consciously exclude material because it would not fit a procrustean ideological bed.

38. Ryckmans 508: Smith, "Events," p. 464.
39. Moberg, ed., *Book of the Himyarites*, p. cxxiii.
40. Ibid.
41. Ryckmans 507–508.
42. Irfan Shahîd, *The Martyrs of Najarn: New Documents* (Brussels: Societé des Bollandists, *Subsidia Hagiographica #49*, 1971). The major sources for the martyrological account are A. Moberg, ed., *Book of the Himyarites*, and the list of Greek, Ethiopic, Armenian, Arabic, and Latin sources of the martyrdom of St. Hârith cited on p. xxiv; the letters of Simeon of Bêth Arsham discussed by Shahîd; and the secular sources cited in Irfan Shahîd, "Byzanto-Arabica: The Conference of Ramla, A.D. 524," *J.N.E.S.* 23 (1964): 115–131. Recommended are I. Guidi, "La Lettera di Simeono vescovo di Beth-Arsham sopra i martiri omeriti," *Atti della R. Accad. dei Lincei, Memorie della classe di scienze morali, storiche e filologiche* 7 (Rome, 1881): 471–515, and the more available translation of the letter by A. Jeffery in *Muslim World* 36 (1946): 204–16. The most detailed narrative, which is not complete, is in *The Book of the Himyarites*. One tantalizing chapter, which is only named by title, is chapter 2, "Account Telling of the . . . Himyarites, Who They Are and Whence They First Re[ceived] Judaism."
43. Moberg ed., *Book of the Himyarities*, p. cv.
44. Ibid., p. cvii.
45. Ibn Ishâq, *Life of Muhammad*, pp. 18f., although this story may be an etiological formation from an existing Yemenite proverb: Not like Daus and not like the things he carried in his saddlebag.
46. Moberg, ed., *Book of the Himyarites*, p. cii.
47. Ibid., p. cix.
48. Ibid., p. cix.
49. This letter is missing in the extant version of *The Book of the Himyarites*, but versions are found in the Letters of Simeon and in the *Martyrium Arethae*. Irfan Shahîd's analysis in "Byzanto-Arabica: The Conference of Ramla, A.D. 524," makes the most cogent sense of the various versions.
50. Irfan Shahîd, "Byzanto-Arabica," p. 115.
51. Irfan Shahîd, *The Martyrs of Najran*, p. 269.
52. Or anti-Diophysite and anti-Monophysite, for he may have been Nestorian according to some readings of the sources.
53. Irfan Shahîd, "Byzanto-Arabica," p. 116.
54. Moberg, ed., *Book of the Himyarites*, p. cvii.
55. Ibid., p. cix.
56. Ibid., p. cv.
57. Irfan Shahîd, *The Martyrs of Najran*, p. 67.
58. Ibid., p. 208.
59. Moshe Gil cites some of the traditions for this in his article "The Origins of the Jews of Yathrib," *J.S.A.I.* 4 (1984): 208 n.
60. S. D. Goitein, *Jews and Arabs* (New York, Schocken Books, 1964), pp. 48–49.

61. Haim Zev Hirschberg, "Concerning New Jewish Inscriptions Discovered in South Arabia," *Tarbîz* (1974–75), pp. 151ff., discusses discoveries reported by Gruntfest and comes to the conclusion that the presence of lists of priestly wards supports the presence of a priests in Arabia.
62. Palestinian Talmud Ta'aniyôt, iv, 60b.
63. Procopius, *History of the Wars*, vol. 1, bk. 20, 11.3–8.

Chapter 5

1. This is the traditional date and linked in the Muslim traditions with the failure of the Abyssinian Abraha to invade Mecca. It is usually arrived at by counting back from the known date of the Hijrah, the change of residence of Muhammad and his community from Mecca to Medina. The date assumes that Muhammad was really forty years of age at the time of the beginning of Islam. That date is suspiciously symbolic, but, lacking evidence to the contrary, historians have generally accepted it.
2. J. Kister, "Al-Hîra," *Arabica* 15 (1968): 145–49, shows that the once subservient tribe of B. Khazraj had assumed the role of tax collectors for the Persians, replacing the B. an-Nadîr and the B. Qurayza as their power waned.
3. Michael Lecker, "Muhammad at Medina: A Geographical Approach," *J.S.A.I.* 6 (1985): 29–62.
4. Moshe Gil reports in "Ha-mîfgash ha-bablî," *Tarbîz* 47 (1979): 57, that the exilarch Bustanay was in the city of Medina sometime around 623 C.E., and M. J. and Menahem Kister detail both political and religious contacts between the Jews of the Hijâz and Israel in their article, "'Al yehûdê 'arab-he'arôt," *Tarbîz* 48 (1979): 230–47.
5. I. Lichtenstadter, "Jews in Pre-Islamic Arabic Literature," *American Academy for Jewish Research* 10 (1940): 185–94, has a short list derived from a sampling of pre-Islamic Arabic literature. Her sample, however, shows the diversity of occupations present in Arabia.
6. A. Jaussen and R. Savignac, *Mission archeologique en Arabie,* (Paris: E. Leroux, 1909), vol. 1, p. 242.
7. Ibid., p. 149.
8. Israel Friedlander, *J.Q.R.* 1 (1910): 251, 451.
9. H. Hirschfeld, "Some Notes on 'Jewish Arabic Studies,' " *J.Q.R.* 1 (1910): 447–48.
10. Ella Landau-Tasseron, "Asad from Jâhiliyya to Islâm," *J.S.A.I.* 6 (1985): 1–28.
11. Ibid., p. 25.
12. By a "pastoral" literary topos, I am referring to the tendency in later Islamic philological literature to overvalue bedouin values, language, etc. Most of the scholars were urban, and some appear to have yearned for the excitement in what they saw as a survival of former greatness and purity. Such a yearning for the "simple, rugged' life can be found associated with the American "Western" and its associated frontier literature. For a discussion of the effects of this sort of "pastoralism" on Islamic historical scholarship, see G. Newby, "Ibn Khaldun and Frederick Jackson Turner: Islam and the Frontier Experience," in *Ibn Khaldun and Islamic Ideology*, ed. B. Lawrence (Leiden: E. J. Brill, 1984), pp. 122–33.

13. Michael Lecker, "Muḥammad at Medina: A Geographical Approach," *J.S.A.I.* 6 (1985): 29–62.

14. Ibid., p. 40. Lecker analyzes the position of the Jews of Ḥusayka, the "strongest Jewish group at that time," at the time they are defeated by the B. Salima, a subgroup of the B. Khazraj.

15. Ibid., p. 43: "Zuhra: *wa-kânat bi-zuhra jummāᶜ mina l-yahûd*, and Yathrib: *ahl yathrib, wa-kânû jummāᶜan mina l-yahûd; jummāᶜ* means: people from various tribes who have the same status, or, what seems more appropriate in our case: groups from various tribes."

16. Ibid., p. 42n.

17. Muhammad b. Isḥâq, *The Life of Muhammad*, trans. A. Guillaume, (Oxford and Lahore: Oxford University Press, 1955), pp. 482–84; G. Newby, "Observations about an Early Judaeo-Arabic," *J.Q.R.*, (1971): 212–21. Sallâm's house was accessible only by means of a ladder, according to the sources, which leaves the impression that it was in the heart of the city.

18. An additional observation about Medina should be made. Yathrib, usually regarded as the older name for the city of Medina, was merely a subsection of the urban locale. It was said to have been inhabited by the best and most noble of the Jews; cf. *Kitâb al-Aghânî*, vol. 19, p. 95. In other traditions, however, Ḥusayka was the center of Jewish power. Apparently "neighborhoods" had separate rivalries and claims to superiority.

19. Moshe Gil, "The Origins of the Jews of Yathrib," *J.S.A.I.* 4 (1984): 210f.

20. Ibid., p. 210.

21. Samhûdî, *Wafâʾ al-Wafâʾ*, vol. 1, pp. 114–16; cf. W. M. Watt, *Muhammad at Medina* (Oxford: Clarendon Press, 1956), pp. 192ff; *Kitâb al-Aghânî*, vol. 19, p. 95.

22. M. Gil, "The Origins of the Jews of Yathrib," p. 211.

23. For a discussion of conversion in early Islam, see M. Shaban, "Conversion to Early Islam," in Nehemia Levtzion, *Conversion to Islam* (New York: Holmes & Meier, 1979), pp. 24–29. This volume also has a good introductory bibliography on the general subject of conversion throughout the wide context of Islam.

24. Shabbat 6:6.

25. Oholot 18:10.

26. The name al-ʾAblaq is usually translated as "piebald" and applied to a horse. One tradition cited in Yâqût's *Muʿjam al-Buldân* (ed. Wüstenfeld; 1:94) attributes the name to the fact that the stonework was alternately red and white. My colleague S. Thomas Parker has called my attention to a Jordanian parallel to banded stonework at the site of Qasir Hallâbât, north of Amman. It is a second-century Roman watchtower rebuilt ca. 213 C.E. as a *castellum* with bands of black and white stone. Rebuilt in 529 C.E. by Justinian, it became a villa with a mosque in the Umayyid period. It would not be surprising if we had a reminiscence of a Syrian architectural style in Taymâ, given the connection between as-Samawʾal and the Ghassânids mentioned in the literary sources. The name al-ʾAblaq can also mean "impenetrable." In the basic stem, the root means "He opened the door wholly," implying hospitality if the name is taken from that meaning. All the meanings—"piebald," "impenetra-

ble," and "open"—are fitting terms for a castle of someone regarded as noble among the Arabs.

27. Abû Faraj al-ʾAṣbahânî, *Kitâb al-ʾAghânî*, ed. Ṣalâḥ Yûsuf al-Khalîl (Beirut: Dâr al-Fikr, reprinted from Bûlâq edition, 1970), vol. 19, p. 98.

28. Ibid., pp. 98–102.

29. Ibid.; Th. Nöldeke, *Beitraege zur Kenntniss der Poesie der alten Araber* (Hannover: Carl Ruempler, 1864), pp. 57–72; Josef Horovitz, "Judaeo-Arab Relations in Pre-Islamic Times," *I.C.* 3 (1929): 173–76; J. W. Hirschberg, *Der Dîwân des as-Samauʾal ibn ʾAdijâʾ* (Kracow, 1931).

30. D. S. Margoliouth, "A Poem Attributed to al-Samauʾal," *J.R.A.S.* (1906): 363–71.

31. See the arguments in A. J. Arberry, *The Seven Odes* (New York: Macmillan, 1957); and I. Shahîd, "Arabic Literature to the End of the Umayyad Period," *J.A.O.S.* 106 (1986): 530.

32. Hartwig Hirschfeld, "A Poem Attributed to alSamauʾal," *J.Q.R.* 17 (1905): 431–40. For Margoliouth's criticism, see "A Poem Attributed to al-Samauʾal," *J.R.A.S.* (1906): 363–71; Hirschfeld's reply is found in the same issue, pp. 701–4.

33. The following is Hirschfeld's translation of the poem:

1. O . . . whom my lords blame(?),
   Hear my voice, I am not unmindful of thee.
2. Let me recount the high qualities of a people which
   Their God has chosen with signs and miracles.
3. He chose them from (?) a barren . . .
   Whom my Lord distinguished on account of their pure descent (?).
4. From fire and sacrifice and trials to which
   They submitted from perfect love of God (?).
5. The one is a friend around whom the fire produced fragrant odours which covered the flexible twigs.
6. The other is . . . sacrifice which he redeemed by his lamb which he created, but which was not the child of the mountain goats.
7. Then there is a prince whom he chose and distinguished.
   And named him Israel the first-born
8. God exalted them . . .
   . . . in this world and the next
9. Did not religion attach to them to guide them,
   And he covered (?) them with bounties and gifts.
10. . . . a glory which overflows the heart (/)
    And kindles an inextinguishable fire in the bosom.
11. And it inspires whisper and illumines . . .
    And casts into his vitals something akin to disquiet (?)
12. Are we not the people of Egypt which was chastised; we
    For whose sake Egypt was struck by ten plagues?
13. Are we not the people of the divided sea, we
    For whose sake Pharaoh was drowned on the day of (his) arduous enterprise?
14. The Creator took the people out on the road
    That it might behold his wonders . . .(?)

15. And that they might carry off the booty of its people, gold over . . . of the girdles.
16. Are we not the people of the sanctuary . . .
    To whom clouds descended which shaded them the whole journey?
17. From sun and rain they were their guard
    Protecting their hosts from the fierce hot wind.
18. Are we not the people of the quails and the manna
    And they to whom the stone poured forth the sweetness of water?
19. . . . . . .
    . . . . . .
20. Its springs flowed according to the number of the tribes
    [Uniting] into a sweet, cool stream whose taste was not changed.
21. They tarried in the desert for renewed life [generation?]
    The Creator sustained them with the choicest of food.
22. The garments of their bodies did not wear out, nor
    Did they require repairs (?) for their shoes.
23. He appointed a light, like a pillar, in front of them
    Which illumined the horizon without departing.
24. Are we not the people of the holy mount . . .
    Which crumbled to dust on the day of the earthquake?
25. Did not the mighty one humble itself completely?
    But the Creator exalted it above every high position.
26. And his servant to whom he spoke, prayed upon it. . .

34. Th. Nöldeke, *Beitraege zur Kenntniss der Poesie der alten Araber* (Hannover: Carl Ruempler, 1864), pp. 53–54.
35. Ibid., pp. 72–76.
36. Abû Faraj al-ʾAsbahânî, *Kitâb al-Aghânî*, ed. Salâh Yûsuf al-Khalîl (Beirut: Dâr al-Fikr, after the Bûlâq edition, 1970), vol. 19, pp. 94f.
37. Nöldeke, *Kenntniss*, p. 76. ʾAws puns with the Arabic *hadâ*, to be guided rightly, and *hâda*, to be or to become Jewish.
38. Ibid., pp. 77f.
39. Ibid., pp. 80f.
40. It has been argued by some that the very secular nature of the pre-Islamic Jewish poets speaks to the fact that they were not Jews or, at least, that they were not very strong Jews, having been converted from paganism. This argument seems wrong on several counts. In the first place, the difficulties of preservation of literary examples means that the collections will, perforce, be selective. It is likely that a Muslim collector of literary lore would choose to preserve some and not other of the material at hand. One has only to experience the modern editor to appreciate that each work has such selections and biases. The fact that a viable Jewish community did not survive in Arabia can be understood as contributing to the selective survival of Arabian Jewish verse. The second objection to the argument is that the presence of secular verse by Jews does not mean that they were not identified with Judaism. An examination of modern Diaspora communities will provide models for secular Jews strongly identified with their faith. Finally, an argument that the convert is

less than a full Jew is an argument that has to be made for each individual case, since many prominent converts can be cited among the sages of Israel, Ben Hê-Hê, for example.

41. For a thorough discussion of Kaʿb's life, see Israel Wolfensohn (Israel Ben-zeev), "Kaʿb al-Aḥbâr und seine Stellung im Ḥadîth und in der islamischen Legenden-literatur," Inaugural dissertation, Johann Wolfgang Goethe University, Frankfurt am Main, 1933. See also M. Lidzbarski, *De Propheticis, Quae Dicuntur, Legendis Arabicis* (Leipzig: G. Drugulini, 1893; B. Chapira, "Legendes bibliques attribuees a Kaʿb el-Aḥbar," *R.E.J.* 69 (1919): 86–107, and 70 (1920): 37–43; M. Perlmann, "A Legendary Story of Kaʿb al-Aḥbâr's conversion to Islam," *Conference on Jewish Relations: Joshua Starr Memorial Volume* (New York: Jewish Social Studies Publications, 1953), pp. 85–99.

42. Muḥammad b. Jarîr aṭ-Ṭabarî, *Tafsîr*, vol. 3, p. 326, *apud* Qurʾân 3:79.

43. Ibid., vol. 6, p. 250, *apud* Qurʾân 5:44.

44. Baba Batra 38b.

45. Baba Batra 75a.

46. Kiddushin 33b.

47. Qurʾân 7:157.

48. H. Hirschfeld, *Beitraege zur Erklaerung des Koran* (Leipzig: O. Schutze, 1886), p. 40, where he also contrasts the term ʾaḥbâr with the Hebrew ʿam ha-ʾarez.

49. It can be noted that Muhammad Marmaduke Pickthall's usually reliable, if somewhat conservative, translation, *The Meaning of the Glorious Koran*, is wrong when he translates ʾaḥbâr as "priests at Qurʾân 5:44 and 5:63.

50. See M. J. Kister, "...illâ bi-ḥaqqihi... A Study of an Early ḥadîth," J.S.A.I. 5 (1984): 43.

51. Steven Wasserstrom, "Species of Misbelief: A History of Muslim Heresiography of the Jews," dissertation, University of Toronto, 1985, pp. 54f.

52. Ibid.

53. Sukkot 20a.

54. In Assyrian rather than Samaritan characters; Sanhedrin 21b.

55. Heb. ha-sôfer.

56. 4 Ezra 14:50.

57. 2 Enoch 22:11.

58. L. Ginzberg, *Legends of the Jews, vol. 6, p. 446.*

59. 4 Ezra 14:9, 50.

60. David Halperin in a private communication, to appear in *Faces of the Chariot* (Tübingen: J. C. B. Mohr, 1987). The best translation of 3 Enoch is by P. Alexander in James H. Charlesworth, *The Old Testament Pseudepigrapha* (New York: Doubleday, 1983) pp. 303–315, which I have used here.

61. 1 Enoch 71:1, etc.

62. 1 Enoch 105:2.

63. Ezra 7:28; 13:32; 14:9 (where Ezra will live with God's Son).

64. E. G. Hirsch, "Son of God," *Jewish Encyclopaedia* (New York: Funk and Wagnalls, 1912), vol. 11, pp. 460–61.

65. In an appendix to his dissertation, Steven Wasserstrom shows how the tradition of God's filiation are used in the polemics against the Jews. The legends associated with Ezra are treated in Haim Schwarzbaum, *Biblical and Extra-Biblical Legends in Islamic Folk-Literature* (Walldorf-Hessen: Verdag für Briertkunde Dr. H. Vorndran, 1982). Because of his asynchronic approach, Schwarzbaum does not, however, set forth a causal relationship between the Enochid traditions and the Qur'ânic accusation. He seems to share the attitude of many that any notion of divine filiation is patently non-Jewish.

66. See D. Halperin and G. Newby, "Two Castrated Bulls: A Study in the Haggadah of Ka'b al-Ahbâr," *J.A.O.S.* 102, no. 3 (1982): pp. 631–38.

67. Chaim Rabin, *Qumran Studies* (Oxford: Oxford University Press, 1957), pp. 112–130.

68. One of the main supports of Muslim apologetics has been the notion that the Qur'ân is the completion and the perfection of previous revelations from God, which revelations were thought to predict Muhammad's advent, just as Christians read the passages in Isaiah to foretell the coming of Jesus. Post-Qur'ânic discussions tell of individuals, usually Jews or Christians, who discover pages stuck together in old books, or rediscover old scrolls that verify that view. While that view becomes a literary topos, its origins appear to be found among the Arabian Jews who claimed to be awaiting a prophet to deliver them.

69. For the most recent and thorough study of the traditions and legends surrounding Ibn Sayyâd, see David J. Halperin, "The Ibn Sayyâd Traditions and the Legend of al-Dajjâl," *J.A.O.S. 96.* no. 2 (1976): 213–25.

70. Ibid., p. 216.

71. Arab. *rasûl al-ummiyyin* (ibid.).

72. Ibid., p. 217.

73. Qur'ân 73:1; 74:1.

74. Arab. *saj'*, regarded as the speech of the *Kâhin*, a word etymologically related to the Hebrew *côhên*, and used of the pre-Islamic mantic seers who practiced divination and theurgy. On the occasion of his first revelation, Muhammad feared that he was becoming a *kâhin*, and was accused by al-Walîd b. al-Mughîra of that. See Ibn Ishâq, *Sîrat rasûl Allâh*, ed. and trans. A. Guillaume, (Lahore: Oxford University Press, 1955), pp. 106, 121.

75. Ibn Ishâq, *Sîrat*, pp. 181ff. Note here how the account of Muhammad's journey to heaven follows an account of his wrestling a mysterious individual, a literary representation that equates Muhammad with the biblical Jacob.

76. Halperin, "The Ibn Sayyâd Traditions," p. 220.

77. Ibn Ishâq, *Sîrat*, p. 121, where Guillaume translates the word for "source," *'asl*, as "root" in keeping with the tree image.

78. Arab. *ad-Dajjâl*.

79. Ibn Ishâq, *The Life of Muhmmad*, p. 252.

80. This "recovered" Midrash was first published by G. Newby in "Arabian Jewish History in the *Sîrah*," *J.S.A.I.* 7(1986): 136–38.

81. Ed. Buber, Lekh Leka 21, p. 39a.

143

82. Abû Qâsim Maḥud b. ʿUmar b. Muhammad b. ʾAhmad al-Khawarizmî az-Zamakhsharî, *Al-Kashshâf ʿan haqâʾ iq at-tanzîl wa-ʿuyûn al-ʿaqawîl fî wjûh at-taʾwîl* (Cairo: Mustafa al-Halabi & Sons, 1966), vol. 2, p. 270. The *isnâd* is incomplete in this account, and it is not possible to tell how this reached az-Zamakhsharî, although it is a reasonable assumption that he received the information through literary rather than only oral means.
83. Nabia Abbott, *Studies in Arabic Literary Papyr* (Chicago: University of Chicago Press, 1967), vol. 2, p. 9.
84. G. D. Newby, "Observations about an Early Judaeo-Arabic," *J.Q.R.* 61 (1971): 220.
85. The term *hibr* is often translated as "rabbi."
86. Nabia Abbott, *Arabic Literary Papyri*, vol. 2, p. 9.
87. Ibid.
88. One of the usual *isnâds* found in the material collected by Ibn Ishâq and reported by aṭ-Ṭabarî is from Ibn Ḥumayd from Salamah from Ibn Ishâq from the Ahl al-Yaman from Wahb b. Munabbih. Wahb is credited with writing a *Qisas al-ʾAnbiyâʾ* and a *K. al-Mubtadaʾ*, both likely collections of Jewish stories and commentaries. At this point, it is not possible to identify the Ahl al-Yaman quoted by Wahb, but from the content of the quotations, it is likely that he was in touch with a group of Yemenite Jews from whom he was obtaining this material.
89. Nabia Abbott, *Arabic Literary Papyri*, (Chicago: University of Chicago Press, 1957), vol. 1, pp. 87ff., describes the extensive literary activity of the early Islamic period. Much work needs to be done to determine the exact nature of the early works from which the Muslim exegetes like Ibn Ishâq were drawing so much detail for their own works.
90. Khayr ad-Dîn az-Ziriklî, *Al-Aʿlam* (Beirut: private printing, 1969), vol. 10, p. 150.
91. Midrash Rabbah: Genesis, ed. and trans. H. Freedman et al. (New York: Soncino Press, 1977), vol. 1, p. 293.
92. The translation is that of the Soncino edition.
93. See Pirke R. Eliezer and Origen on Genesis 9:25.
94. This text was provided to me by my colleague Dr. J. C. Vanderkam.
95. I have written about this subject in "Observations about an Early Judaeo-Arabic," *J.Q.R.*, (1971), and "Arabian Jewish History in the *Sîrah*," *J.S.A.S.* 7 (1966): 132–35.
96. Ibid., and Muhammad b. ʿUmar b. Wâqidî al-Wâqidî, *Kitâb al-Maghâzi*, (London: Oxford University Press 1966), vol 1, pp. 391–92.
97. Newby, "Observations about an early Judaeo Arabic," J.Q.R. 61 (1971): 214–21, and Gordon J. Bahr, "The Seder of Passover and the Eucharistic Words," in H. A. Fischel, ed., *Essays in Greco-Roman and Related Literature* (New York: Ktar, 1977), p. 182.
98. H. Schauss, *Guide to the Jewish Holy Days* (New York: Schocken, 1962), p. 81.
99. Taanit 20b; Ignaz Goldziher, "Notes sur les Juifs dans les poesies arabes de l'epoque ancienne de l'Islam," *Revue des études Juifs* 43 (1901): 10–14.
100. Pesah 99b.
101. Pesah 86a.
102. See S. Stein, "The Influence of the Symposia Literature on the Literary Form of the Pesah Haggadah," *Journal of Jewish Studies*, reprinted in Fischel, ed., *Essays* p. 215.

Apparently the original meaning of the term *apikoman* was to go from place to place, drink wine, toast each other, etc.

103. Bernard Heller, 'Youscha' Al-Akbar et les Juifs de Kheybar dans le Roman d'Antar: un mouvement messianique dans l'ancienne Arabie," *Revue des études Juives* (1927): 113–37. The term ʿîd an-nudhûr is thought by Heller to be *Yôm Kippûr*, but the actions seem more appropriate for Pesaḥ. While it is possible that we have a conflation of the two holidays, the name *nudhûr* may also refer to offerings or dedicated sacrifices, a more appropriate designation for Pesaḥ's festive meal.

104. Ibid. Joshua is apparently regarded here as a "military" Messiah, most likely following the first verse of the third chapter of Zechariah: "And he showed me Joshua the high priest standing before the angel of the Lord."

105. Ibid., p. 130, where the Jews are said to have recited the exclamation *khûṭṭnâ bayna yadayka wa-ilayka*, which represents the Hebrew *khaṭanû lifanekha v-lekha*.

106. S. D. Goitein, *Studies in Islamic History and Institutions* (Leiden: E. J. Brill, 1966), p. 97.

107. This in contrast to Goitein's assertion denying that this could be Jewish: "However, anyone familiar with the technique of the Muslim traditions derived from Jews or Christians is aware of the fact that they more often than not contain fanciful accretions to an authentic core. Muhammad's dictum connected with ʿA.: 'We are closer to (or: have more right to) Moses than you' may well have been genuine and remembered by some of his adherents. The explanation provided for the saying is manifestly spurious." Goitein's skepticism about later traditions does not, in my experience, apply as generally when dealing with the Qurʾân and the earliest material, which can often be understood as accurately representing the "authentic core" to which *later* accretions are sometimes made.

108. Heller, "Youscha' Al-Akbar et les Juifs de Kheybar," p. 132.

109. Ibid., p. 121.

110. See Qurʾân 2:65; 4:47, 154; 7:163; 16:124, where there are references to a number of Jewish haggadic tales about the fate of Sabbath-breakers.

111. J. Charlesworth, *The Old Testament Pseudepigrapha* (Garden City, N.Y.: Doubleday, 1983), vol. 1, p. 949n.

112. Ibid., p. 948.

113. See Heller, "Youscha' Al-Akbar et les Juifs de Kheybar," p. 119.

114. In the case of converts, the question is then asked to what extent the naming pattern represents only partial assimilation to the culture. This is seen in the Islamic period, where names like Isḥâq, Ibrâhîm, and Mûsâ could be thought to be Muslim, Jewish, or Christian, depending on the circumstances. For a discussion of this, see R. Bulliet, *Conversion to Islam in the Medieval Period* (Cambridge, Mass.: Harvard University Press, 1979).

115. We do not have evidence of an "inside-outside" naming pattern in the Ḥijâz such as is common in the United States where the Hebrew name and the legal name have only euphonic or conventional relationship. That does not mean that such a naming pattern did not exist, however.

116. Heller, "Youscha' Al-Akbar et les Juifs de Kheybar," p. 130.

117. Ibid., p. 132.

118. Heller equates this with the legend of al-Fityawn and the *jus primae noctis* and refers to Hartwig Hirschfeld's article in *Revue des études Juif* 7 (1883): 172.
119. Fermented beverage, Arabic *Khamr*, was produced not only from grapes but also from dates. In a tradition cited by Bukhârî (Tafsîr,al-*Quaʾân* 5:15), *we are informed that "khamr* is from five [things]: grapes, dates, honey, wheat and barley."
120. Goldziher, "Notes sur les Juifs dans les poesies arabes de l'epoque ancienne de l'Islam," *Revue des études Juifs* 43 (1901): 10–14.
121. Cf. Ibn Ishâq, *Life of Muhammad*, p. 515: "When the people of Khaybar surrendered on these conditions they asked the apostle to employ them on the property with half share in the produce, saying, 'We know more about it than you and we are better farmers.' The apostle agreed to this arrangement."
122. M. J. Kister, "The Market of the Prophet," *Journal of Economic and Social History of the Orient* 8 (1965): 272–76; Ibn Ishâq, *Life of Muhammad*, pp. 363, 751.
123. S. D. Goitein, *Studies in Islamic History and Institutions* (Leiden: E. J. Brill, 1968), p. 111–25.
124. Ibid., p. 115.
125. Ibid., p. 129.
126. Sûrah 5:43: "Why did they come to you for judgement when they have the Torah in which is God's judgement?" Note that the Arabic word for judgment, *hukm*, is related to the Hebrew hakam, "wisdom." For the discussion of the *ʾumma* agreement of Medina, see below.
127. Goldziher, "Notes sur les Juifs dans les poesies arabes de l'epoque ancienne de l'Islam," *Revue des études Juifs* 43 (1901): 10–14: al-Hutayʾah, a poet from the end of the Jâhiliyyah and the beginning of Islam, recited: "Comme si les Juifs y avaient entendu leurs etoffes de soie, leurs echarpes chatoyantes."
128. Ibid.

Chapter 6

1. I have written elsewhere about the nature of the biographical traditions of Muhammad, particularly as found in the *Sîrah*, and, while this is not the place to discuss that subject at length, it is appropriate that a few remarks be made. The *Sîrah*, written by Muhammad b. Ishâq, and epitomized by Ibn Hishâm, was written a little over a century after Muhammad's death at the behest of the ʿAbbâsid caliph al-Mansûr, as a textbook for his son, the prince al-Mahdî. As mentioned above, its literary model was the Christian Scripture, with the Old Testament portion covering the history of the world from creation to Muhammad, and the life of Muhammad as the New Testament portion. In that sense, it was hagiographic, fitting Muhammad into the pattern of not only Jesus, but also Moses, Jacob, Adam, Noah, and all the prophets and holy men claimed by Islam. The work abounds with stories of those prophets, the contents of which are derived from the trove of rabbinic haggadic and midrashic literature. It functions as a commentary on the Qurʾân and expands the stories of the biblical figures found there, but it also goes beyond the rabbinic material to link Muhammad and Islam to the Jewish and Christian past. So, when the *Sîrah* mentions the "foretelling" of Muhammad by rabbis in Arabia, it is offering

after-the-fact justification for Islam's doctrinal and political positions toward Judaism after the period of the expansion of Islam, particularly in areas of Iraq.

2. Some sources imply that the name *Yathrib* referred to the valley and that *al-Madînah* referred to the city. Later Islamic sources call the city *Madînatu n-Nâbî*, "the city of the Prophet," but given the Jewish character of the city, the name could be Aramaic as well as Arabic.

3. An excellent analysis of the life of Muhammad, reflecting both Western scholarship and Arabic sources, is the two volumes by W. Montgomery Watt, *Muhammad at Mecca* and *Muhammad at Medina*. As has been mentioned above, the *Sîrah* of Ibn Ishâq in the form epitomized by Ibn Hishâm has been translated into English by Alfred Guillaume as *Life of Muhammad*. Ibn Sa'd's *Tabaqât al-Kubrâ* and al-Wâqidî's *Kitâb al-Maghâzî* have not been translated. Muhammad b. Jarîr at-Tabarî's *Ta'rîkh ar-Rusul wa-Mulûk* is still in the process of being translated, but not from a critical edition of the Arabic text. The French translation by H. Zotenberg was made from an abridged Persian edition and cannot be relied on. The monumental ten-volume *Annali dell' Islam* by L. Caetani (Milan: University of Hoepli, 1905–26), supplies a chronological arrangement of the major textual sources.

4. See al-Isfahânî, *Kitâb al-'Aghânî (Beirut: Dâr Al-Fikr reprint of Bûlâg edition, 1970)* vol. 19, p. 95; I. Ben-Zeev, *Ha-Yehûdîm Ba'Arav* (Jerusalem: Achiasaf, 1957), 1957), p. 22. The timing would place their migration from the south around the time of the rise in fortunes of the Jews in the Himyar and the beginning of intense proselytization of the peninsula. It would not be surprising to find evidence of much more movement of peoples and tribes in this turbulent periiod.

5. The usual word for a contractual obligation under treaty in the early texts is *'ahd*, meaning "obligation," "pledge," "vow," "promise," or the act of making the treaty, "oath." This could be further subdivided into two general types, a *juwâr*, a mutual nonaggression pact, and a *hilf*, a pact that was sworn by oath and implied more than just mutual military assistance or abstinence from assault. It appears that new tribal groups could be formed by a *hilf* arrangement, implying a rearrangement of the genealogies of the individuals to conform to a new eponymn for the group.

6. Muhammad b. Jarîr at-Tabarî, *Jâmi' al-Bayân 'an Ta'wîl 'Ayy al-Qur'ân*, 30 vols. (Cairo: Al-Halabî & Sons, 1954), vol. 4, p. 34 *apud* Qur'ân 3:103: In a tradition cited on the authority of Ibn Humayd, from Salamah, Muhammad b. Ishâq said: "'Asim b. 'Amr b. Qatâdah told me on the authority of some elders of his people, that when the Messenger of God, may the prayers and peace of God be upon him, met them [a group from the Khazraj], he said to them, 'Who are you?' They said, 'A group from the Khazraj.' He said, "Are you clients [Arab. *mawâlî*] of Jews?' They responded, 'Yes.' He said, 'Won't you sit down so that I can talk with you?' They said, 'Yes.' So they sat with him and he called them to God, presented Islam to them, and recited the Qur'ân to them." The story then goes on to tell about how the Jews used to threaten their pagan clients with the coming of a prophet who would give the Jews power. The Khazrajites identified Muhammad with the promised prophet and joined him, taking "the women's pledge" to support Muhammad without fighting.

7. Muhammad was called a *kâhin* in Mecca by some of his detractors. Not only did this imply that he was a mantic seer, capable of giving minor prophecies in *saj'*,

"rhymed prose"; it also meant that he could act as an intermediary in disputes as he had done when he cleverly solved the problem of replacing the cornerstone in the Kaʿba by having a representative of each tribe lift the stone in place while holding onto a blanket in which it was wrapped, thus preventing any one of them from claiming priority over another.

8. ʿAbd al-Mâlik b. Hishâm, As-Sîrah an-Nabawiyyah, ed. Muṣṭafâ ash-Shaqâ, et al. (Cairo: Al-Ḥalabî & Sons, 1955), vol. 1, pp. 501–504.

9. Muḥammad b. ʿAmr b. Wâqid al-Wâqidî, Kitâb al-Maghâzî, ed. Marsden Jones (London: Oxford University Press, 1966), vol. 1, p. 186.

10. It is a usual tendency in the early Muslim biographies of Muhammad to distort what we should see as causal development and try to show that Muhammad, as God's agent, was endowed with a predestined power and position, even when the facts belie that construct.

11. Moshe Gil, "The Constitution of Medina: A reconsideration," Israel Oriental Studies 4 (1974): 44–65.

12. Ibid., p. 45.

13. In a tradition cited by Muslim, Ṣaḥîḥ, "Kitâb aṣ-Siyâm," (Cairo: 1963), p. 51, Muhammad was asked about fasting on Monday, to which he replied, "That is the day on which I was born, on which I was sent, and on which I was inspired." In Jewish tradition, Moses descended from heaven on Monday and Thursday were the days the patriarchs visited the Messiah; Monday and Thursday were the days for reading the Torah, holding court, and fasting. See 1: 94 (ed. Buber) Midrash Genesis Rabbah 76:3; and Luke 18:12.

14. See Nabia Abbott, Studies in Arabic Literary Papyri, vol. 2, Qurʾanic Commentary and Tradition (Chicago: University of Chicago Press, 1967), p. 9, where Abû Jald of Basrah claimed that divine benefit derived from both the Qurʾân and the Torah.

15. G. R. Hawting, "The Origins of the Muslim Sanctuary," Studies on First Century of Islamic Society, ed. G. H. A. Juynboll (Carbondale, Ill.: University of Southern Illinois Press, 1982), pp. 23–47.

16. Ibid., pp. 28–29.

17. See the details for this argument in Gordon Newby, "Observations about an Early Judaeo-Arabic," J.Q.R. 61 (1971): 214–21.

18. ʿAbd al-Mâlik b. Hishâm, As-Sîraht an-Nabawiyyaht Muṣṭafâ ash-Shaqâ, et al. (Cairo: Al-Ḥalabî & Sons, 1955), vol. 1, p. 517; A. Guillaume, trans., Life of Muhammad (London: Oxford University Press, 1955), pp. 240f. It should be noted that one of the purposes of this "conversion" story is to show that Muhammad was foretold by Jewish Scripture and that Jewish rejection of Muhammad was based on perversity rather than scriptural foundation. This common theme in Islamic literature, when combined with the notion of tahrîf, or the corruption of Scripture, allows the silence of Jewish and Christian writings in reference to Muhammad's advent and Islam's foundation to be an argument for Muhammad's authenticity.

19. The reader might analogize the situation in Medina with reactions among Jews today when faced with the "Jews for Jesus" missionaries.

20. Ibn Hishâm, As-Sîrat, vol. 1, pp. 527–29; A. Guillaume, trans., Life of Muhammad, p. 246. The term in Arabic for those who falsely join Islam is munâfiq, a word with an

interesting semantic range. As a verb, it means "to sell well, to be a successful merchant." One of the nominal forms means "the hole of a rat or a mouse," and a verbal form from that means "to undermine" or "to tunnel." Muhammad's use of the term for the opposition in Medina was probably playing on the double meaning of the word as both merchants and rats undermining his efforts. One is also reminded by this image of the traditional Muslim commentary on Qur'ân 34:15ff., the story of the breaking of the Dam of Ma'rib, where a mouse undermined its foundations, causing a break and a destructive flood. M. J. Kister, "The Massacre of the Banû Qurayẓa," *J.S.A.I.* 8 (1986): 88, observes that the *munâfiqûn* were "in fact a group of Medinans who had outwardly converted to Islam, but who had remained loyal to their former allies, faithful to their Jâhilî ideals and their tribal relations." Quoting Ibn al-ʿArabî: "The *munâfiqûn* used to aid the Jews of Qurayẓa and the Christians of Najrân because they were people of cultivated land and used to supply them with provisions and lend them money. Therefore they said: 'How are we to sever the bonds of friendship with a people who make our dwellings spacious when we are afflicted by a year of drought and are in need of them?' "

21. Gabriel is usually depicted in Jewish sources as a friend of the Jews, but in some passages he is described as an angel of death. The argument that Gabriel is an enemy of the Jews seems to be a development from the Judeo-Islamic polemic.

22. Ibn Ishâq, *Sîrah*, pp. 256f.

23. W. M. Watt, *Muhammad at Medina* (Oxford: Oxford University Press, 1956), pp. 204ff.

24. Ibn Hishâm, *As-Sîrat vol. 2, pp. 44f.*

25. Abû al-Faraj al-ʾIsfahânî, *Kitâb al-Aghânî*, vol. 6, pp. 99f. Here is evidence that the Jews were making fermented beverages from more than just grapes and dates, but there is no indication that they were practicing distillation in addition to fermentation.

26. Ibn Hishâm, *As-Sîrat*, vol. 2, p. 47.

27. Ibid., pp. 47f.

28. Watt, *Muhammad at Medina*, p. 209.

29. Barakat Ahmad, *Muhammad and the Jews: A Reexamination* (New Delhi: Vikas, 1979), pp. 55–62.

30. Ibn Hishâm, *As-Sîrat*, vol. 2, p. 49.

31. Barakat Ahmad, *Muhammad and the Jews*, p. 60.

32. Ibn Hishâm, *As-Sîrat*, vol. 2, p. 48.

33. Ibid., p. 47.

34. Maxime Rodinson, *Mohammed*, trans. A. Carter (New York: Pantheon 1971), p. 194.

35. At-Ṭabarî, *Ta'rîkh*, ed. M. J. De Goeje, (Leiden: E. J. Brill, 1882), p. 1369.

36. Ibn Ishâq, *Sîrah*, p. 366.

37. Kister, "The Massacre," p. 90.

38. Ibn Ishâq, *Sîrah*, p. 200.

39. Ibid., p. 301.

40. Ibid., p. 453.

41. Ibid., p. 368.

42. Ibid., p. 369.

43. Ibid., p. 372; Watt, *Muhammad at Medina*, p. 22.
44. Barakat Ahmad, *Muhammad and the Jews*, p. 64.
45. Ibn Ishâq, *Sîrah*, p. 437.
46. Ibid.
47. Ibid.; Ibn Hishâm, *As-Sîrat*, vol 2., p. 191, where the word is *nijâf*, variously translated as "lintel" and "bar of a door." This unusual action on the part of the B. an-Nadîr is undoubedly their compliance with the talmudic injunction that the mezuzah inscription, prescribed in Deuteronomy 6:9, not fall into the hands of the unclean lest the name of God be desecrated. While we cannot be sure, it would seem that the practice among the Arabian Jews was not to use the small case containing the twenty-two Deuteronomic lines but, rather, to use the entire door-post. Ahmad's assertion that wood was expensive, while true, seems an inadequate explanation.
48. Ibn Hishâm, *As-Sîrat*, p. 191.
49. Watt, *Muhammad at Medina*, p. 36.
50. Al-Wâqidî, *Kitâb Al-Maghâzî*, p. 445; M. J. Kister, "The Massacre," p. 85.
51. Ibn Ishâq, *Sîrah*, pp. 459f.
52. Ibid., p. 461.
53. In what appears to be an apochryphal story, Ibn Ishâq, *Sîrah*, pp. 461–62, tells us that Ka'b b. 'Asad outlined their plight by offering them three choices: (1) becoming Muslim, (2) killing the women and children and committing suicide, and (3) violating the Sabbath and attacking Muhammad. The Jews reject all three options by plausible arguments consistent with Jewish ideals.
54. Ibn Ishâq, *Sîrah*, p. 463.
55. Ibid.
56. Ibid., p. 464.
57. Barakat Ahmad, *Muhammad and the Jews*, p. 85; Watt, *Muhammad at Medina*, p. 216.
58. Al-Wâqidî, *Kitâb Al-Maghâzî*, pp. 521–24.
59. See Watt, *Muhammad at Medina*, pp. 215, 238.
60. W. N. Arafat, "New Light on the Story of Banû Qurayza and the Jews of Medina," *J.R.A.S.* (1976): 100–107.
61. Barakat Ahmad, *Muhammad and the Jews*.
62. Kister, "The Massacre."
63. Ibid., p. 83.
64. Ibn Hishâm, *As-Sîrat*, vol. 1, p. 501: "qâla-bnu 'ishâqa wa-kataba rasûlu-llâhi sl'm kitâban bayna-l-muhâjirîna wa-l-'ansâri wâda'a fîhi yahûda wa-'âhadhum wa-'aqarrahum 'alâ dînahum wa-'amwâlahum wa-sharata lahum wa-shtarata 'alayhim."
65. Ibn Ishâq, *Sîrah*, pp. 482ff.
66. Ibid., pp. 504ff.
67. Ibid., pp. 510ff.
68. Ibid., p. 515. Date-palms, for example, are often hand pollinated in a desert climate in order to produce a full yield, a job requiring both dexterity and skill.
69. Ibid., p. 523.
70. Ibn Hishâm, *As-Sîrat*, vol. 2, p. 589.

150

71. Ibn Isḥâq, *Sîrah*, p. 525.

Chapter 7

1. The question of whether or not Muhammad appointed a successor and who that successor should be is a point debated between the Sunnî ad Shiʿî factions in Islam to this day. Most Western scholars are of the opinion that Muhammad had not designated a successor, and that Abû Bakr's acquisition of power was a result in part of his personality and in part because he represented the strongest and most organized group, those of the Qureish who had claims to nobility in the pre-Islamic period. Muhammad's closest living relative, ʿAlî, apparently had a following, but was a more controversial personality, and his "party" did not develop until later. See W. M. Watt, *Islamic Political Thought*, Islamic Surveys, no. 6 (Edinburgh: Edinburgh University Press 1968), p. 31.

2. The Arabic term *khalîfah*, "successor," has the original sense of riding behind someone on an animal or following behind someone. It starts as an indistinct term, for there was no designated "office" of caliph. The political history of Islam after Muhammad is, in large part, an attempt to define and legitimize the office.

3. At-Ṭabarî, *Taʾrîkh*, ed. M. J. de Goeje (Leiden, 1890), ser. 1, vol. 4, p. 1848. This report of Abû Bakr's resoluteness is transmitted through the family *isnâd* of az-Zubayr, who opposed Abû Bakr, was a member of the party supporting ʿUmar, and was himself an accomplished military commander under Muhammad. For our purposes, though, whatever tendentious shaping may have taken place in this narrative, it seems not to have involved the report about the Jews and Christians.

4. For a careful analysis of the sources for this period, see E. S. Shoufani, *Al-Riddah and the Muslim Conquest of Arabia* (Toronto: University of Toronto Press, 1973).

5. Muhammad b. Saʿd (Kâtib al-Wâqidî), *At-Ṭabaqât al-Kabîr*, ed. E. Sachau, (Leiden: E. J. Brill, 1904), vol. 3, pt. 1, p. 203: "wa-huwa ʾakhraja -l-yahûda mina -l-hijâzi wa-ʾajlâhum min jazîrati -l-ʿarabi ilâ-sh-shaʾmi wa-ʾakhraja ʾahla najrâna wa-ʾanzalahum nâhîyata -l-kûfati."

6. At-Ṭabarî, *Taʾrîkh*, Ser. 1, vol. 5 pp. 2594–95. The text concerning Fadak is confused here, indicating, according to the editor of this volume, E. Prym, that some material has been excised. My translation follows his reconstruction in the notes. It is greatly to be regretted that the new translation of at-Ṭabarî's Taʾrikh will not be based on a much needed new critical edition of the Arabic text.

7. *Himâ* territory is land under a patron, in this case the caliph, who leases the land for a fixed sum to tenant farmers. Terms vary according to locale, but this is different from the *ʾiqṭâʿ* system, where land was granted under terms similar to feudal tenure, with the payment in military service, Even at this early date, it was a clear advantage to the caliph to have a source of income separate from a landed military aristocracy.

8. M. J. Kister, "Some Reports concerning al-Ṭâʾif," *J.S.A.I.* 1 (1979): 13.

9. Israel Ben-Zeev (Israel Wolfensohn), *Ha-Yehûdîm Ba-ʿArav* (Jerusalem: Achiasaf, 1957), p. 227. R. Sharîrâ died ca. 1000 C.E. and R. Hai ca. 1038. In their reply to the

questions, the two authorities make much of the growing of dates, an agricultural feature appropriate for the region.

10. Itzhak Ben-Zvi, *The Exiled and the Redeemed*, trans. Isaac Abbady (Philadelphia, Pa.: Jewish Publication Society, 1957), p. 176.

11. Benjamin of Tudela, *Travels, apud I tzhak*, Ben-Zvi, *The Exiled*, pp. 177ff.

12. Ibid., p. 178.

13. Israel Ben-Zeev (Wolfensohn) (Abû Dhuʾayb), *Taʾrîkh al-Yahûd fî Bilâd al-ʿArab* (Cairo: 1927/1345).

14. Itzhak Ben-Zvi, *The Exiled*, p. 180.

15. Ibid., p. 182.

16. Ibid., p. 184.

17. Al-Isfahânî, *Kitâb Al-Aghânî*, vol. 3, p. 18. In this story, it is implied but not stated that the Jew Shaʿbah b. Ghurayd had converted to Islam.

18. Itzhak Ben-Zvi, *The Exiled*, pp. 185f.

19. Ibid., p. 186.

20. Jacob Sapîr, *Eben Sapîr*, (Lyck: I. Silbermann 1866), translation here by Ben-Zvi, *The Exiled*, p. 187. This story is reminiscent of earlier narratives about the bedouin Jews of Arabia raiding *hajj* caravans and extracting taxes, but what is most striking is the notion that Jews would go on the pilgrimage caravans to the *hajj*. If one believes this story, then the tradition in the *Kitâb al-ʾAgânî*, vol. 3, p. 18, where Muʿâwiyya encountered a Jew at Mecca's sacred mosque should be read as telling us that a Jew from Taymâ was praying at the site.

21. Charles M. Doughty, *Travels in Arabia Deserta* (New York: Dover Publications, 1979), vol. 1, p. 328.

22. Ibid., vol. 2, p. 146, for example.

23. Ben-Zvi, *The Exiled*, p. 190.

24. Ibid., p. 193.

25. Bernard Lewis, *The Jews of Islam* (Princeton, N.J.: Princeton University Press, 1984), p. 74.

26. Ibid.

27. We do not even need to consider the assumption implied in the title of Geiger's work, that religious and cultural systems, once formed, can "lend" ideas or can be plundered as though they were great treasuries of jewels and precious coins. The metaphor of money for the dynamic interaction of peoples and cultures is too devalued to help us much.

28. S. D. Goitein, *Jews and Arabs: Their Contacts through the Ages* (New York: Schocken Books, 1970), pp. 7–8.

29. This study has concentrated, for the most part, on the Jews of the northern portion of Arabia except for the period of King Yûsuf Dhû Nuwâs. Recently Reuben Ahroni has written a clear account of the Jews of the Yemen in the medieval and modern periods, bringing their story up to the 1980s. I recommend this book to those interested in that subject: *Yemenite Jewry: Origins, Culture and Literature* (Bloomington: Indiana University Press, 1986).

Chapter 8

1. I. Goldziher questioned the reliability of Hadîth in the second volume of his *Muhammedanische Studien*, and much controversy surrounded the question of the authenticity of the pre-Islamic Arabic Odes. Starting with Theodor Nöldeke's *Beiträge zur Kenntniss der Poesie der alten Araber* (1864) through the acerbic article by D. S. Margoliouth, "The Origins of Arabic Poetry," *J.R.A.S.* (1925), pp. 417–46, and the recanted statement of Taha Husayn in his *fî-l-shiʿri-l-jâhiliy* (1926), pre-Islamic poetry has been suspected of being created by later hands. Although scholars of the stature of A. J. Arberry, *The Seven Odes* (1957), have argued for the authenticity of the poems and most students of the poetry accept their early character, the verses do not remain free from the suspicious gaze of the modern historian.

2. Patricia Crone and Michael Cook, *Hagarism* (Cambridge: Cambridge University Press, 1980).

3. Ibid., p. 3.

4. P. Crone, *Slaves on Horses* (Cambridge: Cambridge University Press, 1980), p. 6.

5. See below.

6. Crone, *Slaves on Horses*, p. 7.

7. As we shall see below, their epistemological stance has been a part of Western thought since Descartes and Hume, if not Plato.

8. Douglas Stewart, "Mythomorphism in Greco-Roman Historiography: The Case of the Royal *Gamos*," *Bucknell Review* 22, no. 1 (1976): 188–89.

9. Ibid.

10. John Wansbrough, *Qurʾânic Studies: Sources and Methods of Scriptural Interpretation* (Oxford: Oxford University Press, 1977).

11. John Wansbrough, *The Sectarian Milicu: Content and Composition of Islamic History* (Oxford: Oxford University Press, 1978).

12. Ibid., pp. 1–2.

13. Ibid.

14. Ibid. p. ix.

15. Ibid., pp. 144–48.

16. Ibid., p. 143.

17. Ibid., chap. 1 and passim; and *Quranic Studies*, pp. 122–28 and passim.

18. Barakat Ahmad, *Muhammad and the Jews: A Re-examination* (New Delhi: Vikas, 1979). From Wansbrough's point of view, Barakat Ahmad's work would still be too positivist because he sees the texts as reflecting a recoverable historical reality as well as a literary bias. Thus Ahmad is able to question the historicity of the slaughter of the B. Qurayza without also denying the existence of the group. Nevertheless, Ahmad sees literary structure, in this case hagiography, and authorial motive as determinants in the final construct, which is then presented as history.

19. Marilyn Robinson Waldman, *Toward a Theory of Historical Narrative: A Case Study in Perso-Islamicate Historiography* (Columbus: Ohio State University Press, 1980), pp. 140–41. The first chapter reviews some of the major arguments against the traditional approaches to historical texts and provides a good introduction to this subject.

20. Ibid.
21. It is outside the scope of this work to consider the structure and function of the *Sîrah* in detail, but an examination of Jewish historiographic questions among Jews in the Islamic world after the rise of Islam shows that Islam and Islamic issues helped condition the nature of the questions asked about the Jewish past. Jewish communities under Islamicate domination received the Muslim cultural stamp in this area just as they became Hellenized in the areas of philosophy and science. I intend to explore this in detail in a future study of the effects of Islamic textualization on Jewish historical perspectives.
22. Ibn Ishâq, *The Life of Muhammad*, trans. A. Guillaume (London: Oxford University Press, 1955), p. 68.
23. Ibid.
24. Ibid., p. 72.
25. Ibid., pp. 62–68.
26. G. D. Newby, "Abraha."
27. Genesis Rabbah 55:7.
28. A consequence of this equation of Muhammad's grandfather with Abraham is that Muhammad must be understood as Jacob. By the time of Ibn Ishâq, a body of literature had developed around the first verse of Sûrah 17, which represented Muhammad as having made a heavenly ascension from the Temple Mount in Jerusalem, from the Rock that was Jacob's Pillow. This trip to heaven is called *mi'râj* in Arabic, meaning "ladder" and referring to Jacob's vision of a heavenly ladder. Of course, following the bias of the hagiography, Muhammad does Jacob one better by actually ascending to heaven.
29. Jonathan Culler, *Structuralist Poetics* (Ithaca, N.Y.: Cornell University Press, 1975), p. 3.
30. For a philosophical discussion of the notion of "speech acts," see John R. Searle, *Speech Acts* (Cambridge, England: Cambridge University Press, 1969).
31. Culler, *Poetics*, p. 249.
32. Wansbrough, *Sectarian Milieu*, p. 31.
33. Ibid., p. 39.
34. D. C. Phillips, "On What Scientists Know," *Learning and Teaching the Ways of Knowing*, ed. Elliot Eisner (Chicago: University of Chicago Press, 1985), p. 40.
35. Thomas S. Kuhn, "Logic of Discovery or Psychology of Research," *Criticism and the Growth of Knowledge*, ed. Imre Lakatos and Alan Musgrave, Proceedings of the International Colloquim in Philosophy of Science, London, 1965 (Cambridge, England: Cambridge University Press, 1970), vol. 4, p. 2.
36. Phillips, "On What Scientists Know," p. 41, and J. Fodor, "Observation Reconsidered," *Philosophy of Science* 51, no. 1 (March 1984): 23–43.
37. Israel Scheffler, *Science and Subjectivity* (Indianapolis, Ind.: Hackett Publishing Co., 1982), p. 44.
38. Karl Popper, "Normal Science and Its Dangers," *Criticism and the Growth of Knowledge*, ed. Imre Lakatos and Alan Musgrave (Cambridge, England: Cambridge University Press, 1970), pp. 56–57.
39. Phillips, "On What Scientists Know," p. 43.

40. Thomas S. Kuhn, *The Structure of Scientific Revolutions*, (Chicago, Ill.: University of Chicago Press, 1970) pp. 111ff.
41. Walter Weimer, *apud* Phillips, "On What Scientists Know," p. 50.
42. Thomas S. Kuhn, "Reflections on My Critics," *Criticism and the Growth of Knowledge*, ed. Lakotos and Musgrave, pp. 266ff.
43. Burleigh Taylor Wilkins, *Has History Any Meaning?* (Ithaca, N.Y.: Cornell University Press, 1978), p. 125.
44. Ibid., p. 126.
45. For a more extended discussion of this definition of the role of the historian, see Wilkins, *Has History Any Meaning?* pp. 57ff.
46. See Thomas S. Kuhn, *The Structure of Scientific Revolutions*.
47. Carl Hempel, *apud* Phillips, "On What Scientists Know," p. 45.

BIBLIOGRAPHY

Abbott, Nabia. *Aisha the Beloved of Muhammad*. Chicago: University of Chicago Press, 1942.

_____. *Studies in Arabic Literary Papyri* University of Chicago Oriental Institute Publications. Vol. 1: *Historical Texts*, 1957. Vol. 2: *Qur'anic Commentary and Tradition*, 1967. Chicago:

_____. "Wahb b. Munabbih: A Review Article." *Journal of Near Eastern Studies* 36 (1977): 103–12.

Ahmad, Mirza Bashir. *Sources of the Sirat*. Qadian: Nazir Dawat-o-Tabligh, n.d.

Ahmad, Barakat. *Muhammad and the Jews: A Reexamination*. Indian Institute of Islamic Studies. New Delhi: Vikas, 1979.

Ahroni, Reuben. *Yemenite Jewry: Origins, Culture and Literature*. Bloomington: University of Indiana Press, 1986.

Al'Asbahânî, Abû Faraj. *Kitâb al-'Aghânî*. Ed. Salâh Yûsuf al-Khalîl. Beirut: Dâr al-Fikr, reprinted from Bûlâq edition, 1970.

Al-Assouad, M. R. "Dhû Nuwâs." *Encyclopaedia of Islam*, 2nd edition. 2: 244.

Al-Azraqî, Abû-l-Walîd Muhammad b. 'Abdullâh. *Kitâb 'Akhbâr Makka*. Ed. F. Wüstenfeld. Beirut: Khayyât reprinted 1964.

Al-Baghdâdî, Abû Bakr Ahmad b. 'Alî. *Ta'rîkh Baghbâd*. 14 vols. Cairo: 1931/1349.

Al-Baghdâdî, 'Alâ ad-Dîn 'Alî b. Muhammad b. Ibrahîm al-Khazân. *Lubâb at-Ta'wîl fî Ma'ânî at-Tanzîl*. 4. vols. Cairo:, 1955.

Al-Balâdhurî, Ahmad b. Yahyâ, *Futûh al-Buldân*, Ed. M. J. de Goeje. Leiden: E. J. Brill, 1866.

Al-Bukhârî, Abû 'Abdullâh Muhammad b. Ismâ'îl. *Kitâb at-Ta'rîkh al-Kabîr*. Hyderabad: 1361-77.

_____. *Sahîh*. 9 vols. Bulaq: 1311-13

'Alî, Jawâd. *Târîkh Al-'Arab Qabla Al-Islâm*. 3 Vols. Baghdad: Al-Tafîd, 1950–53.

Al-Kisâ' î, Muhammad b. 'Abdullâh. *Vita Prophetarum*. Ed. Isaac Eisenberg. Leiden: E. J. Brill, 1923.

Al-Maqdisî, Abû Naṣr al-Mutahhar b. Tâhir. *Kitâb al-Badʾ wa-t-Taʾ rîkh. Ed. Cl. Huart.* 5 vols. Paris: 1899.

Al-Masʿûdî, Abû al-Hasan ʿAlî b. al-Husayn b. ʿAlî. *Murûj adh-Dhahab.* 4 vols. Cairo: Dār Al-Rijāʾ, 1965/1384.

Altheim. F., and Ruth Stiehl. *Die Araber in der alten Welt.* 1 (1964); 2 (1965); 3 (1966); 4 (1967); 5, no. 1 (1968); 5, no. 2 (1969).

———. *Finanzgeschichte der Spaetantike.* Frankfurt am Main: Vittorio Klosterman, 1957.

———. *Geschichte der Hunnen.* Berlin: Walter de Gruyter & Co., 1960.

Al-Wâqidî, Abû ʿAbdullâh Muhammad b. ʿUmar. *Kitâb al-Maghâzî.* Ed. Marsden Jones. 3 vols. London: Oxford University Press, 1966.

Andrae, Tor. *Der Ursprung des Islams und das Christentum.* Uppsala and Stockholm: Almguist and Wiksells, 1926.

———. *Mohammed: The Man and His Faith.* Trans. T. Menzel. New York: Harper and Row, 1960.

Arafat, W. N. "New Light on the Story and of Banû Qurayẓa and the Jews of Medina." *J.R.A.S.* (1976): 100–107.

Arberry, A. J. *The Seven Odes.* New York: Macmillan, 1957.

———. "The *Sîra* in Verse." Ed. Georges Makdisi. *Arabic and Islamic Studies in Honor of H. A. R. Gibb.* Cambridge, Mass.: Harvard University Press, 1965; pp. 64–72.

As-Samhûdî, ʿAlî b. ʿAbdullâh b. ʾAhmad. *Kitâb Wafâʾ al-Wafâʾ.* Cairo: Al-Saʿârah, 1955/1374.

As-Sijistânî, Abû Hâtim. *Kitâb al-Muʿammarîn . . . ,* Cairo: 1961.

Ath-Thaʿ labî, Ibn Ishâq Ahmad b. Muhammad. *Qiṣṣaṣ al-Anbiyâʾ,* Cairo: n.d. (1950?).

Atiya, Aziz Suryal. *History of Eastern Christianity.* Notre Dame, Ind.: University of Notre Dame Press, 1968.

At-Tabarî, Abû Jaʿfar Muhammad b. Jarîr. *Taʾrîkh Ar-Rusul wa Al-Mulûk (Annales).* M. J. de Goeje et al. Leiden: E. J. Brill, 1879-98.

———. *Jâmiʿ al-Bayân ʿan Taʾwîl ʾAyy al-Qurʾ ân.* 30 rols Cairo: Mustafa al-Halabî & Sons, 1954/1383.

Az-Zamakhsharî, Abû Qâsim Mahmûd b. ʿUmar b. Muhammad b. ʾAhmad al-Khawarizmî. *Al-Kashshâf ʿan haqâʾ iq at-tanzîl wa-ʿuyûn al-ʾaqawîl fî wujûh at-taʾwîl.* Cairo: Mustafa al-Halabi & Sons, 1966.

Az-Ziriklî, Khayr ad-Dîn. *Al-Aʿlam.* Beirut: 1969.

Babylonian Talmud, The. Trans. with notes and glossary by R. I. Epstein et al. London: Soncino Press, 1948

Bacher, W. "Johanan b. Zakkai." *The Jewish Encyclopedia,* vol. 7. New York: Funk & Wagnalls, 1912.

BIBLIOGRAPHY

Bahr, Gordon J. "The Seder of Passover and the Eucharistic Words." In H. A. Fischel, *Essays in Greco-Roman and Related Literature*. New York: Ktav, 1977.

Baumstark, A. "Das Problem eines vorislamischen Christlich-kirchlichen Schrifttums in arabischer Sprache." *Islamica* 4 (1931): 562–75.

_____. "Eine altarabische Evangelienuebersetzung aus dem Christlich-Palaestinenseben." *Zeitschrift für Semitistik*, 8 (1923): 201–9.

Becker, C. H. "Christliche Polemik und islamische Dogmenbildung." *Z.A.* 26 (1912): 175–95.

_____. *Islamstudien, vom Werden und Wesen der islamischen Welt.* 2 vols. Leipzig: Quelle and Meyer, 1924-1932.

_____. "Prinzipielles zu Lammens' Sîrastudien." *Der Islam* 4 (1913): 263-69.

Beeston, A. F. L. "Two Bi'r Ḥimâ Inscriptions Re-examined." *B.S.O.A.S.* 48, no. 1 (1985): 42–52.

Bell, R. *Introduction to the Qur'ân.* Edinburgh: Edinburgh University Press, 1963.

_____. "Muhammad and Previous Messengers." *M.W.* 24 (1934): 330–40.

_____. *The Origin of Islam in Its Christian Environment.* London: Cass. 1968.

_____. *Kaʿb al-Ahbâr und seine Stellung im Hadîth und in der islamishchen Legendenliteratur.* Inaugural dissertation, Johann Wolfgang Goethe University, Frankfurt am Main, 1933.

_____(Abû Dhuʾayb). *Taʾ rîkh al-Yahûd fî Bilâd al-ʿ Arab.* Cairo: 1927/1345.

Ben-Zvi, Itzhak. *The Exiled and the Redeemed.* Trans. Isaac Abbady. Philadelphia: Jewish Publication Society, 1957.

Blachere, R. *Le probleme de Mahomet, essai de biographie critique du fondateur de l'Islam.* Paris: Presses Universitaires de France, 1952.

_____. "Regards sur la litterature en Arabe au Ier siecle de l-Hegire." *Semitica* b (1956).

Bowersock, G. W. *Roman Arabia.* Cambridge, Mass.: Harvard University Press, 1983.

Brauer, Erich. *Ethnologie der jemenitischen Juden.* Heidelberg: Carl Winters, 1934.

Bravmann, M. M. *The Spiritual Background of Early Islam.* Leiden: E. J. Brill, 1972.

Brockelmann, Carl. *Geschichte der arabischen Literatur.* 2 vols. 2nd edition. Leiden: E. J. Brill, 1943, 1949.

_____. *Supplement* [to *Arabischen Literatur*]. 3 vols. Leiden: E. J. Brill, 1937–42.

Bulliet, Richard. *The Camel and the Wheel.* Cambridge, Mass.: Harvard University Press, 1975.

_____. *Conversion to Islam in the Medieval Period.* Cambridge, Mass.: Harvard University Press, 1979.

158

Burton, J. *The Collection of the Qur'ân*. Cambridge, Eng.: Cambridge University Press, 1977.

Caetani, L. *Annali dell'Islam*. 10 vols., Milan: University of Hoepli 1905–26.

Carra de Vaux, B. "Bilkîs." *Shorter Encyclopedia of Islam*. Ed. H. A. R. Gibb and J. Kramers. Leiden: E. J. Brill, 1961; p. 63.

Caskel, Werner. "The Bedouinization of Arabia." *Studies in Islamic Cultural History*. Ed. G. E. von Grunebaum. Memoirs of the American Anthropological Association 76. Menshasha, Wis: George Banta, 1954; pp. 36–46.

———. *Entdeckungen in Arabien. Arbeitsgemeinschaft fuer Forschung des Landes Nordrhein-Westfalen: Geisteswissenschaften*. Vol. 30. Cologne: Westdeutscher Verlag, 1954.

———. *Lihyan und Lihyanisch. Arbeitsgemeinschaft fuer Forschung des Landes Nordrhein-Westfalen: Geisteswissenschaften*. Vol. 4. Cologne: Westdeutscher Verlag, 1954.

Chapira, B. "Legendes bibliques attribuées a Ka'b el-Aḥbar." *R.E.J.* 69 (1919): 86–107: 70 (1920): 37–43.

Charlesworth, J. *The Old Testament Pseudepigrapha*. 2 vols. Garden City, N.Y.: Doubleday, 1983.

Cheikho, L. "Quelque legendes musulmanes anteislamique." *Actes du XVe Congres International des Orientalistes*. Copenhagen, 1908.

Cook, Michael. *Muhammad*. Oxford: Oxford University Press, 1983.

Crone, P. *Slaves on Horses*. Cambridge, Eng.: Cambridge University Press, 1980.

———, and Michael Cook. *Hagarism*. Cambridge, Eng.: Cambridge University Press 1980.

Culler, Jonathan. *Structuralist Poetics*. Ithaca, N.Y.: Cornell University Press, 1975.

Dilman, A. *Lexicon Linguae Aethiopicae*. New York: Frederick Unger, 1955.

Dinur, Ben Z. *Yisrael be-Golah*. Tel Aviv and Jerusalem: Dabir, 1972.

Diodorus Siculus. *The Library of History*. Trans. C. H. Oldfather. Loeb Classical Library). Cambridge, Mass.: Harvard University Press; sec. 19.

Dougherty, R. P. *Nabonidus and Belshazzar*. New Haven, Conn.: Yale University Press, 1929.

———. "Nabonidus in Arabia." *J.A.O.S.* 42 (1922): 305–16.

———. "The Sealand of Arabia." *J.A.O.S.* 50 (1930): pp. 1–25.

Doughty, Charles M. *Travels in Arabia Deserta*. New York: Dover Publications, 1979.

Dozy, R. *Die Israeliten zu Mekka von David's Zeit*. Trans. from Dutch original. Leipzig: W. Engelmann, 1864.

BIBLIOGRAPHY

Encyclopaedia of Islam, 4 vols. and Supplement. Ed. Th. Houtsma et al. Leiden and London: E. J. Brill, 1913–38.
_____. New edition. Ed. H. A. R. Gibb et al. London and Leiden: E. J. Brill, 1954–.

Fischel, W. J. "The Region of the Persian Gulf and Its Jewish Settlements in Islamic Times." *Alexander Marx Jubilee Volume.* New York: Jewish Theological Association, 1950, pp. 203–30.

Fodor, J. "Observation Reconsidered." *Philosophy of Science* 51, no. 1 (March 1984): 23–43.

Freedman, David Noel, "The Prayer of Nabonidus," *B.A.S.O.R.* 145 (1957): 31–32.

Friedlander, Israel. "Jews of Arabia and the Gaonate." *J.Q.R.* 1 (1910): 249–257.
_____. "Jewish–Arabic Studies." *J.Q.R.* 1 (1910): 183–215.

Fück, Johann W. *Muhammad ibn Isḥâq; literarhistorische Untersuchungen.* Frankfurt am. Main: 1925.
_____. "Muhammad-Persoenlichkeit und Religions-stiftung." *Saeculum* 3 (1952): 70–93.

Gadd, C. J. "The Harran Inscription of Nabonidus." *Anatolian Studies* 8 (1958).

Geiger, Abraham. *Was hat Mohammed aus dem Judenthume aufgenommen?* New York: Ktar, 1970.

Gibb, H. A. R. "Pre-Islamic Monotheism in Arabia." *Harvard Theological Review* 45 (1962): 269–80.

Gil, Moshe. "The Constitution of Medina: A Reconsideration." *Israel Oriental Studies* 4 (1974): 44–65.
_____. "Ha-mîfgash ha-bablî." *Tarbîz* 47 (1979).
_____. "The Origins of the Jews of Yathrib." *J.S.A.I.* 4 (1984): 203–24.

Ginzberg, Louis. *Legends of the Jews.* 7 vols. Philadelphia: Jewish Publication Society, 1967.
_____"Akiba Ben Joseph." *The Jewish Encyclopedia*, vol. 1. New York: Funk & Wagnalls, 1901; pp. 304–8.

Glaser, Eduard. *Skizze der Geschichte und Geographie Arabiens.* Reprint. Hildesheim: 1976.

Glueck, Nelson. *Rivers in the Desert: A History of the Negev.* New York: Farrar, Straus & Cudahy, 1959.

Goitein, S. D. *Jews and Arabs: Their Contacts through the Ages.* New York: Schocken Books, 1970.
_____. "Muhammad's Inspiration by Judaism." *Journal of Jewish Studies* 9 (1958): 149–62.

160

A History of the Jews of Arabia

────── . *Studies in Islamic History and Institutions*. Leiden: E. J. Brill, 1966.

Goldziher, Ignaz. *Abhandlungen zur arabischen Philologie*. 2 vols. Leiden: E.J. Brill, 1896, 1899.

────── . "Lâ Misâsa." *Revue Africaine* 268 (1908): 23ff.

────── . *Muhammedanische Studien*. 2 vols. Halle: 1889. Trans. C. R. Barber and S. M. Stern, as *Muslim Studies*. 2 vols., Chicago: Aldine, 1968, 1971.

────── . "Notes sur les Juifs dans les poesies arabes de l'epoque ancienne de l'Islam." *R.E.J.* 43 (1901): 10–14.

Graham, W. *Divine Word and Prophetic Word in Early Islam*. The Hague: Mouton, 1977.

Gregoire, H. "Mahomet et le Monophysisme." *Melange Charles Diehl* Paris: E. Leroux, 1930: 107–19.

Groom, Nigel. *Frankincense and Myrrh*. London: Longman, 1981.

Grünbaum, Max. *Neue Beitraege zur semitischen Sagenkunde*. Leiden: E.J. Brill, 1893.

Guidi, I. "La Lettera di Simeono vescovo di Beth-Arsham sopra i martiri omeriti." *Atti della R. Accad. dei Lincei, Memorie della classe di scienze morali, storiche e filologiche* 7 (Rome 1881): 471–515.

Guillaume, Alfred "The Biography of the Prophet in Recent Research." *Islamic Quarterly* 1 (1954): 5–11.

────── . "The Pictorial Background of the Qur'ân." *Annual, Leeds University Oriental Society* 3 (1961–62): 39–59.

────── . "Some Aspects of the Prophet Muhammad in Tradition." chap. 3 of *The Tradition of Islam*. Oxford: Oxford University Press, 1924.

────── . "The Version of the Gospel Used in Medina circa 700 A.D." *Al-Andalus* 15 (1950): 289–96.

Halevy, Joseph. "Voyage au Nedjran." *Bulletin de la Société de Geographie de Paris* 6 (1873).

Halperin, David. "The Ibn Sayyâd Traditions and the Legend of al-Dajjâl." *J.A.O.S.* 96, no. 2 (1976): 213–25.

Hamadeh, Muhammad Maher. *Muhammad the Prophet: A Selected Bibliography*. Ph. D. dissertation, University of Michigan, 1965.

Hamidullah, M. "The Christian Monk Abu 'Amir of Medina of the Time of the Holy Prophet." *Journal of the Pakistan Oriental Society* 7 (1959): 231–40.

────── . "Two Christians of Pre-Islamic Mecca, 'Uthman ibn al-Huwairith and Waraqa ibn Naufal." *Journal of the Pakistan Oriental Society* 6 (1958): 97–103.

Hawting, G. R. "The Origins of the Muslim Sanctuary." *Studies on the First Century of Islamic Society*. Ed. G. H. A. Juynboll. Carbondale, Ill.: University of Southern Illinois Press, 1982; pp. 23–47.

Heller, Bernard. "La legende biblique dans l'Islam." *R.E.J.* 98 (1934): 1–18.

BIBLIOGRAPHY

_____. "Youscha⁾ Al-Akbar et les Juifs de Kheybar dans le Roman d'Antar: un mouvement messianique dans l'ancienne Arabie." *R.E.J.* 84 (1927): 113–37.

Herzberg, H. Z. "Arabia." *E.J.*, 1: 232–36.

Hirsch, E. G. "Son of God." *The Jewish Encyclopaedia*, vol. 11. New York: Funk & Wagnalls, 1912; pp. 460–61.

Hirschberg, J. W. [Haim Zev]. "Concerning New Jewish Inscriptions Discovered in South Arabia." *Tarbîz*, 44 (1974–75).

_____. *Der Dîwân des as-Samau⁾ al ibn ⁾Adijâ⁾*. Kracow: Polish Oriental Society, 1931.

_____. *Juedische und christliche Lehren in vor- und fruehislamischen Arabien*. Krakow: Polish Oriental Society, 1939.

_____. "The Name of the Last Judaizing King in Himyar." *Tarbîz* 15 (1944): 130ff.

_____. *Nestorian Sources of North-Arabian Traditions on the Establishment and Persecution of Christianity in Yemen*. Krakow: Nakladem Polskiego Towarzystwa Orientalistycznego z. Zasitku Ministerstwa Oswiaty, 1949. This is detached from Rocznik Orientalistyczny vol. 15, pp. 321–38.

_____. "On Some New Jewish Inscriptions in Yemen." *Tarbîz* 44 (1974–75): 151.

_____. *Yisrael ba-⁾Arab*, Tel Aviv: 1946.

_____. *New Researches into the Composition and Exegesis of the Qoran*. London: Royal Asiatic Society, 1902.

Hirschfeld, Hartwig. *Beitraege zur Erklaerung des Koran*. Leipzig: O. Schulze 1866.

_____. *Juedische Elemente im Koran: Ein Beitrag zur Koranforschung*. Berlin: 1878.

_____. "A Poem Attributed to alSamau⁾ al." *J.Q.R.* 17 (1905): 431–40.

_____. "Some Notes on 'Jewish Arabic Studies.'" *J.Q.R.* (1910): 447–48.

Hitti, P. K. *A History of the Arabs*. London: Macmillan, 1951.

Horovitz, Josef "Biblische Nachwirkungen in der Sira." *Der Islam* 12 (1922): 184–89.

_____. "Der Ursprung des Islams und das Christentum." *Orientalische Literaturzeitung* 29 (1926): cols. 841–45.

_____. "The Growth of the Mohammed Legend." *M.W.* 10 (1920): 49–58.

_____. *Jewish Proper Names and Derivatives in the Koran. Hebrew Union College Annual*. vol. 2. Cincinnati: Hebrew Union College, 1925: 145-227.

_____. "Judaeo-Arabic Relations in Pre-Islamic Times." *I.C.* 3 (1929): 173–76.

_____. *Koranische Untersuchungen*. Berlin: W. de Gruyter, 1926.

"Zur Muhammad-Legende." *Der Islam* 5 (1914): 41–53.

A History of the Jews of Arabia

Horst, H. "Israelitische Propheten im Koran." *Zeitschrift für Religions- und Geschichte* 16 (1964): 42–57.

Huart, Clement. "Wahb ben Monabbih . . . ." *Journal Asiatique* 10, no. 4 (1904): 331–50.

Husayn, Taha. *Fî-l-shiᶜ ri-l-jâhiliy*. Cairo: Dâr Al-Maktabah Al-Miṣriyyah, 1926.

Ibn Abû Hâtim, ᶜAbd ar-Rahmân ar-Râzî. *Al-Jarh wa-t-Taᶜ dîl*. 4 vols. Hyderabad: Dâr Al-Maᶜârif, 1952–53.

Ibn al-Kalbî, Hishâm. *Kitâb al-Aṣnâm*. Trans. N. A. Faris, as *The Book of Idols*. 35 Princeton, N. J.: Princeton University Press, 1952.

Ibn an-Nadîm. *Kitâb al-Fihrist*. 2 vols. Ed. G. Fluegel. Halle: F.C.W. Vogel, 1872.

Ibn ᶜAsâkir, ᶜAlî b. al-Hasan. *At-Taʾ rîkh al-Kabîr*. 7 vols. Damascus: 1911–12.

Ibn Chabib, R. Jacob. *ʾAgadah ᶜEn Yaᶜ qob (En Jacob)*. Trans. and ed. S. H. Glick. New York: Hebrew Publishing Co., 1921.

Ibn Hajar al-ᶜAsqalânî. *Tahdhîb at-Tahdhîb*. 12 vols. Hyderabad: Nizâmiyyah, 1907–09/1325–1327.

Ibn Hishâm, Mahammad b. ᶜAbd al-Malik. *As-Sîrat an-Nabawiyyat 1-Ibn Hishâm*. Ed. Muṣtafâ ash-shaqâ, et al. Cairo: Al-Halabî & Sons, 1955.

———. *Das Leben Muhammeds*. 3 vols. Ed. F. Wüstenfeld. Göttingen: Dieterich, 1860.

———. *Kitâb at-Tijân*. Hyderabad: Dâr al-Maʾârif, 1928/1347.

Ibn Ishâq. *The Life of Muhammad*. Trans. A. Guillaume. Oxford and Lahore: Oxford University Press, 1955.

Ibn Saᶜd, Muhammad b. Saᶜd Kâtib al-Wâqidî. *At-Ṭabaqât al-Kabîr*. Ed. E. Sachau. Lieden: E. J. Brill, 1904.

Jastrow, Marcus. *A Dictionary of the Targumim, The Talmud . . . .* 2 vols. New York: Pardes, 1950.

Jaussen, A., and R. Savignac. *Mission archeologique en Arabie*. Vol. 1. Paris: E. Leroux, 1909. Vol. 2. Paris: Paul Geuthner, 1914.

Jeffery, Arthur. *The Foreign Vocabulary of the Qurân*. Baroda: Oriental Institute, 1938.

———. "The Letter of Simeone of Beth Arshan," *M.W.* 36 (1946): 204–16.

Josephus. *Antiquities of the Jews*. Trans. Wm. Whiston. Philadelphia: John Winston Co., 1922.

Juynboll, G. H. A. *Studies on the First Century of Islamic Society*. Papers on Islamic History 5. Carbondale, Ill.: Southern Illinois University Press, 1982.

Kister, M. J. "Al-Hîra: Some Notes on Its Relations with Arabia." *Arabica* 15 (1968): 143–69.

_____. "The Campaign of Hulubân: A New Light on the Expedition of Abraha." *Museon* 78, nos. 1–2 (1965): 425–36.

_____. "Haddithû ʿan banî isrâʾ îla wa-lâ haraja: A Study of an Early Tradition." *Israel Oriental Studies* 2 (1972): 215–39.

_____. ". . . . illâ bi-haqqihi . . .: A Study of an Early Hadîth." *J.S.A.I.* (1984): 43.

_____. "The Market of the Prophet." *Journal of the Economic and Social History of the Orient* 8 (1965): 272–76.

_____. "The Massacre of the Banû Qurayza." *J.S.A.I.* 8 (1986).

_____. "Mecca and Tamîm (Aspects of Their Relations)." *Journal of the Economic and Social History of the Orient* 8 (1965): 113–63.

_____. "On the Wife of the Goldsmith from Fadak and Her Progeny: A Study in Jâhilî Genealogical Tradition." *Museon* 92 (1979): 321–30.

_____. "Some Reports concerning al-Tâʾ if." *J.S.A.I.* 1 (1979): 1–18.

_____. "Some Reports concerning Mecca from Jâhiliyya to Islam." *Journal of the Economic and Social History of the Orient* 15 (1972): 61–93.

_____. *Studies in Jâhiliyya and Early Islam*. London: Variorum Reprints, 1980.

_____, and Menahem Kister, "ʿAl yehûdê ʿarab—heʿ arôt." *Tarbîz* 48 (1979): 230–47.

Krauss, S. "Talmudische Nachrichten über Arabien." *Z.D.M.G.* 70, nos. 3–4 (1916).

Kuhn, Thomas S. "Logic of Discovery of Psychology of Research." *Criticism and the Growth of Knowledge*. Ed. Imre Lakatos and Alan Musgrave. Vol. 4 of the Proceedings of the International Colloquium in Philosophy of Science, London, 1965. Cambridge, Eng.: Cambridge University Press, 1970.

_____. "Reflections on My Critics." *Criticism and the Growth of Knowledge* Ed. Imre Lakatos and Alan Musgrave. Vol. 4 of the Proceedings of the International Colloquium in Philosophy of Science, London, 1965. Cambridge, Eng.: Canbridge University Press, 1970.

_____. *The Structure of Scientific Revolutions*. 2nd edition. Chicago, Ill.: University of Chicago Press, 1970.

Lakatos, Imre, and Alan Musgrave, eds. *Criticism and the Growth of Knowledge*. vol. 4 of the Proceedings of the International Colloquium in the Philosophy of Science, London, 1965. Cambridge, Eng.: Cambridge University Press, 1970.

Lammens, H. *La Mecque a la veille de l'hegire; Melange de l'Universite Saint-Joseph* 9, fasc. 3. Beirut: Catholic Press, 1924.

Landau-Tasseron, E. "Asad from Jâhiliyya to Islâm." *Jerusalem Studies in Arabic and Islam* 6 (1985): 1–28.

Lecker, Michael. "Muhammad at Medina: A Geographical Approach." *J.S.A.I.* 6 (1985): 29–62.

Leszynsky, Rudolf. *Die Juden in Arabien*. Berlin: Mayer & Mueller, 1910.

Levi della Vida, G. "Pre-Islamic Arabia." *the Arab Heritage*. Ed. N. A. Faris. Princeton, N.J.: Princeton University Press, 1944.

———. "Sîra." *Shorter Encyclopaedia of Islam*. Ed. H. A. R. Gibb. Leiden: E.J. Brill.

Lewis, B. *The Jews of Islam*. Princeton, N.J.: Princeton University Press, 1984.

Lichtenstadter, I. "Jews in Pre-Islamic Arabic Literature." *American Academy for Jewish Research* 10 (1940): 185-194.

Lidzbarski, M. *De Propheticis, Quae Dicuntur, Legendis Arabicis*. Leipzig: G. Drugulini, 1893.

Lieberman, S. *Hellenism in Jewish Palestine*. New York: Jewish Theological Seminary 1962/5711.

Margoliouth, D. S. "A Poem Attributed to al-Samau' al." *J.R.A.S.* 83 (1906): 363–71.

Midrash Rabbah. 5 vols. Ed. and Trans. H. Freedman et al. London: Soncino Press, 1977.

Milik, J. T. "Priere de Nabonide." *Revue Biblique* 63 (1956): 407–15.

Moberg, Axel, ed. *The Book of the Himyarites*. Skrifter Kungliga Humanistika Vetenskapssamfundet i Lund, vol. 7. Lund, Sweden: Gleerup, 1924.

Mommsen, Theodor. *The Provinces of the Roman Empire from Caesar to Diocletian*. Trans. W. P. Dickson. New York: Chas. Scribner's Sons, 1887.

Moubarac, Youakim. *Abraham dans le Coran*. Paris: J. Vrinn, 1958.

———. *Moise dans le Coran*. Paris: J. Vrinn, 1954.

Newby, G. D. "Abraha and Sennacherib: A Talmudic Parallel to the Tafsir on Surat al-Fil." *J.A.O.S.* 94 (1974): 431–37.

———. "An Example of Coptic Literary Influence on the *Sirah* of Ibn Ishaq." *J.N.E.S.* 31 (1972): 22–8.

———. "Ibn Khaldun and Frederick Jackson Turner: Islam and the Frontier Experience." *Ibn Khaldun and Islamic Ideology*. Ed. B. Lawrence. Vol. 40 *International Studies in Sociology and Social Anthropology*, ed. K. Ishwaran. Leiden: E. J. Brill, 1984; pp. 122–33, and also in *Journal of Asian and African Studies* 18, nos. 3–4 (1983): 274–85.

———. "Observations about an Early Judaeo-Arabic." *J.Q.R.* 61 (1971): 214–21.

———. "Review of *Mekorot Yehudim baQuran* by Andre C. Zaoui." *Journal of Reform Judaism* 33 (Fall 1986).

_____. "The Sirah as a Source for Early Arabian Jewish History." *J.S.A.I.* 7 (1986): 121–38.

_____. "Tafsir Isra'iliyat: The Development of Qur'ân Commentary in Early Islam." *Journal of the American Academy of Religion* 47, no. 4 (December 1979): 685–97.

Nöldeke, Theodor *Beiträge zur Kenntniss der Poesie der alten Araber*. Hannover: Carl Ruempler, 1864.

O'Leary, DeLacy. *Arabia Before Muhammad*. London: Kegan Paul, 1927.

Ong, W. *Orality and Literacy*. New York: Methuen, 1982.

Paret, Rudi. "Das Geshichtsbild Mohammeds." *Welt als Geschichte* (1951): 214–24.

Perlmann, M. "A Legendary Story of Ka'b al-Ahbâr's Conversion to Islam." *Conference on Jewish Relations: Joshua Starr Memorial Volume*. New York: Jewish Social Studies Publications, 1953; pp. 85–99.

Peters, Frances. *The Harvest of Hellenism* New York: Simon & Schuster, 1970.

Philby, Harry St. John Bridger. *Arabian Highlands*. Ithaca, N.Y.: Cornell University Press, 1952.

Phillips, D. C. "On What Scientists Know." *Learning and Teaching the Ways of Knowing*. Ed. Elliot Eisner. Eighty-Fourth Yearbook of the National Society for the Study of Education, Part II. Chicago, Ill.: University of Chicago Press, 1985.

Pickthall, Muhammad Marmaduke. *The Meaning of the Glorious Koran*. New York: Mentor, n.d.

Pigulevskaya, N. V. *Al-' Arab 'alâ Hudûd Bîzantah wa-' Irân min al-Qarn ar-Râbi' 'ilâ -l-Qarn as-Sâdis al-Milâdî*. Trans. Salâh ad-Dîn 'Uthmân Hâshim. Kuwait: Ministry of Publications 1985/1405.

Pliny. *Natural History*. Trans. H. Rackham. Loeb Classical Library. Cambridge, Mass.: Harvard University Press, 1945.

Popper, Karl. "Normal Science and Its Dangers." *Criticism and the Growth of Knowledge*. Ed. Imre Lakatos and Alan Musgrave. Vol. 4 of the Proceedings of the International Colloquium in the Philosophy of Science, London, 1965. Cambridge, Eng.: Cambridge University Press, 1970.

Procopius. *History of the Wars*. Trans. H. B. Dewing. Cambridge, Mass.: Harvard University Press, 1961.

Rabin, Chaim. *Qumran Studies*. New York: Schocken, 1975.

Rodinson, Maxime. *Mohammed*. Trans. A. Carter. New York: Pantheon, 1971.

Rölig, W. "Nabonid und Tema." *Compte Rendu de l'Ileme Recontre Assyriologie Internationale, 1962*. Leiden: E.J. Brill, 1964; pp. 21–32.

Rosenthal, F. "The Influence of Biblical Tradition on Muslim Historiography." *Historians of the Middle East*. Ed. B. Lewis and P. M. Holt. London: Oxford University Press, 1964: pp. 35–45.

Rudolph, Wilhelm. *Die Abhaengigkeit des Qorans von Judentum and Christentum*. Stuttgart: W. Kohlhammer, 1922.

Ryckmans, G. "Graffites sabéens relevés en Arabie sa'udite." *Revista degli Studi Orientali* 32 (1957): 550–67.

———. "Inscriptions sud-arabes." *Le Muséon* 64 (1951): 93–106.

Ryckmans, J. "Les corégents du roi Himyarite Abûkarib As'ad d'après le texte Rossi 24." *Revista degli Studi Orientali* 37 (1962): 243–57.

———. "Inscriptions historiques Sabéennes." *Le Muséon* 66 (1953): 319–42.

Sack, Ronald H. "The Nabonidus Legend." *Revue d'Assyriologie* 77 (1983): 59–67.

Sapir, Jacop. *Eben Sapir*. 2 vols. Lyck: 1, Silbermann, 1866.

Schapiro, I. *die Haggadischen Elemente im erzaehlenden Teil des Korans*. Leipzig: H. Itz Kowski, 1907.

Schauss, H. *Guide to the Jewish Holy Days*. New York: Schocken, 1962.

Scheffler, Israel. *Science and Subjectivity*. 2nd edition. Indianapolis, Ind.: Hackett Publishing Co., 1982.

Schwarzbaum, Haim. *Biblical and Extra-Biblical Legends in Islamic Folk-Literature*. Vol. 30 of *Beiträge zur Sprach- und Kulturgeschichte des Orients*. Ed. O. Spies. Walldorf-Hessen: Verlag für Orientkunde Dr. H. Vorndran, 1982.

Searle, John R. *Speech Acts*. Cambridge, Eng.: Cambridge University Press, 1969.

Serjeant, R. B., "Professor A. Guillaume's Translation of the Sîrah." *B.S.O.A.S.* 21 (1958): 1–14.

Sezgin, F. *Geschichte des arabischen Schrifttums*. Vol. 1. Leiden: E.J. Brill, 1967.

Shaban, M. "Conversion to Early Islam." In Nehemia Levtzion, *Conversion to Islam*. New York: Holmes & Meier, 1979; pp. 24–29.

Shahîd, Irfan. "Arabic Literature to the End of the Umayyad Period." *J.A.O.S.* 106 (1986): 529–38.

———. *Byzantium and the Arabs in the Fourth Century*. Washington, D.C.: Dumbarton Oaks, 1984.

———. "Byzanto-Arabica: The Conference of Ramla, A.D. 524," *J.N.E.S.* 23 (1964): 115–31.

———. "A Contribution to Koranic Exegesis." *Arabic and Islamic Studies in Honor of H. A. R. Gibb*. Ed. G. Makdisi. Cambridge, Mass.: Harvard University Press, 1965.

———. *The Martyrs of Najran: New Documents*. Subsidia Hagiographica, no. 49. Brussels: Société des Bollandists, 1971.

BIBLIOGRAPHY

_____. *Rome and the Arabs: A Prolegomenon to the Study of Byzantium and the Arabs*. Washington D.C.: Dumbarton Oaks, 1984.

_____. "Pre-Islamic Arabia." *The Central Islamic Lands*, vol. 1 of the Cambridge History of Islam. Cambridge. Eng.: Cambridge University Press, 1970; pp. 3–29.

Shoufani, E. S. *Al-Riddah and the Muslim Conquest of Arabia*. Toronto, Canada: University of Toronto Press, 1973.

Smith, S. "Events in Arabia in the 6th Century A.D.." *B.S.O.A.S.* 16, no. 3 (1954): 424–68.

Speyer, Heinrich. *Die biblischen Erzaehlungen im Qoran*. Reprint. Hildesheim: Georg Olms, 1961.

Stein, S. "The Influence of the Symposia Literature on the Literary Form of the Pesah Haggadah." Reprinted from *Journal of Jewish Studies*, in Henry Fischel, *Essays in Greco-Roman and Related Literature*. New York: Ktar, 1977.

Stewart, D. "Mythomorphism in Greco-Roman Historiography: The Case of the Royal Gamos." *Bucknell Review* 22, no. 1 (1976): 188–89.

Strabo. *Geography*. Trans. Horace Leonard Jones. Cambridge, Mass.: Harvard University Press, 1930.

Strack, H. *Introduction to the Talmud and Midrash*. Philadelphia: Jewish Publication Society of America, 1931.

Torrey, C. C. *The Jewish Foundations of Islam*. New York: Jewish Institute of Religion, 1967.

Von Wissmann, Herman. "Die Geschichte des Sabaeerreichs und der Feldzug des Aelius Gallus." *Aufstieg und Niedergang der römischen Welt* 2. 9.1. Ed. Hildegard Temporini. Berlin: Walter de Gruyter, 1976; pp. 308–544.

Waldman, Marilyn R. *Toward a Theory of Historical Narrative: A Case Study in Perso-Islamicate Historiography*, Columbus: Ohio State University Press, 1980.

Wansbrough, John. *Quranic Studies: Sources and Methods of Scriptural Interpretation*. Oxford: Oxford University Press 1977.

_____. *The Sectarian Milieu: Content and Composition of Islamic Salvation History*. Oxford: Oxford University Press, 1978.

Wasserstrom, S. "*Species of Misbelief: A History of Muslim Heresiography of the Jews*." Ph. D. dissertation, University of Toronto, 1985.

Watt, W. M. "The Condemnation of the Jews of the Banû Qurayẓah." *M.W.* 42, no. 3 (1952): 160–71.

_____. "The Early Development of the Muslim Attitude to the Bible." Transactions of the Glasgow Oriental Society 16 : 50–62.

168

A HISTORY OF THE JEWS OF ARABIA

1961.

———. *Islamic Political Thought*. Islamic Surveys, no. 6, Edinburgh: University of Edinburgh Press, 1968.

———. *Muhammad at Mecca*. Oxford: Oxford University Press, 1953.

———. *Muhammad at Medina*. Oxford: Oxford University Press, 1956.

Weber, Otto. *Arabien vor dem Islam*. Leipzig: J.C. Hinrich, 1904.

Wellhausen, Julius. *Skizzen und Vorarbeiten*. vol. 3. Berlin: Georg Reimer, 1887.

Wensinck, A. J. "Mohammed und das Judentum." *Der Islam* 2 (1911): 286–91.

Wilkins, Burleigh Taylor. *Has History Any Meaning?* Ithaca, N.Y.: Cornell University Press, 1978.

Wittgenstein, Ludwig. *The Blue and Brown Books*. New York: Harper & Bros., 1960.

———. *Tractatus Logico-Philosophicus*. Trans. D. F. Pears and B. F. McGuiness. Introduction by Bertrand Russell. London: Routledge & Kegan Paul, 1961.

Wolfensohn, Israel. *See* Ben-Zeev, Israel.

Wolff, H. J. "Römisches Provinzialrecht in der Provinz Arabia." *Aufstieg und Niedergang der römischen Welt* 2, no. 13 (Berlin, 1980): 763–806.

Wüstenfeld, Ferdinand, "Geschichte der Stadt Medina," *Abhandlungen der Königlichen Gesellschaft der Wissenschaften zu* Göttingen. 9 (1860): 1–156.

Yadin, Yigael. *Bar Kochba*. New York: Random House, 1971.

———. "Expedition D—The Cave of Letters." *Israel Exploration Journal* 12 (1962): 227–57.

———. "the Nabataean Kingdom, Petra and En-Geddi in the Documents from Nahal Hever." *Ex Orientis Lux* 17 (1963): 227–41.

Yâqût ar-Rûmî, Ibn 'Abdullâh. *Kitâb Irshâd al-Arîb* . . . . Ed. D. S. Margoliouth. 10 vols. Leiden: E.J. Brill, 1907–27.

———. *Muʿ jam al-Buldân*, Ed. F. Wüstenfeld. 6 vols. Leipzig: F. A. Brockhaus, 1866–73.

Zayyât, Habîb. "Al-Yahüd fî Al-khilâfah Al-ʿAbbâsiyyah," *Mashriq* 36 (1938): 155–157.

Zwettler, Michael. *The Oral Tradition of Classical Arabic Poetry*. Columbus, Ohio: Ohio State University Press, 1978.

INDEX

169

INDEX

176